SEVENTY-FIVE YEARS IN OLD VIRGINIA

WITH SOME ACCOUNT OF THE LIFE OF THE AUTHOR AND SOME HISTORY OF THE PEOPLE AMONGST WHOM HIS LOT WAS CAST,—THEIR CHARACTER, THEIR CONDITION, AND THEIR CONDUCT BEFORE THE WAR, DURING THE WAR AND AFTER THE WAR

BY

John Herbert Claiborne, M. A., M. D.

Honorary Alumnus of the University College of Medicine, Honorary Fellow and ex-President of the Medical Society of Virginia, Corresponding Member of the Gynecological Society of Boston, Fellow elect of the Victoria Institute of Great Britain, Member of the First Pan-American Congress, Formerly Member of the House of Representatives and Senate of Virginia, Lately Major and Surgeon of the 12th Virginia Infantry, Mahone's Brigade—Subsequently Surgeon on the General Medical Staff of the Confederate Army, and Executive Officer in charge of all Military Hospitals at Petersburg, Va., etc., etc.

HERITAGE BOOKS
2012

HERITAGE BOOKS
AN IMPRINT OF HERITAGE BOOKS, INC.

Books, CDs, and more—Worldwide

For our listing of thousands of titles see our website
at
www.HeritageBooks.com

A Facsimile Reprint
Published 2012 by
HERITAGE BOOKS, INC.
Publishing Division
100 Railroad Ave. #104
Westminster, Maryland 21157

Copyright © 1904 John Herbert Claiborne

— Publisher's Notice —
In reprints such as this, it is often not possible to remove blemishes from the original. We feel the contents of this book warrant its reissue despite these blemishes and hope you will agree and read it with pleasure.

International Standard Book Numbers
Paperbound: 978-0-7884-0010-0
Clothbound: 978-0-7884-9261-7

To my only Sister,

Mrs. Mary Augusta Thomas,

of Marion, Alabama,

who as comrade of my early years will read with more interest than others this record of personal reminiscences, and who, as to the rest, will doubtless prove my most lenient critic, this volume is affectionately inscribed.

CONTENTS

CHAPTER I. - - - PERSONAL AND FOR MY PERSONAL FRIENDS.

My Birth—The Character of the People Amongst Whom I Was Born—At School at Leasburg, North Carolina—My Mother—At Ebenezer Academy—I Attend Randolph-Macon College—Emory & Henry College—Again at Randolph-Macon—I Matriculate at University of Virginia—To Philadelphia, Where I Take Diplomas From Jefferson Medical College, the Pennsylvania Hospital, and the Philadelphia Obstetrical Institute—On Staff of Jefferson Medical College—I Return to Virginia and Look for a Location—Decide on Petersburg—Some First Experiences, ... 17

CHAPTER II. - - - - - - - - PETERSBURG IN THE FIFTIES.

The City as I Found It—Some Early History—The Population and a Comparison—The Society—The Fourth of July—Hospitality and Liberality—The Business Interests—Growth of the City—Its Hotels and Taverns—A Professional adventure—Principal Resources and Finances—Its Municipal Government—The Churches and their Pastors—The Colored Congregations—The Press of Petersburg in 1850 and Later—The Schools and Teachers—The Petersburg Bar and Some Reminiscences of Its Honored Members—The Physicians of Petersburg—Recollections of Many Notable Members of the Profession Before and During My Time—Petersburg's Rise After the War, ... 40

CHAPTER III. - - - - POLITICS OF THE ANTE-BELLUM PERIOD.

Politics in the Past—The Two Parties of the Day—The Alliance of the Whig and Know-Nothing Parties to Fight the Democratic Party—The Wreck of the Whig Party—

My First Vote Cast With the Democratic Party—Nominated by the Democratic Party for the House of Delegates—An Unwilling and Unexpected Launch Upon the Sea of Politics—Everything Goes Democratic—Some Account of Events in the Exciting Sectional Drama Leading to the Outbreak of Hostilities—A Nefarious Mission—The John Brown Raid the First Gun of the Fight—I Decline Re-election, but Am Renominated Against My Wish and Elected—Serve in 1857-'58 and Again in 1859-'60—An Account of Events and Measures Immediately Preceding the War—My Position Made Clear—Speeches in the Senate and Elsewhere—The Nominations of the National Conventions—The Secession Convention—The Peace Conference—The Call For Troops From Virginia by the Government the Last Straw—The Union Men of Virginia—A Visit to Washington and Some Things Heard and Seen—Opinions of Eminent Men North and South—Governor Letcher's Proclamation, ... 128

CHAPTER IV. - - - - - - - - - - - - - The War.

The Fourth Virginia Battalion Receives Orders—Quartered in Norfolk—The Companies and Officers—I Accompany the Battalion as Captain and Assistant Surgeon—Am Again Elected to the Senate—Ordered to Take My Seat by the Secretary of War—Obey the Order and Resign, and Apply For Orders For the Army—An Interview—Ordered to Open Hospitals in Petersburg and Made Surgeon in Charge—Appointed Post Surgeon—How Some Supplies Were Acquired—Events Preceding Siege of Petersburg—Arrival of the Enemy—Incidents of the Siege—Ordered to Remove the Hospital Patients and Correspondence with General Lee—The "Fiasco of the War"—An Adventure Before the Lines of the Enemy—"In Vinculis"—The Crater—General Mahone's Part in the Crater Affair—I Am Visited By a Shell at Night—More Incidents of Our Great Generals, And Another of Mahone in Particular—What Manner of Man Was He? What Manner of Men Were They?—Five Forks—Evacuation and Events Immediately Following, ... 191

Contents. xi

CHAPTER V. - - - THE SURRENDER AND EVENTS FOLLOWING.

The 2nd of April, 1865—I Prepare to Evacuate—A Pathetic Scene—I Note the Absence of My Dog Jack—A "Borrowed" horse—On to Amelia Court House—An Invitation From Mahone—Romulus Given His "Free Papers"—A Brave Quartermaster—I Lose All My Possessions Through a Yankee Cavalry Raid—The Asset of a Broken Concern—"A Swig From the Same Canteen"—The Best Forager I Ever Saw—Signs of Demoralization—Fall Into the Hands of the Enemy—I Give Away a Pair of Spurs—Interview With General Devlin—An Invitation to a Much-Needed Breakfast—I Show the "Sign of Distress"—Ordered To Be Paroled—A Night Adventure—Mahone Again and a Parole Blank—An Inhospitable Reception and the Very Opposite—A Question of Boots—With My Wife and Children Once More—A disagreeable incident—The Finale of The Old Regime, ... 259

CHAPTER VI. - - - - - - - EVENTS FOLLOWING THE WAR.

My Dog Again—I Am Warned to Leave Petersburg—Make A Purchase and Start for Louisburg, N. C.—Back Again and to Work—The Condition of the South Before the War An Anomaly of Content and Happiness—The Military Government—The Carpet-Bag Government and Its Curse—Opinions of Some Eminent Northerners On the Reconstruction Period—Will History Reproduce Itself in the Philippines—The Evidence of Robbery, ... 311

APPENDIX.

The Last Fight at Five Forks—Mr. Granier—What Manner of Man Was He—In the Interest of Justice to Mahone—Old Blandford Church—Personal Ancestry—American Bastiles—Dahlgren's Raid—"Who Fired the First Gun?" 330

PREFACE

In February, 1900, the author received a request, through Mr. F. B. Sanborn, of Massachusetts, to read a paper on the "Changes in the Sociology of Old Virginia During the Last Half of the Last Century," before the National Sociological Society of America, to convene in Washington on May 2, 1900. He acknowledged the compliment, and accepted the invitation; but circumstances made it impracticable for him to fill the engagement.

In gathering data for the fulfilment of that task, the author filed many of the facts recited in the first chapter of this volume. Becoming more interested in the subject, he continued to write, until reminiscences grew and multiplied, and crowded one upon another, and the whole scope and design of the original intention of the writer was lost in that law of association which the poet puts into classic verse:

> "Lulled in the countless chambers of the brain,
> Our thoughts are linked by many a hidden chain,
> Awake but one, and lo! what myraids rise!
> Each stamps its image as the other flies."*

In the meantime the author saw that his reminiscences had run, in length at least, into a book; and as custom ordains that every book should have a preface, he followed the precedent. In the preface, as is usual, he furnishes his readers with the reasons which induced him to appear before them, and, unbidden, to parade his wares.

---

* Rogers, "Pleasures of Memory," Part II.

Primarily, he wishes to say that he wrote these "Reminiscences," in good part, to please himself—*Cacoethes scribendi* if the reader chooses so to characterize it.

Secondarily, he desires to publish the book for the information of his children and grandchildren, and in their interest to record some account of his early life, as well as some of the revolutionary scenes and times in which his long and eventful life was cast; and to some extent to give a rehearsal of the part which he played in the exciting drama.

He confesses that since the commencement of his task the wish has grown that he could catch the ear of the great public of the present generation, that he might impress their minds with some lasting memory of the heroism of their fathers, and of the heroism of their mothers, during four years of a cruel and relentless war, waged to their very doors, and of the patience and fortitude with which the former, when disarmed, bore for eight years the contumely, humiliation, and oppression of the carpetbagger and the scalawag.

And now, once and for all, he disclaims any personal bitterness or any rankling in his heart of a revenge which he is content to leave to Him who says "vengeance is mine."

For the Northern soldier who struck for the right as he saw it, and who leveled his blows at men, not at women and children, and who, when victor, extended his hand in help to his fallen foe and generously divided his own thin rations with him, the author has no feeling but that of honor and admiration of his manhood. But for the soldier who boasted that he had "cut a swath through two States a mile in breadth, marked by the chimneys of burned mansions and desolated homes;" for the soldier who proclaimed that a "crow flying over the fairest portion of the Valley of Virginia would have

Preface

to carry his rations with him to avoid starvation;" for the soldier who ordered that "any grain left as food [for the helpless inhabitants] should be scattered in the fields and trampled in the dust;" for the soldier who made chloroform and opium contraband of war, and directed all medicine to be swept away or confiscated when found in a Southern home; for the soldier who ordered the capture and imprisonment of the unarmed surgeon, refusing to leave his post and giving humane help to friend and foe alike; for the soldier who could drive out from their homes the women and children of a whole city, and send them into the wilderness without food or shelter in the midst of the rigors of winter, and turn a deaf ear to their cries—for all these the author feels a contempt which words cannot measure, and an undying wish to pillory to posterity some names that to-day desecrate the Temple of Fame.

And as to the present government of the United States, he recognizes and accepts the change in the construction of the Constitution—a construction born of arms and not of law, but he took his oath of allegiance to the same, and he has kept the faith; and, more, he has given hostages of his fealty: he sent a son, a volunteer and an officer of the line, to the Spanish-American War, and has a grandson who, in the Philippines and elsewhere, has been upholding for several years, as an officer in the Regular Army, the flag of the tradition of the "Land of the free, and the home of the brave"—and as long as it represents the tradition, so long may it wave.

As to the style of the text and its literary character, whilst he feels that no author has a right to foist upon the public crude and incorrect writing, he owes it to himself to say that these pages were written mostly after the fatigue of days of labor, and at night when others were asleep; and when, perhaps, some of his readers may think that he ought to have been also. "What I have writ I have writ"—would it were worthier.

And as to the criticism which may follow his work.—He has reached an age where applause does not greatly exalt, nor abuse depress. He is content to have written the truth as he saw it and found it, and recognizes his responsibility; and, following the words of a better man,* in writing of a different matter, he adopts the somewhat defiant family motto which was copied from the entrance hall of Marischal College, Aberdeen: "Thay haif said: Quhat say thay: Lat thame say."

---

* Geo. S. Keith, in Preface to a "Plea for a Simpler Life."

Seventy-five Years in Old Virginia

CHAPTER I

Personal and For My Personal Friends.

My Birth—The Character of the People Amongst Whom I was Born—At School at Leasburg, North Carolina—My Mother—At Ebenezer Academy—I Attend Randolph-Macon College—Emory & Henry College—Again at Randolph-Macon—I Matriculate at University of Virginia—To Philadelphia Where I Take Diplomas from Jefferson Medical College, the Pennsylvania Hospital, and the Philadelphia Obstetrical Institute—On Staff of Jefferson Medical College—I Return to Virginia and Look For a Location—Decide on Petersburg—Some First Experiences.

I was born in Brunswick County, Virginia, on the 10th of March, 1828. So says the record in the old Family Bible; and it must be correct, as the birth of the first boy in the house was an event of note at that day, and it is not probable that there would be a mistake. It is true that the law of primogeniture and entail had been abolished for perhaps a third of a century, as incompatible with the genius and unfavorable to the simplicity of republican institutions; but enough of English custom and English thought still leavened social life in the Old Dominion to cause the first son to be considered the master of the house and the representative of the family. Whilst it is not probable, therefore, that a mistake was made in the registry, yet it is due to truth to say that it does not accord with traditional history. I was told, as far back as I can remember, that I was born on the day and at the hour of a very severe earthquake which traversed this portion of the State in the early twenties—an earthquake so severe that in some places there were no inconsiderable chasms made in the earth. But this occurred in 1829, instead of 1828; and there is no record, traditional or otherwise, of an earthquake at all in 1828. I accept, however, the record. Yet if the seismic convulsions occurring about that time augured anything of the troubled and tempestuous life which was awaiting me, I should rather incline to tradition.

The section of the country in which I was born was known as "The Red Oak Neighborhood." This was about fifteen miles north of Lawrenceville, the county seat, and was distinguished as a locality for the wealth, culture, refinement, and hospitality of the families who occupied it. They were literally the F. F. V's—a term which had not been used up to that time as a covert sneer, and, as it has been so often used since, to decry a race of men whom their critics would have us, of this day, believe were a pretentious and bloated aristocracy, resting their claims to eminence upon ancestral merit. They were large slave-holders, owning large plantations, which had been their heritage for years, and which gave with guaranteed wealth a leisure that furnished opportunity for culture, a culture that insured refinement and made the gentleman. The owning of slaves established and cultivated the habit of command, and fitted the master to lead—as the Southern man did ever lead—in society, in politics, and in war.

The F. F. V's, descendants of the cavalier* elements which settled that State and wrested it from the savage by their prowess, introduced a leaven in the body politic, which not only bred a high order of civilization at home, but spread throughout the Southern and Western States, as the Virginian, moved by love of adventure or desire of preferment, migrated into the

---

*See Appendix.

Personal and for my Personal Friends

new and adjoining territories. And from this sneered-at stock was bred the six millions of Southrons who for four long years maintained unequal war with thirty millions of Northern hybrids, backed by a hireling soldiery brought from the whole world to put down constitutional liberty—a war waged to free four million of servile blacks and to enslave six million of proud and cultivated whites; a war waged to place the foot of the menial upon the neck of the master; an unequal war, in which the same Southron stock struck undaunted for honor and the right, until its cohorts of starved and ragged heroes perished in their own annihilation. And this same stock, after the disaster of a defeat worse than death, and a decade of years of humiliation and torture, sprang up again, Phoenix-like, from the ashes of its desolation; and thirty years after, the same despised and damned stock sits again in the Halls of the Congress of a nation that had affixed on it the stigma of Felon, and its brigadiers are called to command armies which were sent to suppress it as a traitorous faction.

This is a digression. But I make no apology for it. I am proud to record that I was born and reared amongst such a people; and I regard this as the highest heritage that I can hand down to my children and my children's children.

From my grandfather, Captain John Herbert Claiborne, who, as a member of the "Surry Troop," a company of young gentlemen who armed and equipped themselves, and fought without pay in the famed legion of "Light Horse Harry" Lee, I learned the story of war and drank in the lesson that "resistance to tyrants is obedience to God." Little did he surmise that his grandsons, under Robert E. Lee, the son of his old commander, would ever be called to draw their swords in defense of home, and of the holy soil of Virginia—

assailed not by alien hands, but by the hired hordes of
a government which had been founded on principles
enunciated by Virginia statesmen and established by
the prowess of Virginia soldiers.

But to return.   Until nine years of age I lived on my
father's plantation the life of a Virginia boy,—roving,
hunting, fishing, riding, driving cattle,—always followed by two or three negro boys of about the same age,
my satellites and companions, partners in any mischief,
and with whom I cheerfully divided any good fortune
which came to me in the way of cakes, fruit, or other
edibles. Thus was established that good feeling and
mutual trust which characterized the relationship of
master and slave. The negro of that day was proud
of his master, devoted to his interests, and would lay
down his life for him or his family.

The doors of the mansion house were rarely locked
at night, and its inmates were as safe from alarm or
intrusion as if surrounded by a cordon of police. What
a travesty the present condition of things presents,
since freedom has come with its blessings of Northern
civilization and education!

When I became nine years of age my father concluded that it was best for me to break up this free and
semi-nomadic life, and to send me from home to
school. I had picked up the rudiments of education in
a female school which had been established at home
for the education of my two sisters, and which was
taught by two Northern ladies, one a Miss Parsons, of
Massachusetts, and the other a Miss Draper, of New
York. Miss Draper was a sister of Dr. Draper, who
subsequently became the famous professor and savant
of the University of New York, but who, at that time,
was Professor of Chemistry at Hampden-Sidney College in this State.

At that date it was almost the invariable custom to employ female teachers from the North, as Southern ladies were debarred by social status from engaging in such work. My sister's education having been completed just at this era in my life, the school at home was adjourned *sine die*—another reason which made it imperative that I should seek other tutelage.

There were several male schools or academies in my native county,—schools long established and of good repute,—one of them, the Ebenezer Academy, founded by Bishop Asbury (and to which, as will be seen, I finally drifted); but my father, for some reason, doubtless satisfactory, but which I never understood, selected a large boarding-school in Western North Carolina, in Leasburg, Caswell County, and taught by an excellent scholar and gentleman, the Rev. Lorenzo Lea. And to this school, on the 1st of January, 1838, two months before I entered on my 10th year, I was taken by my father and committed to the Rev. Mr. Lea, with many charges to him as to the care and management of his hopeful son, and much good and varied advice to me as to my conduct and behavior.

I had never left home before, or slept out of my mother's chamber; was known as a "mother's boy," and was petted and spoiled by her and my sisters, and colored mammy, and, barring my father, who alone held sway over me, considered myself Lord Proprietor of the house and its happenings. Only he who has jumped from such surroundings into the dormitory of a big boarding-school for boys can imagine the cold and icy plunge which engulfed my babyhood!

Well, after one session's buffeting I came out of that bath no longer a baby, but a boy, almost a man; if not in strength, yet in the wisdom of this world's ways, and —shall I add?—in wickedness. One lesson I learned, however, and for which I shall be ever grateful: It

taught me, in the future that awaited my manhood—
a most exciting and eventful future—to fall on my feet.
And whether in peace, in politics, in war, or in prison,
I always managed to stand on my feet and to keep my
head above water.

I was utterly ignorant of what awaited me "at
school," and left home with a lighter heart than I would
have carried had I been aware of all that was before
me. Besides, I was to ride a race-horse all the way to
school, and that was the climax of my boyish ambition.
My father, as was the habit of many gentlemen of Virginia of that day, bred racing stock, and he promised
me, as an inducement to go, that I might ride a beautiful Lusborough filly,—of an imported sire,—an animal
of great spirit, but kindly and gentle, and a splendid
riding-horse. I was a young rider, but accustomed to
horses, and to horseback exercise, from early recollection, and my father knew of my staying qualities and
had no fear of my mount. He accompanied me in his
gig—a two-wheeled concern, a homely analogue of the
cart of to-day—upon which was strapped my little
trunk, in which my mother, with many tears and misgivings, had packed my clothes and belongings. The
butler (known then as dining-room servant) followed
on another horse—both to add dignity to the cavalcade
and to render any attention or service that we might
require.

It was more than an hundred miles from my father's
to Leasburg, the place of our destination, and it was in
January, with the winter roads of mud and water; but
we made our journey in three days, not uncomfortably,
and to me without fatigue. Indeed the trip to me was
enjoyable, and the memory of that ride lingers amongst
my pleasant things of the past. But not until I had
been conducted from the village tavern, in Leasburg,
to the boarding department of the academy, and saw

my father file away on the road which looked toward home, followed by the butler leading my filly riderless, did the utter desolation of my condition strike me. I was no longer a man, but a child again, as I was only a child in form and in years, and I gave vent for the first time to a child's feelings and to a child's tears. But this only continued a little while, and it was the last paroxysm of grief to which I gave exhibition. As young as I was, I soon discovered that one's sorrow was his own, and that there was no place and no pity for such demonstration amongst the bright or busy or bad boys about me. I knew that with such show of myself I should be called "baby," and I would "have died and made no sign" before I would have asked or accepted consolation or borne that soubriquet for an hour.

One object which my father had in taking me so far from home was to take me from my "mother's apron strings," as he called it, and to wean me from my dependence on, and my adoration of, her. In that object he failed. My love for her was intensified, if such a thing were possible; she was never out of my thoughts by day or my dreams by night. I never laid down upon my bed, or even stood at rest upon the play-grounds, but that I religiously turned my face in the direction of that Mecca, that home which her life and her presence consecrated. And I looked forward to meeting her, when the session of the school ended and I should be permitted to go back, as the one idea of happiness which nothing could crown and nothing could displace. I wish to record right here that always thereafter, though life brought me success, and a loving and beloved wife, and a devoted family, and applause and honor from men, yet nothing ever relit in my heart the fire which went out one tempestuous night in January just twenty years from that date, when, laying in my arms, she breathed her last; and again I wish to record here, that whatever has come to me since of pleasure, of interest, of profit, of advancement, there has always been something lacking which life could not fill. Even the physical world has been changed beyond reparation, and places that I knew and connected with her life have fallen out of my existence, and perished as islands sunken in some unknown sea. Of all the precious memories which hallow my past, her last words linger as fresh to-day as when they fell from her dying lips: "My son, when I close my eyes to-night I do not care to awaken again, and before I sleep I wish to say to you, that as boy or man you have never grieved or distressed me." When the morning came the tempest was over, and the sun revealed all that was left of the most beautiful, the most affectionate, and the most unselfish woman I ever knew; but it brought none of the old joyous light to me* From that hour I have kept and cherished in my heart the hope that sometime, somewhere in the Great Beyond, I shall yet meet her again, and once more hold her again to my breast.

But whilst this love of mother and of home was perhaps morbid, as some might think, I soon made friends of my schoolmates and enjoyed their association. The boys were like boys are everywhere—disposed to lord it over the smaller ones and the new scholars, but they never were guilty of the foolish and cowardly system of hazing such as prevails at the Virginia Military Institute and at West Point, and some other State-fed and self-asserting establishments. I never suffered an indignity to be put upon me without repelling it to the best of my ability, and though I always came off worsted, as the smallest and weakest boy in school, yet I

---

*See Appendix.

always came off likewise with the decided respect of my adversary, and after a little while had no further personal affrays. Indeed, in a very short time my friends grew in numbers and in grace, and as it was always my pleasure to meet them with courtesy and kindness, I was soon dubbed with the soubriquet of "Gentleman John Claiborne." I had forgotten this complimentary appellation until, some two years ago, I saw an article in a Raleigh paper, reminiscences of one of the "Old Boys" of the Leasburg Academy, in which he referred to me by that name.

When my first session of six months was ended, my father sent a servant and horse for me, and I turned my face homeward—no longer a child, though only ten years and a few months old—with a heart so happy at the prospect of again meeting my mother, that my joy was almost delirious. The first night after leaving Leasburg I stopped at Roxborough, North Carolina, and riding up to the hotel (tavern), called for rooms for self and servant. The old gentleman who kept the hostelry was sitting on the long piazza, which seemed an organic part of every tavern of that day. He did not seem at all overcome by my presence, or abashed by my precocious audacity, but received me more than civilly, and, asking me to be seated near him, entered into conversation with me. I can not recall after sixty years the general subjects which engaged our attention, but one remark of his is fresh in my mind, as upon that soft summer afternoon in June, on my asking for some water, he startled me by saying that he had "never tasted a drop of water in twenty years"; that "water gave him the headache," and he was "compelled to drink whiskey in the place of it." His face attested the accuracy of his statement, and I was not surprised to hear some few years afterwards that even whiskey could not relieve his headache, and that the village tavern had fallen into other hands and my village boniface had fallen into the grave.

But another incident indelibly fixes that visit to Roxborough in my mind. Going out on the street (there was but one street in Roxborough at that time) I noticed on the counter of one of the stores a collection of hats, one of them quite tall and stylish-looking to me, and it at once occurred to me that that hat would not only add manly grace to my general get-up, but that it would be a revelation to the folks at home when they saw me approaching with so grand a head-piece. But to give completeness to the picture I should explain. It was the fashion of the boys at the Leasburg Academy to wear their hair cut short behind—shingled, it would be called now—and long in front, coming down, when parted, below the ears, sometimes as far as the collar. These were called "soap locks," the name being derived from the saponaceous material which was not infrequently applied to paste them in position. Some of the fellows had full ambrosial locks worthy of Jove, and were the envy of the school. Not so, all of them—mine were thin and yellow, and obedient only to generous pasting. It was above these locks that I had set the crowning grace of my tall chapeau. So attired, I rode up on the evening of that day, after a day's journey, to a hotel in Boydton, Virginia, on my way home. But my mother was at the hotel awaiting me, having come partly with that object, and partly that my two sisters, just turned out, might attend the commencement exercises of Randolph-Macon College, which was then established near Boydton.

I will pass over the first glad greeting with which she received me and held me to her heart. This was in the public-room of the hotel. Almost immediately she ushered me into her private apartments, and, holding me off at arm's length, with a countenance in which a sense of horror and a sense of the ludicrous seemed striving for the mastery, she exclaimed: "My son, my son, where did you get that hat? And that hair?" Without a moment's delay, and with as much gentleness, perhaps, as the occasion called for, she removed the hat from my head. Calling for a pair of scissors, the hair soon followed the hat—my precious, long-trained locks. What became of hat or hair I never knew, for I never saw either afterwards.

After adjusting other parts of my attire more in accordance with what she deemed suitable for a boy of ten years of age than for a man of twenty-five,—in which it seems I had glorified myself with a view of impressing the natives at home with my rapid strides to manhood,—she presented me to her friends, in evident pride of her boy. But for myself, I must confess that I felt shorn of my gains; and as I contemplated my image in the mirror I recalled the picture of a young rooster that I had seen plucked of his feathers and slinking away to the barnyard.

After my vacation was ended (the vacation at that time covered four weeks), I returned to Leasburg, where I spent two more sessions of five months each without incident worth recording. At the expiration of that time, my health, which was never strong, became very feeble, and my father entered me as a scholar at the Ebenezer Academy, an institution to which I have before referred. This was five miles distant from home, and I rode horseback every morning, carrying my dinner in a little basket and my horse's dinner in a wallet or bag which was tied behind my saddle, returning every afternoon after school was "let out," as it was expressed at that day. As I was very fond of horseback riding, this arrangement was not only very agreeable to me, but was conducive to my health, which soon became quite robust.

For the first two sessions of the school after I entered it, Mr. Hogan was the teacher; an old Irishman, of fine classical education, and a good teacher and disciplinarian. He was a true believer of the old school in corporal punishment, not only for disobedience and mischief, but when he failed to impress a lesson on a boy's mind as he thought he should, he applied the birch without fail—to that other portion of the body which has not been considered the seat of intellect.

After two sessions of my stay at the Ebenezer, Mr. Hogan left, and the school was taken charge of by a gentleman named Thompkins Rice. Mr. Rice was a Virginian and a native of Brunswick County, but he had been abroad for many years, and was educated at Oxford, England. He was also a fine scholar, and, with the exception of Prof. R. E. Rogers, and Prof. J. S. Davis, to whom, after some years, I recited at the University of Virginia, the best teacher that I ever met. He was, moreover, a very genial man, and was greatly beloved by the boys; but he never abated a jot of his dignity. He also was a strict disciplinarian, and insisted upon perfect obedience to all rules of conduct and of study, and announced in the beginning that he would not tolerate a dunce or a dullard. If he appointed a task—and I must confess he was not a hard master in the number or length of the lessons—he saw that the task was completed perfectly; and if it was not, the boy who failed knew what to expect and his anticipations were certainly realized. Mr. Rice never lost his temper or his equilibrium, but with great grace and good humor he could plant a birch, without ever missing the mark, upon that portion of a boy's anatomy which the short jackets of that day seemed to expose for the especial purpose.

Personal and for my Personal Friends   29

After two years, Mr. Rice succumbed to the charms of a handsome widow, whose ample means permitted him to retire from the chair of the pedagogue, and the Academy was again left without a teacher.

Our next master was a Mr. Lanier, a mild-mannered gentleman, no great scholar, but a good teacher—a man who made himself a companion to the boys in their sports, who won their love and ruled by love. Under his domination the rod ceased to appear.

At the expiration of two sessions I think another change was made in the teachers, but at that time, January, 1843, I was sent to Randolph-Macon College to enter the freshman class, half advanced.

I should add to this part of my narration that about the year 1840 or 1841 a young relative of mine, John R. Claiborne, having lost his father and mother, he, with his sister, S. Josephine Claiborne, several years younger than himself, was adopted into my father's family, and John Claiborne attended the Ebenezer Academy with me and went with me from there to college. They were the children of Dr. Jas. B. Claiborne, of Brunswick County, who was not very closely related to my father; but Dr. Claiborne married my mother's sister, Jane Weldon, of Roanoke, and these children were my mother's nephew and niece. They were to me as brother and sister. John, when he grew up to manhood, went to Central America, and died there in two years after he left home, at San Juan del Sur, on the Pacific Coast, in the service of the Nicarauguan Transit Company. Josie lived to take care of, and to rear, my children after the death of their own mother, and, after they were grown, to comfort my father in his second widowhood, and until he died, in extreme old age, at my home in Petersburg. She survived him many years, and died under my roof, which had been her home virtually for

twenty years, endeared to me as a sister, faithful and
affectionate, and to my children as a mother, loving and
dutiful—the only mother whom they ever remembered.

Our life at the Ebenezer Academy was rather quiet
and humdrum. One enlivening incident is impressed
upon my mind quite indelibly. There were some six or
eight boys who rode on horseback to school, retaining
their horses at the Academy and riding home after
school was "let out" in the afternoon. This number
made a very respectable company of cavalry, which we
organized and trained as such. But in an evil hour,
and led by that spirit of mischief which is born in every
boy, we charged the infantry of the school one day as
they formed for drill or play, and routed them with such
serious consequences, riding over several of them, that
a meeting of the Board of Trustees was called and we
were disciplined. My father was president of the Board
of Trustees, but though a stern man himself, he had a
keen eye for the picturesquely ludicrous, had been a
lover of fun in his young days, and seeing more to
amuse than to condemn in the heartrending details of
the encounter, we escaped any serious infliction. Our
cavalry company was disbanded, however, and we rode
no more in company of fours, nor fell any more upon
the flanks of the infantry. But how many of our little
band, twenty years afterwards, rode with Fitz Lee, and
with Stuart, and with Rosser,—rode upon the serried
squares of alien marauders on their homes and their
country,—I know not. As the war waged I would meet
one of them sometimes, with the same firm seat in the
saddle, the same spirit of dash and deviltry—but how
many were left to tell to their children the story of
battle and of bivouac **is not** recorded. I only know
that I can not recall a **single** living one to-day. As far
as I can learn, every one has responded to the last Long

Roll, and every one has answered *adsum*—here—to the black sergeant—Death.

At the termination of the session of Randolph-Macon College, in June, 1845, my health had again become so impaired that my father concluded that it was best for me not to return to college. But as my health improved somewhat after a month's vacation, he sent me to Emory & Henry College, in Washington County—not only on account of the salubrity of the climate, but as that institution had been conducted as a labor school, he wished me to combine manual labor with the course of the institution. At the time of my matriculation the manual labor feature of the school had been abandoned, and I only remained there about three months, and returned home. I made some warm friends, however, amongst them two young gentlemen from Alabama, named Clayton, one of whom became a general in the Confederate Army, but with whom I was never fortunate enough to meet. They were my room-mates.

It may be of interest to note that it took me, at that time, three days and nights of continuous staging to make the trip. It was not a dream of that day that an iron horse would climb the Blue Ridge and Allegheny Mountains and speed his way at the rate of forty miles an hour.

At the commencement of the session of 1846 at Randolph-Macon College my health was so much improved that I again matriculated, and after two years was graduated with the degree of A. B. at the head of my class. The faculty, being unable to determine upon whom the first honor should be conferred,—Mr. J. C. Granbery and myself having stood with equal grade for two years,—settled the matter by lot. He drew the longest straw, and, I may remark, has kept it ever since. For some years he has been a distinguished divine and a

Bishop of the Methodist Episcopal Church, South. As far as I can learn, he and I are the only surviving members of the graduating class of 1848.

After graduation came the momentous question of a choice of profession—a question that gave me great trouble. My tastes, my inclination, and my ambition led me to prefer the law. But my father, who had been educated at William & Mary College for the bar, and had practised law up to middle life, and laid it aside after having achieved success, for reasons which seemed pertinent and powerful to him, bitterly opposed my following the same profession, urgently advising me to study medicine.

In obedience to his wishes, therefore, I matriculated at the University of Virginia in October, 1848, and took the medical ticket. I had by no means made up my mind to practise medicine, but I was young enough to give a year to the study of the profession, and I knew that by earnest application I could take the degree of M. D. in that time, which would not only be quite an addendum to a polite education but would greatly gratify my parents. I succeeded in my effort, and in July, 1849, was graduated with the degree of M. D. At that day a student was not asked how long he had studied medicine, or if he had studied it at all, but at the expiration of the session an examination was placed upon the boards, and the candidate for graduation was required to write his replies to the questions. If he could answer correctly a certain per centum he was given his degree. And, forsooth, he was entitled to it. His knowledge of anatomy, of physiology, of materia medica, of chemistry, of medical jurisprudence, and of the theory of practise was tested and drained to the last drop; and the little piece of parchment—diploma —which was presented him, if successful, was a ready witness to his proficiency anywhere thereafter that he chose to take it. Of course there were few graduates —many throwing up the game in discouragement, as not worth the candle. Eleven, I think, were graduated in the class of seventy-two students of which I was a member.

From the University of Virginia I went to Philadelphia, spending the remainder of the year 1849, and a good part of 1850-'51, in seeking practical knowledge of the profession. I took a diploma from the Jefferson Medical College, from the Pennsylvania Hospital, and from the Philadelphia Obstetrical Institute, but I had no more trouble with examinations.

After graduating at the Jefferson Medical College, Dr. Thomas D. Mutter, Professor of Surgery in that institution, one of the most skilful surgeons and most accomplished gentlemen I ever knew, offered me a place on the staff of the surgical clinic of the college, one of my confreres being Dr. J. M. DaCosta, a young Spaniard or Cuban, who subsequently settled in Philadelphia, and rose to the head of the profession. I had just taken my place when my father summoned me home. He had met with unexpected reverses, and as I had one profession there was no time to consider the question of acquiring another, but pressing occasion to put into practise one which had cost me no little money and the elements of which I had pretty well mastered. So it is "that there is a divinity which shapes our ends, rough hew them as we may."

The next earnest and important question was, where to locate. That was a matter involving not only life's labor, but life's success or life's failure, possibly. Certain gentlemen in the town of Farmville and its vicinity, moved by what consideration I never knew, proposed to guarantee me the sum of twelve hundred dollars a year if I would settle in that section. One of these was Mr. Joseph E. Venable, who afterwards moved to

Petersburg, and who was one of our most upright and
honored citizens, and, to his death, one of my best patrons and most faithful friends. I visited Farmville and
called on and thanked my stranger friends—for they
were all strangers to me; but I had pretty well determined to settle in some city, and the choice lay between Petersburg and Norfolk, as I had more friends
and acquaintances in those cities than in any others of
the Commonwealth. I visited Norfolk, which about
that time was a sleepy burgh of some 12,000 to 15,000
people, lacking in enterprise, but abounding in social
pleasures and distinguished for its hospitality and high
living. I had letters to a Doctor Andrews, whom I
found was not only considered the Nestor of the profession in that city, but almost the profession itself. I
had never heard one man referred to so universally as
head and shoulders above all others in the same line,
and I suspect he deserved the distinction.

Unfortunately I met with quite a severe accident a
few days after getting to Norfolk, and was compelled
to trespass upon his time and consult his skill. He impressed me as a man thoroughly conversant with both
medicine and surgery (I had recourse to him as a surgeon), but I was especially struck with the simplicity
of his manner and of his treatment. In that perhaps
consisted his true worth as a doctor, and to that he
owed his undisputed and distinguished success.

I had two very good friends—old college chums—
in Norfolk, Prof. O. H. P. Corprew and Mr. E. T.
Hardy. Both received me kindly and hospitably, but
I concluded that I would not like Norfolk as a place of
residence. A fortunate conclusion. Four years afterwards Norfolk was swept with a fearful epidemic of
yellow fever, more than half the local physicians dying,

paying the penalty of their faithfulness with their lives. One of my classmates at the University and in Philadelphia, Dr. Junius Briggs, fell an early victim.

After leaving Norfolk I concluded to locate in Petersburg, and on the 1st day of January, 1851, I left my father's house in Brunswick County, and, making the trip of forty-five miles in one day, drove up to Powell's Hotel in the evening and registered my name and "at home." I came with two horses, driving one given me by my father, to a fine sulky, which had been made for me a few months before, costing $100, by Mr. Jno. H. Atkinson, whose carriage factory was located on Sycamore Street, just where Lewis & Bro. now have their stand. The other horse was ridden by my body-servant, Preston, a fine young negro man, given me by my grandfather. I placed my horses in Ragland's Livery Stable, which occupied the locality where the China Palace and adjoining store now stand, and next to Powell's Hotel, which stood on the site the Iron Front building recently occupied. I engaged board for myself and servant at the above-named hostelry, then kept by Mr. Wm. N. Friend, the father of our esteemed citizen, Mr. Alfred Friend, Sr.—kept with prodigal munificence of store and larder which characterized the old tavern, where I made my pleasant home until two years afterwards, when I married and made my own home.

A few days afterwards I rented an office over the store of Todd & Christian, druggists, then occupying the store at the corner of Sycamore and Lombard streets, now occupied by Mr. John Trusheim as a confectionery and lodging-house. In doing so I bought out Dr. R. M. Anderson, who wished me better luck than he had had, saying that he had not been able to make a living there. This, I confess, was discouraging, as the doctor was a man not only of some experience in the profession, but a man of more than ordinary merit and acquirement. He moved to Dinwiddie County soon afterwards, where he was more successful, accumulating quite a competency to cheer and support the ripe old age to which he attained.

After three or four months of patient occupancy of my quarters, my clientele did not crowd my reception-room, as I had vainly imagined would be the case; and I began to fear that Dr. Anderson's fate awaited me.

I found it convenient, in order to eke out my failing finances, to sell one horse, as two horses were only a luxury, not a necessity demanded by my overcrowded work. Then, after another short interval I concluded that the constant attention of my servant in the ante-room was scarcely entirely necessary for the reception of the callers, whom I succeeded in apprising of my presence or absence by an ingenious reversible card—the invention, I suspect, of some impecunious person. On one side of this card, posted upon the door, was written "IN," on the other "OUT," with the hour of return noted. This device was so happy that I dispensed with the servant, hiring him out, thereby not only feeding him, but utilizing the wages of his hire for my own daily bread.

At the expiration of six months, reading one morning in the Scriptures that "a horse was a vain thing for safety," I began, in a moment of abundant leisure, to make a sort of an exegesis of the text, and, amongst other ideas suggested by reflection, it occurred to me that a horse was also a vain thing for a man to keep whose provender was exhausted. I could not send my horse to follow my servant, and make his own living, for two reasons: Firstly, he had a glass eye, by which he became generally well known, but which would not have militated against his usefulness had he not—secondly—manifested to all observers the most conspicuous habit of insubordination, so that it became the general remark that he was a horse that would allow no man to ride or drive him except the doctor who owned him. I sent him, therefore, to the country, to my father's, to spend the summer, my father kindly offering to take care of him until the exigencies of my practise demanded his recall. I did not send for him again until the following winter. Practise began to improve, and in addition I formed a co-partnership with Dr. R. L. Madison, an old college-mate of mine, who had settled in Petersburg some months after I did, and between us we felt that, jointly, we could bear the expense of a horse. But we only kept him a short time. During his long idleness he had "waxed fat," and was more incorrigible than ever in his deviltry, and I had to sell him. I sold him to a gentleman who was engaged, I think, in hauling railroad iron, but Glass Eye had made up his mind that he would submit to no such humiliating service as the drawing of a dray, and like an illustrious character in Scripture (Deuteronomy 32: 15) who had "waxed fat" before him, he "kicked," and cutting a large artery in his leg, lost his life.

However, we soon secured a more docile Rosinante, business improved rapidly, and we felt that we were on the up grade. But as Dr. Madison and I were only together for a year or so, and now are about to part company, I can not leave this part of my story without testifying that a more honest, faithful, loyal friend, and a more genial, generous, great-hearted, and accomplished gentleman I never met. He was a great-nephew of President Madison, of the proudest and purest of old Virginia stock, modest and sensitive as a woman, but as brave as and a type of the Chevalier Bayard. He was a physician of high attainment, but ambitious to be and do more than was open before him in so limited a field as Petersburg. Dr. Madison married, on the 3rd of May, 1853, a lady of great accomplishments, and

as ambitious as himself—a Miss Leigh, of Orange
County, Virginia—and removed to Philadelphia, where
his talents and energy soon brought him into most
favorable notice. His wife lived only a year, I think,
after reaching Philadelphia, and two years afterwards
he married Miss Helen Bannister of this city, a most
estimable lady, a beauty, and a belle. He remained in
Philadelphia until the breaking out of the war between
the States—the War of the Rebellion, as it was termed
there, the especial home of hate and bitterness against
the South, and the home of one Rev. Brooks, who afterwards became a bishop of the Protestant Episcopal
Church, but who bore the savory reputation then, and
there, of being a persecutor of any unfortunate rebel—
man, woman, or child—who came under his power, and
with a cruelty and malignity only measured by his opportunity of giving them distress. It is to be hoped
that before he was called upon for the rendition of his
final account he stumbled upon a text which he might
have found in the great sermon of Paul, to the
Athenians, on Mars Hill when he was declaring to them
the Unknown God (Acts 17:30).

I enter no apology for this little digression.*

At the breaking out of the war Dr. Madison came
South, as did all its loyal sons—came home and struck
with them for fireside and altar. He was elected Surgeon and Professor at the Virginia Military Institute,

---

*To the Hon. Edwin G. Booth, of Philadelphia, formerly a citizen of Virginia, Southern prisoners, wherever they could be reached by him, were indebted for great kindness, and most liberal contributions of clothes, blankets, etc. And there may have been other friends in the City of Brotherly Love as kind as he, but I never heard of them. God knows who even gave a cup of cold water in his name—and God reigns, even yet, and there. Any one wishing to enquire further into this subject is referred to "United States Bonds," a book published by Rev. I. W. K. Handy, D. D., of Augusta County, Virginia, a journal of fifteen months' confinement as a prisoner at Fort Delaware.

JOHN HERBERT CLAIBORNE
Of the Surry Troop
Light Horse Harry Lee's Legion, 1776

filling his place in war and in peace with distinguished credit to himself. He died some ten years subsequent to the restoration of the Union, in Thomasville, Georgia, whither he had gone trying to evade the Nemesis consumption, which had pursued to death his first wife, and her two lovely daughters, just as they budded into womanhood. A loving letter from him as he was entering the dark scenes of the Great Unknown told me of the fearlessness with which he was meeting his last and only enemy, and of his perfect confidence in a higher and better life. In a few days came the announcement of his death.

> "Green be the turf above thee,
> Friend of my better days;
> None knew thee but to love thee,
> None named thee but to praise."

Dr. Madison was not a native of Petersburg, but of Orange or Madison County, Virginia. Having lost his father at an early age, he came to Petersburg with his mother, who was a Miss Strachan, of this city, and with her lived with Mr. Robert Strachan on a farm near Butterworth's Bridge, at the head of Halifax Street. But he was educated in Petersburg, and his name should be listed upon the roll of the many sons of the old Cockade City whose virtuous and distinguished lives have given her preeminence amongst the cities of the Commonwealth.

CHAPTER II

PETERSBURG IN THE FIFTIES.

The City as I Found It—Some Early History—The Population and a Comparison—The Society—The Fourth of July—Hospitality and Liberality—The Business Interests—Growth of the City—Its Hotels and Taverns—A Professional Adventure—Principal Resources and Finances—Its Municipal Government—The Churches and Their Pastors—The Colored Congregations—The Press of Petersburg in 1850 and Later—The Schools and Teachers—The Petersburg Bar and Some Reminiscences of Its Honored Members—The Physicians of Petersburg—Recollections of Many Notable Members of the Profession Before and During My Time—Petersburg's Rise After the War.

At the time when I settled in this city, on the 1st of January, 1851, it was a town of 103 years of age, having been incorporated by the House of Burgesses, with the Town of Blandford, in 1748, and directed to be laid off—the Town of Petersburg from the lands of one Abraham Jones, and the Town of Blandford from the lands of one William Poythress. These acts of incorporation were probably passed at the instance and by the influence of Col. William Byrd, of Westover, who, in 1733, determined that two citites should be founded in Virginia—one at the falls of James River, to be called Richmond, and one at the falls of the Appomattox River, to be called Petersburg.

This town was named for Captain Peter Jones, appointed by the Council commander-in-chief of Fort Henry. It was also called Peter's Point. At this point was erected the first trading house on the river, just opposite Bath Island, the former situation of the Southside Railroad shops, and probably on the spot now occupied by Dunlop's factory. This was in the year 1675.

Petersburg in the Fifties 41

In 1720 Captain Peter Jones's name appears on the Register of Bristol Parish, with that of one John Bannister, both said to have been companions and comrades of that gallant and enterprising gentleman Col. William Byrd, who about the year 1733 was employed as one of the commissioners to run the dividing line between Virginia and North Carolina. Bristol Parish at that time extended from Charles City County to Petersburg and Blandford, including those two corporations, which corporations or towns must have had some population, for from the same Registry we read that in 1733 the old "Ferry Chapel," whose site was somewhere in the neighborhood of Pocahontas Bridge, "was out of repair, and too small to hold the congregation," and that the church wardens were instructed to purchase an acre of land from John Low, on Wells' Hill, Blandford, as a site for a new church; and further that Robert Bolling and Wm. Poythress were appointed superintendents of the new building, "plans and specifications prepared,". and that they contracted with one Thomas Ravenscroft to build the church for 485 pounds, current money of Virginia. The church was completed in 1737, and in the month of August of that year the vestry held its first meeting in it. This was called the New Brick Church on Wells' Hill, and is to us of to-day the Old Blandford Church, of sacred heritage and precious memories. Though dismantled and unused for worship now, it still stands, its roof and walls in perfect preservation, a silent sentinel over the graves of the sleepers of two hundred years. There are few who enter its ever-open portals, or who tread its vacant aisles, that do not feel a solemnity which silences all save consecrated thought. "A Stranger," whose name has never been known, whilst visiting this hallowed structure some time about the beginning of

the last century, penned on its walls certain striking and
beautiful lines, which can never be reproduced too
often.*

In 1752 a town was ordered to be laid off from the
lands of Richard Wittom, on the northern side of the
Appomattox River, just opposite Petersburg—said
town to be called Pocahontas; and John Bolling,
Richard Eppes, Augustine Claiborne, and Roger Atkinson were appointed trustees. Amongst the ordinances formulated by these worthy gentlemen for the
government of this town is one of interest so singular,
if not so curious, that it is worth noting, viz: That no
wooden chimney should be erected to any house within
the precincts of this town. And the sheriff was vested
with full power to pull down any such structure.

At this time, and indeed until the War of the Revolution, Blandford was the most prosperous, if not the
most populous, of the three corporations which finally
coalesced into one city. Socially it was the court end.
Its merchants were thrifty, enterprising, and wealthy,
carrying on direct trade with the Old Country, their
vessels landing their cargoes at Bates' Spring, on the
river, just below Blandford. And some of its citizens
were men of note, amongst them George Keith Taylor,
one of the most eminent jurists of his day, and Dr. John
Shore, one of the most eminent physicians.

In 1850 Petersburg, with its purlieus, Pocahontas and
Blandford, became a city, under a charter granted by
the General Assembly of Virginia, with power to elect
a mayor, common council, and other municipal officers,
by the people, with a *viva voce* vote, under the system
designated as manhood suffrage, or universal suffrage, which had been adopted by the Convention
of 1850 in the place of homestead suffrage. And

---
*See Appendix.

Petersburg in the Fifties

here was the entering wedge, as it was predicted at the time, for the introduction of methods and management at the voting precincts which have oftener suppressed than expressed the popular will. I do not refer to its effects on this city alone, or this commonwealth alone, but on every city and every commonwealth where free suffrage, as it is now called, is adopted. And in some of the cities of this great country, under this same license of free suffrage, municipal government has not only been a failure or a fraud, but the municipal offices are often filled by men vicious and corrupt, who pluck, to their own repletion, the body politic as their lawful prey.

In the charter of March, 1850, the mayor was still elected by the council, but afterwards it was changed by vote of the people. On November 5, 1850, the polls were opened on the question whether the mayor should be elected by the council or the people. The vote stood for electing the mayor by the people, 208; for electing the mayor by the council, 59—only 267 votes in all. This can easily be understood by reflecting that a qualified voter at that date had to be a "freeholder" of lots within the city, and own property to the value of $150. Free suffrage has increased the number of suffragans greatly out of proportion to population.

The population of Petersburg at this time—census of 1850—was 14,603. The first mayor elected by the people was John Dodson, Esq., attorney at law, a most courteous and elegant gentleman, and one who is doubtless remembered by some of the citizens of this day. For several years before his election most of the functions of the office of mayor devolved upon a magistrate or police justice—in this instance upon a sturdy and uncompromising old Scotchman known as **Squire Patterson**. The Squire gave the "lar" (law) to all unfortunate offenders without fear, favor, or affection, and was a terror to evil-doers. His executive officers or policemen were only two—Billy Fenn and Billy Williams, sharp, shrewd, courageous, and sleepless guardians of the public safety and the public peace. And though the city embraced at that time within its corporate limits a population of nearly 15,000, I think that law and order were preserved as well and as fully as now with a police corps of 26, and only about 7,000 more souls to superintend. *O Tempora! O Mores!*

The society of Petersburg as I found it was refined, cultivated, and exclusive. There were only about 6,000 whites, but it would have been difficult to find in the same population anywhere a greater number of fine women or brave men. It had proudly borne for forty years the soubriquet of the Cockade City of the Union, a title conferred by President Madison in recognition of the patriotic service of the "Canada Volunteers," a company formed from its best citizens, and who marched from Virginia to the northern frontier of the United States, in the War of 1812, and at Lundy's Lane got their baptism of blood in repelling the British forces.

On visiting the monument in the Blandford Cemetery, erected in memory of these heroes, and reading the names recorded there, one could easily recognize among the citizenship of Petersburg in 1850 many men worthy of their sires, and many women worthy of the men.

I have said of the society of Petersburg at this time that it was exclusive. This does not indicate that it was cold or repellant. A more hospitable and warmhearted people did not live, but a stranger was required to bring character and cultivation as his credentials. Money, with its meretricious adornments and its vulgar display, was not the sesame to open any gentleman's door. There were few people of large fortunes,—none as fortunes are estimated now,—but a large proportion of the population were possessed of comfortable estates and incomes sufficient to insure a generous support. In no portion of the Commonwealth were the people in easier circumstances. And they mingled in their social gatherings with a freedom and elegance born of the old cavalier stock and worthy of their inheritance. Their public gala days were the 22d of February—Washington's Birthday, and the 4th of July, the birthday of National Independence. On both of these days business was virtually suspended, and there was a parade of the military and the firing of national salutes. On the night of the 22d of February there was generally a ball given at one of the prominent hotels, where the beauty and chivalry of the city and surrounding country assembled,

"And chased the glowing hours with flying feet."

Military spirit was rife at that time in Petersburg, as it had been for forty years, and as it was at the breaking out of the Civil War. There were three companies of infantry and one of artillery, all of full ranks and composed of the best material, not only of young men, but of men of any age under forty-five years, the limit of military service. In the ranks were found men of all classes, all grades of social condition, and professions. And this spirit pervaded the community until, when called upon to furnish her quota of volunteer troops for the defense of the South, more soldiers stepped out to the tap of the drum, and filed away to the field, than there was left of the voting population at home.

We have spoken of the gala days. The 4th of July was the great day. The military and civic societies paraded in the morning, and in the afternoon a public

dinner, with refreshments solid and liquid, was served,
either on the Poplar Lawn (now Central Park), or on
the island in the river, between the present locations
of the Norfolk & Western Railroad and the old company shops. A few weeks before the 4th of July a
meeting of the citizens was always called at the Court
House, and an orator was chosen to make the address
at the celebration of the 4th, and a reader to read the
Declaration of Independence.

 Although I had not been a resident of the city quite
eighteen months, and was but little known, a friend of
mine, R. G. Pegram, a young attorney, as I was then
a young doctor, nominated me as orator for the 4th of
July, 1852. He had had the same honor conferred on
him the year preceding, and whether he desired to
share with me the laurels won by himself on that occasion, or was moved by a spirit of mischief, I never
knew. However, I accepted the nomination. Lieutenant Davidson, of the United States Navy, a brother
of the Misses Nora and Virginia Davidson, the well-known educators of this city, and who, I suspect, are
among the few people left that will remember the occasion, was appointed reader of the Declaration of Independence. The exercises were held on Poplar Lawn.
A stand was erected under a large gum tree, still standing by the spring, and the amphitheatre above was fitted with rows of seats in semicircles to the summit of
the hill. After the parade and the firing of the national salute the military was marched to the Lawn
and the orator and the reader were conducted to the
stand. On reaching the stand I found seated on the
rostrum Governor Johnson, then Governor of Virginia,
the Hon. R. K. Meade, the distinguished representative
in Congress from the Petersburg District, and several
other notables of the Commonwealth and of the city,
whilst occupying the seats in the amphitheatre—a great

part being ladies—and standing around the circle was a great crowd, filling the air with patriotic huzzas. I saw that I had an audience before me of more than a thousand, looking into whose faces I could catch the eye of few acquaintances and of fewer friends, whilst seated behind me were public men of great prominence who had won forensic fame on many a hard-fought field. The scene and the surroundings were sufficiently inspiring for any speaker, but for me they were rather awe-inspiring and suggestive of an attack of stage fright.

However, when Lieutenant Davidson had finished the reading of the Declaration I gathered my trembling nerves together and advanced, on call of the master of ceremonies, to the railing in front of the stand, and, as soon as the applause which greeted my appearance subsided, launched out into the patriotic strain peculiar to that day. I was not quite so unaccustomed to public speaking as some of my friends supposed, in fact had often, in the four years of my collegiate course, appeared before the public and aired my young eagles in classic oratory of the schools, but I had never appeared before an audience so large and on an occasion so trying. Of course I did not dare to appear before such an assembly of people unprepared. I was sure of my ground, and took for my subject certain salient points in Washington's Farewell Address, so, accustomed to "thinking on my feet,"—an art that young men should acquire,—never faltered a minute for a word. I had a manuscript buttoned up in the breast of my uniform (I was an officer in the artillery), but I had no recourse to it. Memory did not fail me. And though I have not a line or scratch of pen of one word which I spoke on that day, yet I can as distinctly remember my exordium as when it passed from my lips more than half a century ago:

Fellow Citizens:

    Called by your too-partial kindness to play so conspicuous a part in the celebration of this natal day of American Independence, you must not expect me to wield any mighty weapon in this battled arena upon which I am thrown. Poetry, painting, and eloquence have exhausted their resources in commemorating this day; and I am neither Homer, nor Apelles, nor Tully. I belong to a profession whose fame is not heard in the echoes of the forum, and whose glories are not enshrined amid the records of forensic eloquence. I have only a mite to bring, but, as I lay it on the altar, I pray that its incense may arise with the orisons that go up to-day from ten thousand hearts to heaven that God would bless our country and perpetuate our institutions.

At the conclusion of this sentence there was a great huzza, and an explosion of loud amens from a number of worthy old patriots seated just before me, and on looking down I saw the tears welling from their eyes. Amongst the few that I knew I recognized old Major Lyon, Capt. Daniel Butts, Capt. F. Rives, Rev. Mr. Charlton, and one or two others. I saw at once that I had my audience under my power, and the encouragement was so full that I had no trouble as I proceeded, but held their attention for nearly an hour, when I sat down, overwhelmed by congratulations and deafened by applause. One enthusiastic gentleman—now an old man and a resident of New York—took me by the hand and said, "It is well, young man, that you did not speak in the old theatre to-day [the 4th of July oration was sometimes delivered there when the weather was bad]; that applause would have shaken the house down."

I was greatly elated, of course, and have never scored a success in any manner or time or place, in the fifty years since, which gave me such unqualified pleasure.

Of course a copy of the address was asked for for publication; and then came forward two kindly mentors, sincere and common-sense friends, who said to me: "No, do not print it. It will not read in print as

Petersburg in the Fifties

you spoke it. Besides, there was not so much in it after all. You took the people by surprise, for they did not expect so much of you, and they were agreeably disappointed. Let it end here, and don't let them turn your head."

I accepted their counsel, knowing that it was wise, and feeling that it was kind.

But that day's work was far-reaching in its results. When, in a few years subsequently, political fires of such fierceness were kindled in the community that the whole social fabric felt their baleful force, and neighbor and friend were separated from neighbor and friend, and faces that before had only smiled on meeting now scowled with hate, I was often called to the front; and on the hustings encountered many a throng which bore no semblance to that crowd which I swayed and captured on that happy 4th of July, 1852. My meaning will plainly appear when I write of Petersburg from 1854 to 1861.

In the meantime, let us return to Petersburg as it was when I reached it in January, 1850. According to Mr. E. S. Gregory ("Sketches of Petersburg," published by Campbell & Co.), "no place in this country excelled it for hospitality and liberality. She had a large trade with European ports, which every day added to her growth and wealth. Throughout the whole Union her culture, her cordiality, and her enterprise were commended of all men. The merchants of that day were princes in their profession, exceeded by none for their integrity, their foresight, and their boldness to improve the legitimate opportunities for investment." And these merchants represented every department of trade and commerce. Old Street, as I recall it, was crowded day by day with drays and wagons—country wagons, not the frail and cheap creations of to-day, painted red and marked made in some distant State,

4

and sold by some home business arrangement; but high, long-bodied, covered with white canvas, in fact regular schooners—laden not with small piles of loose tobacco, but three great hogsheads weighing perhaps 1,800 pounds apiece, or with an hundred sacks of corn or wheat, and drawn by six stalwart horses, driven by sable jehus, who, proud of their teams, proud of the masters whom they represented, proud of the music of the jingling bells on their leaders' necks, cracked their long whips in glee, the embodiment of fat, well-fed and contented labor. These wagons were all of home manufacture, in the city or surrounding country, and many of them by a sterling old citizen of Halifax street—price $100; but the buyer could confidently know that he got the worth of his money, the simple inscription "Wells, Maker," being the only guarantee asked or given. Old Mr. Wells—I suspect that few men of to-day remember him; if they do, they remember him as I do—faithful, honest, just and upright, was the type of the mechanic in Virginia of the olden time; and his work was the model work of a workman's hands, not the shoddy output of machinery.

Among the merchants on Old Street who handled these products from the planter's hand, and the factors who bought and sold for him, and managed his town business, was, as I recall the most prominent of them Thomas Branch, general commission merchant, importer of Peruvian guano, buyer of wheat in large quantities for export or for sale, etc., who did probably the largest business of the kind in the city. Mr. Branch was a portly man of fine appearance, cordial in manner, hospitable, and charitable when convinced that the charity was needed. He was a great Methodist, and for years was a power in the church. After the war,

Branch & Sons occupied the same location, and in the early seventies removed to Richmond, where one of the firm, Mr. J. P. Branch, still survives.

Another firm which I recall was Sturdivant, Hurt & Co. These gentlemen did a large grocery and commission business, selling great quantities of groceries adapted to the wants of the surrounding country, and handling on commission tobacco, wheat, corn, and, indeed, all the products of the planter in exchange. They were active, popular, and of excellent credit, and commanded the confidence of their customers to the fullest extent. One of this noted firm yet survives in the person of our venerable and highly respected citizen Mr. S. J. Hurt, though not now engaged in the same business.

Then I can recall on this crowded street a number of other commission merchants and grocers, amongst them Peebles, White & Davis, Jones & Blunt, Hall & Peebles, Heath & Mason, and Mr. Lewis Lunsford, a manufacturer of and a very large dealer in whiskeys, who lived on the south side of Old Street, about opposite Mr. Tarlton Heath's, and whose son has a large feed and grain store on the same street now. On the south side of the Market Square there were a number of Israelitish citizens, dealers in general merchandise,— A. Eichberg, the Cohens, Kulls,—some of whom, or their sons, still survive the half century; and by the thrift, industry, and business capacity peculiar to their race now enjoy deserved prosperity. There were no Jews at that time in business higher up town than the house just below the present stand of Armstrong, the druggist; this was occupied by Marx Robinson, general dealer. There were several families of English Jews, the Davises, living on Bollingbrook Street. These were not merchants, but were generally considered rich.

There were not a great many stores on Bollingbrook Street. Amongst the merchants who did business on that street I readily recall Andrew Kevan & Brother. These were millers, or rather manufacturers of flour, doing a most extensive business, buying probably more wheat in one year than is now brought to the city in twenty years. Mr. Andrew Kevan, the elder partner, was a most public-spirited citizen, taking great interest in municipal affairs, and was, I think, the last mayor of the city under the old regime, when the mayor was selected by the council. Yet Mr. Kevan was not in any measure a politician. He lived to a very advanced age, never losing his interest in public affairs, and keeping to the last that which he merited—the confidence and respect of his fellows.

On the northeast corner of Bollingbrook and Sycamore Streets were Muir & Stevens, wholesale and retail dealers in china, glass-ware, etc.; and adjoining them the large shoe house of Drummond & Wyche. Below them, on the opposite side, was Patrick Booth, afterwards Booth & Grigg; and at the southeast corner of Bollingbrook and Sycamore Streets J. H. Robertson, or Spotswood & Robertson, druggists; and below them on Bollingbrook Street, W. R. Wilkins, merchant tailor, and Mr. Charles Loomis, merchant tailor; and next a lottery office kept by Mr. Granier* and a large confectionery store by Peter Martin. Both of these latter gentlemen had escaped from San Domingo at the general massacre of the whites on that island, and had cast their lots in the United States.

On Sycamore Street, on the west side, and opposite Bollingbrook, were Daniel Perkinson & Co., saddlers and dealers in harness; and, passing up the street, Bragg & Wilson, wholesale and retail druggists, oc-

---

*See Appendix.

Petersburg in the Fifties 53

cupying the stand now held by Wm. E. Armstrong & Co., the location of perhaps the oldest drug stand in the city, kept first by Colonel Bragg, then by Bragg & Sons, then by Wm. Bragg, Jr., & Thomas, and then by Bragg & Wilson. William Wilson will be remembered by many of his old comrades of Co. E, 12th Virginia Regiment. He was a genial, generous gentleman, exempt by law from military service, but he joined the army of Lee when the siege of Petersburg was begun, and was killed at the Battle of Hatcher's Run, the bullet cutting the femoral artery. According to the infantryman who stood next to him in line, Mr. George S. Bernard, he died almost immediately.

Next above Bragg & Wilson came Abrams, Lyon & Davis, large dry-goods merchants, mostly retail; and then Q. & L. Morton, hardware; and Dunn & Spencer, hardware; and Peebles, White & Scott, dry-goods—large assortment of staple and fancy dry-goods, did large country trade; and Mr. John Bradbury, fine and staple dry-goods for same trade; and E. P. Nash, northwest corner Sycamore and Bank Streets, books and pianos and music, did a very large business. Mr. Nash was a most excellent and enterprising gentleman, and was one of the prime movers in founding the Petersburg Female College, the building now owned and occupied by Mr. Robert Gilliam. Of the seventeen original trustees of the college, only one (myself) is living.

There was another book store kept by Col. J. C. Swann, a gallant old Irish gentleman (on Bank Street, I think); and another by Gaines & Riches, which I can not locate. Mr. Riches—an uncle of Dr. Harwood—still survives, in the nineties, the only survivor of the firms which I have enumerated.

On the east side of Sycamore, between Bollingbrook and Bank Streets, I can recall only three stores. These were Echols & Hall, hats, etc.; the large clothing house of Scott, Keen & Co.—the pioneer house for ready-made clothing in the city; Thomas Nowlan, jewelry, watches, etc.; and at the northeast corner of Sycamore and Lombard Streets, then called "Back" Street, Charles Corling, druggist, successor of Brown & Corling, a very old establishment. This corner was known as "Corling's Corner" for many years.

Passing up Sycamore Street on the west were Charles Lumsden, afterwards Stevens & Hopkins, jewelry, watches, silver-ware, etc.; Thomas Royston, clothing; Brodnax, Tanner & Wright, retail dry-goods, did a large town and country business; Samuel Marks, confectioner, who is yet alive, in his nineties; William and Andrew Morgan, gunsmiths, etc.; and John Pollard, saddlery and harness.

On the east side of Sycamore Street, beginning at Lombard, southeast corner, was Thomas H. Rosser, druggist; then A. Bond (father of A. and Thos. Bond), family grocery; higher up the extensive wholesale dry-goods house of Paul & McIlwaine; and of John Stevenson; and the wholesale house of Kerr & Marbury, glassware and crockery, importers and extensive dealers; and the house of Peed & Parson, cabinet makers and manufacturers of furniture generally; and Booth & Sommers, and Turnbull, Morrison & Stone, grocers. Of the latter firm Mr. R. T. Stone is the sole survivor.

Crossing to the west side of Sycamore Street again, on the northwest corner was Mechanics' Hall; and crossing over West Tabb Street to the southwest corner of Tabb and Sycamore was the large grocery establishment of McIlwaine, Brownley & Co., doing the largest business in the city, and probably as large as any in the State. Their building extended from the corner to Powell's Hotel, which occupied the ground recently covered by the Iron Front, Rosenstocks, etc. Above Powell's Hotel was Ragland's Mule and Livery

Stables, then came a long row of one-storied wooden shanties, extending as far as St. Paul's Church, which stood some forty or fifty feet back from the street about the present location of Russell's confectionery, Reinach's shoe store, etc. Between St. Paul's Church and the northwest corner of Sycamore and Washington Streets were several stores, amongst them N. M. Martin & Donnan, I think, grocers and commission merchants. At this corner, now occupied by Beckwith as a drug store, was the entrance to Centre Warehouse.

Returning to East Tabb Street and east side of Sycamore, we find at the southeast corner Lea & Madison, grocers, and Pitman & Cuthbert. Then passing up the street we find a large and popular boarding-house, kept by Mrs. Ariana Smith—to some extent a place of overflow from Powell's Hotel, just opposite. Then "Harness and Saddlery" by P. M. Steward; a most worthy man, and an excellent merchant. Then there were few or no houses, except West Hill Warehouse, until getting to Franklin Street. At the southeast corner of Franklin and Sycamore Streets was the residence of Rev. Minturn Thrift, whose premises and garden extended along the east side of Sycamore to Washington Street. Crossing Washington Street, on the southeast corner of Washington and Sycamore was an old wooden dwelling occupied by a German family. In this family, some two or three years afterwards, I saw the first case of diphtheria that I ever saw or heard of, and perhaps the first case, or amongst the first, of that disease which had been reported since 1757. It soon made itself known to us, however, and for several years subsequently pervaded the city and made sad havoc amongst the people. It did not confine itself especially to children, but claimed its victims amongst young and old.

Following Sycamore Street on the east side there were only two or three houses intervening below Washington and Wythe Streets—one the old brick house, yet standing, and bearing marks of indisputable antiquity. This was owned and occupied by a gentleman named Weeks, and had been used as a tavern, though it was not used for that purpose in 1850-51. Passing Mr. John Dunn's residence there was not another house on the east side of Sycamore between his house and Marshall Street. The whole of the square between the alley running just north of the Petersburg Club House and Marshall Street on the south, and between Adams Street on the east and Sycamore Street on the west, was open, with the exception of the old brick house now standing at the northeast corner of the alley and Adams Street, and was occupied by a Scotchman named McKinsie as a flower garden.

But we have followed this line far enough for our purpose. The growth of the city, counted by houses, since 1850 has been wonderful. A good part of South Market Street, almost all of West Washington, from South Street; the whole of the square between Washington on the north and Shepherd Street on the south; and South Street on the east, and Dunlop Street on the west, was a vacant lot. The square on the opposite side of West Washington Street, bounded by it on the south, by Pearl Street on the north, by South Street on the east, and Dunlop Street on the west, was vacant, with the exception of two or three old wooden shanties on Washington Street—in fact almost all of what is now the western part of the city has been built up since 1850, yet the census of 1900 shows only an increase in population of 7,000 in those fifty years. It is simply incredible.

The hotels of the city have not increased in number *pari passu* with other buildings and with the population.

Petersburg in the Fifties 57

The principal hotels of that day were three. There was "Powell's," occupying the locality where the "Iron Front" stood, and kept by Mr. Wm. N. Friend, the father of our respected fellow citizen, Mr. Alfred Friend. This house was mostly patronized by the people of Brunswick, Lunenburg, Mecklenburg, Nottoway, Dinwiddie and Amelia Counties, and by people who came to the city by private conveyance from the southside country. There were large stables belonging to the hotel for the care of the horses of the visitors. "The accommodation for man and beast," in parlance of that time, was of the first class. The menu was the menu of the table of the old Virginia country gentleman, and the cuisine and the service could not be surpassed. The dishes were not brought in by detail, nor the contents served in dabs around your plate. When the guest appeared at the table he saw before him what there was to eat (the table was long, and not in sections or divisions), and a willing servant stood ready to cater to his choice of food.

At this period almost every one—ladies and gentlemen—was served at the table d'hote; but when, as a boy, I first became acquainted with this house, visiting it with my father and family, when ladies were of the party, we did not sit at the public table, but had a suite of rooms, of which one was always the dining-room. The genius of this room was a courteous old darky, whose bald pate was as polished as his manner, and I shall never forget his reverential obeisance as he took orders for what he should provide for the next meal. Contented, cheery, happy old Sam,—a slave if you choose to call him so—he filled his place perfectly in his day and generation, and passed away, his dust to mingle with the dead of the fine ladies and gallant gentlemen whom he delighted to serve, and who loved to reward and honor him. Man and master, the like, or better, can never be reproduced.

And there were Sam's fellow servants, John Bolling and Sam Bolling, having charge of the rooms of the guests; and Bob Clark in the dining-room, who, with his savings, bought his freedom and opened a livery stable on Lombard Street; and old Jacob, the porter or omnibus man; and others whose names I can not recall—all men whose urbanity, whose faithfulness, and whose integrity might well be copied now by many who look upon their lives as the memories of a degraded humanity.

Another of the principal hotels was "Jarratt's"; still *in situ*, but changed in all else. This was kept by John Jarratt, a born boniface, who knew his business, and who attended to it. His house was always full, and was the hostelry chiefly of the people who came to town by railroad from Greenesville County, Northampton County, and the counties contiguous to the Petersburg Railroad; and from North Carolina, whose citizens at that time formed a large contingent of those who came to Petersburg on business or for pleasure. The terminus of the Petersburg Railroad was at the Union Street Depot. There the passengers left the train, and those wishing to remain in the city found convenient quarters, and comfortable, withal, at "Jarratt's." Those wishing to go farther north were hurried into a long omnibus, and behind four horses were driven rapidly to Pocahontas, where the train of the Richmond & Petersburg Railroad awaited them. The driver was one Henry, a sable personage, but a master of the reins, and with evident pride in his exalted position on the box. I have seen him recently on our streets, but age and freedom have evidently not dealt very kindly with him, and one would hardly recognize in his attenuated

Petersburg in the Fifties   59

form the stately jehu who rattled his pampered team over our rough pavements fifty years ago.

The other principal hotel was the "Bollingbrook," also still *in situ*, and kept well by a worthy man at present; but he who remembers it in the pride of its past feels now, as he treads its corridors, that he

> "Treads alone some banquet hall deserted,
> Whose lights are fled, whose garlands dead,
> And all but he departed."

It was kept at that time by Dr. John Minge, a gentleman of the olden school, and who knew how to keep a hotel for gentlemen. It was mostly patronized by the people in the lower counties—Prince George, Sussex, Surry, Southampton, Isle of Wight; by the people "down the river." It was constantly filled, especially by those on pleasure bent, but its great season was the time of the New Market Races. Virginia at that period, as it had been for many years, was the home of the race-horse and its race tracks were the theatres for the display and for the triumphs of some of the finest coursers which this country has ever produced. Eclipse, Red Eye, Sir Charles, Arabian, Lusborough, Virginius, Baslona, and Andretta were names as familiar to the public as the names of the most prominent politicians and statesmen. Mr. Otway P. Hare, lately deceased in his nineties, was the owner of the New Market grounds, and the owner of some of the finest horses which contended for the prizes, and which won them. At his beautiful home, situate on the hill above the race track, he kept open house, and dispensed the most generous and lavish hospitality. At such times he had for his guests the most famous turfmen of the country, and his stables were the homes of their stock. But the "Bollingbrook" gathered the hundreds who came to the annual display and the annual sport, and "beauty and chivalry" filled its famous halls.

There were other hotels of minor importance in the city. One at the corner of Old and Short Market Streets; another at the corner of the Old Market Square; another on Second Street, below the "Bollingbrook," on the opposite side. These were cheap taverns for the accommodation of people of moderate means. And there were two taverns outside of the corporation, in Dinwiddie County—one at the junction of the Squirrel Level Road and the Court-House Road, at the house now occupied by Mr. Steere; and one at the junction of the Court-House Road and Cox Road. The latter was a long, rambling house of two stories, with a portico running its whole length, and was known by the distinctive title of the "Long 'Onery'" ("Ordinary"), a term formerly applied to any house where the meals were furnished at a common table. Planters coming from the country traversed by the roads before mentioned would time their arrival at these houses so that they could spend the night under their hospitable roofs, and going into town after early breakfast attend to their business and return to their quarters at night, so as to get an early start for their homes the following morning.

At the tavern on Second Street I had a professional adventure which came near proving a very serious one for me. I was summoned one morning after breakfast to see a guest at this hotel, and on going to the office and enquiring for the room of my patient I was addressed by a burly, red-headed man at my side, who informed me that he was the person who wished to see me, and he invited me to his room. On getting there he commenced to ask me a number of desultory and irrelevant questions as to where I was born, where I was educated, whether I had ever matriculated at a school in Berlin or Vienna, how long I had remained there, etc., until I became impatient and said to him

Petersburg in the Fifties

that if he wished to see me professionally I would talk with him, but that I was busy, and if he had nothing more important to say to me I would leave. "No," he answered, "you can't leave. I have something very important to say to you; but this room is not sufficiently private." He then ushered me into an interior and adjoining room, and locking the door put the key in his pocket. This room was bare of furniture, except a large, heavy bench, upon which he motioned me to be seated. Standing before me, he told me that he was from Richmond; that he had gone to the confessional that morning before leaving, but that there was something on his mind which he wished to confess to me alone. Still a little annoyed and impatient, I replied, "Let us have it then." Said he, "I am in love." I was not in the humor to be amused by what I supposed were the fancies of a drunken man, and quickly said, "Open that door; we have had enough of this." He replied that he would only open that door after he had obtained the object for which he had sent for me. "Well, what is it," I said. He replied, "I am informed that you brought with you from abroad a formula for a medicine by the administration of which you can make any woman love you whom you wish to win." I answered, "I am tired of this egregious folly," and was about to seek the door and force it, when he stopped me, saying, "I was prepared for this, and am prepared to enforce my demands," showing at the same time a very ugly revolver. I saw then that I was dealing with a madman, a powerful man with whom I could not cope in strength, and I recognized at once that I would have to resort to strategy to rescue myself, so I replied: "What you have remarked is true. I have a prescription for a love powder which will accomplish all that you wish, but I have never shown it or acknowledged it to any living being before. It is simply priceless;

but you have me in your power, and if you choose to rob me of it I have no means of preventing you." To this he answered: "I do not propose to rob you. I can pay you, and propose to pay you your full price; but it is well for you to understand that I am going to have it, if I have to resort to violence to secure it." "All right," I said, "put up your pistol. Do you read Latin?" "No," he replied. I then wrote a prescription for a most powerful depressant emetic, in two powders; told him to take one, and to administer the other to his enamorata when he returned to Richmond. I thought it possible he might summon a boy and send for it and take it whilst he kept me in durance, but had he done so I should have had no fear of him in fifteen minutes after he swallowed it. However, he simply put the formula in his pocket and opened the door, and I lost no time in leaving the room. He followed me, and when we reached the office an officer was awaiting him, and immediately took him in charge, informing me that he was an escaped lunatic. The officer politely inquired if I had any charges against him or wished to detain him. "No charges," I said, "and I beg that you will not think of detaining him a minute on my account." I did not even give away the love powder story, and could not help hoping that my lunatic would get a little of it before he reached his destination.

In enumerating the business houses of note on the various streets, I omitted to note the establishment of the Leonards, on Old Street, south side, who had a hardware and gun store. It is now greatly enlarged, and conducted by the surviving brother, Mr. Charles Leonard, on Bank Street. On the same side of the street was the saddle and harness manufactory by Mr. B. P. Harrison, a most worthy and excellent Christian man. And on Short Market Street there was a carriage manufactory, by Mr. Slaughter; and on Bank

Petersburg in the Fifties 63

Street another by Mr. Camp; and on Sycamore Street, near West Hill Warehouse, another by Mr. Pope; and on South Sycamore Street, just where the Lewises now have their extensive business, was still another carriage factory by Mr. Atkinson. These mechanics served their day and generation with faithful, honest work, and no man was compelled to go North or elsewhere to find a handsome or substantial vehicle. Good, substantial oak or hickory stock they used, without the plaster of veneer or putty; and their work might have been likened to the work of the one-horse shay of Dr. Holmes, warranted to run an hundred years and a day.

There were in different portions of the city the establishments of such mechanics and contractors in brick or wood as Major Daniel Lyon, Mr. Beverly Drinkard, W. H. Baxter, Lumsden & Shedden, Traylor & Peterson, and others whom I can not recall.

Of the sons of Tubal-Cain,—workers in brass and iron,—Tappey & Lumsden, at the old stand, still kept up on Washington Street; and Uriah Wells, who might be called the father of the foundries here, a man no less noted for his mechanical genius than for his rugged countenance, and his incorruptible integrity. His place of business was just where Dunlop's Factory now stands.

Tobacco, the staple and money crop of the surrounding country then, was a prime article of manufacture in the city, and the source of her wealth and prosperity. Mr. David Dunlop (not the person who owns and conducts a factory now on Old Street) occupied almost a square between the lower part of Bollingbrook and Lombard Streets with his elegant house and capacious factories; Messrs. Osborne and Chieves occupied the factory on the corner of Washington and Jefferson Streets now owned and occupied by Mr. John H. Maclin; Mr. Robert Leslie, the uncle of Messrs. Watson

and McGill, occupied the factory on Washington Street
now owned and occupied by them; Mr. Reuben Ragland had a large factory at the corner of Washington
Street and Jones' Road, and Messrs. Williamson &
Venable, young men, who had just come to Petersburg
to try their fortunes, occupied a factory at the Basin,
on the locality now occupied by Mr. J. E. Routh as a
basket and crate factory. Large quantities of tobacco
were then brought down in hogsheads on batteaux—
long boats—by the river and canal, and the location
was a most convenient one for a tobacco factory. Mr.
J. P. Williamson, the Williamson of that firm, and one
of our most respected and valued citizens, still survives,
and doubtless holds in kindly memory the halcyon days
and nights made merry by the old boatmen of the Appomattox batteaux.

Messrs. McEnery and McCulloch owned and occupied a factory on Washington Street, at the corner of
Guarantee, and did a large business; and the Camerons owned and occupied a large factory on Perry
Street, though not exactly at the location of their present factory.

Twelve years later the most of these buildings were
devoted to very different objects. Large, airy, and well
ventilated, they were admirably suited for hospitals,
and in the spring of 1862 were hired or impressed for
that purpose, and were soon filled with sick or wounded soldiers. The peaceful art of manufacture had given
place to the cruel art of war, and instead of the songs
of the dusky operatives at their cheerful work were
heard only the groans of the sick or the cries of those
who had been wounded in battle. The surgeon had
assumed the position of the manager, and many of the
colored employees were utilized as nurses and servants,
and with the imitativeness, the docility, and kindliness
of the slave, soon became as useful as they had been in

their legitimate employment. One of these factories—that of the Camerons—was named the North Carolina Hospital; another—that of Osborne & Chieves, now Maclin's—was named the South Carolina Hospital; and another—that of Robert Leslie's, on Washington Street, now Watson & McGill's—was named the Virginia Hospital; but they were all organized by order of the Confederate Government. The general orders were that the soldiers of these States, when brought to the city sick or wounded, should be assigned to the respective hospitals bearing the name of their States—which were mostly under charge of surgeons from those States—for the sake of convenience and of comradeship; and this was done so far as practicable, but not fully, as the exigencies of the service made it often impossible.

The only other factories at this period of any importance, or which contributed to any extent to the public interest, were the cotton factories—Matoaca, Ettrick, Battersea, Petersburg Mills, Swift Creek, and Merchants' Mills. These factories represented a capital of between $800,000 and $1,000,000, and employed between 800 and 1,000 hands,—white, all of them,—with a monthly pay roll of about $10,000 or $12,000, and average capacity for turning out sheeting and cotton yarns, etc., of about 200,000 yards per week. This was no inconsiderable industry for the period and for this section. Manufactories in the South employing white operatives were but few, and these in Petersburg, for the few years during which they had been established, were considered a God-send to the poorer classes of people in the city and the surrounding counties, enabling them to secure a decent livlihood, which it was difficult to do by agricultural pursuits, where all the best lands were tilled by planters owning their own labor, who had no necessity to hire other help, even had pride of race and caste permitted the white man to labor in the fields by the side of the negro slave.

Now to conduct the various business pursuits and industries to which we have referred, necessitated capital and money accommodation. This was furnished by men—public-spirited citizens—of fortune, and by the banks. There were three banks in the city at that time, as there are three now—the Exchange Bank, on Bank Street; George W. Bolling, president; Pat Durkin, cashier. The Farmers Bank, on Bollingbrook Street; Wm. Robertson, president; Pleasant Osborne, cashier. And The Bank of Virginia, on Bank Street; Joseph Bragg, president; George W. Stainback, cashier. I do not know what amount of capital was invested in these banks or what amount of deposits was received and utilized by them. They were what were known at that time as State Banks, being banks both of issue and deposit, and their notes of issue were of unexceptionally good credit. Considering the very heavy business which was transacted, not only with the city people, but with the people of the surrounding counties, all of which were then rich and prosperous, we take it for granted that their financial condition was about that of the three banks of to-day; if so, their aggregate capital—stock and undivided profits—must have been about $750,000, their aggregate deposits about $1,850,000, and their gross assets about $2,600,000, which would have enabled them to do an annual volume of business of $75,000,000 to $100,000,000, not far, I suspect, from the true condition of things.

We have no accurate knowledge—that is, no knowledge from statistics compiled at the time—of the amount of money used directly and indirectly in the tobacco trade, but assuming that at least as much tobacco was produced in the surrounding counties tributary to Petersburg at that period as is produced now, and that as much was brought to this market then as is brought now,—by no means a violent assumption,—we shall count fifteen millions of pounds annually bought by manufacturers and shippers. This at an average of eight cents a pound would have required an expenditure of $1,200,000 passing through first hands. Then, as now, this tobacco was manufactured for export and for domestic purposes. And the average number of hands employed in all branches of the trade was about 3,000, with aggregate wages of about $500,000. Tobacco, not cotton, was king in Petersburg in 1850, And to-day, according to the reports of the Internal Revenue office, 80 per cent. of all the tobacco exported from the United States is exported from Petersburg; and when the annual revenue receipts from Petersburg are $4,000,000—we may say that tobacco is yet king.

There were at that time, it is true, two or three grist mills—corn and wheat, of the latter notably the Eagle Mills, and the Kevan Mills, which turned out annually thousands of barrels of flour, not only for home consumption, but for export. But the great industrial interests were tobacco and commerce.

The financial condition of the city was most satisfactory. According to Mr. E. S. Gregory in his "Sketch of the History of Petersburg," "the annual revenue of the town was $20,000 and the annual expenditures about the same." "And yet," remarks the same author, "the long-headed citizens were said to be greatly concerned for fear the town should go to protest and its credit be forever impaired." The rate of taxation was what might be called nominal at this day. During the same year, however, the town was authorized by a vote of the people to subscribe $200,000 to the stock of the Southside Railroad, and the Treasurer of Virginia was required to guarantee the town bonds for the benefit of the Southside Railroad to the amount of $323,000, and the "Town" was required to mortgage its whole property to indemnify the State as security. This was the commencement of the creation of a debt, which by subsequent expenditures and subsequent issues of bonds for municipal and other improvements amounts to-day to $1,261,000.

To that day there had been mostly unsalaried offices, and the same rigid economy exercised by those who had the care and oversight of public affairs which they showed in the conduct of their private affairs. In addition, the exchequer was in the hands of men who held and who owned the property responsible for every outlay of town expenditure, and manhood suffrage had not brought to the surface the hoi polloi who were not so particular about contracting a debt for the discharge of which the tax-gatherer could find no visible assets. What mattered it to Thomas, or Richard, or Henry (late Tom, Dick, or Harry) that his vote should fasten upon the corporation an obligation which he could not be called upon to liquidate! What mattered it that he voted for a scheme involving an hundred, or a thousand, or a million of dollars! He would not be expected to fumble in his pockets for a dime of the principal or interest. But this is old fogyism—worse, it is rank heresy to the new regime and to the eminent domain of young America. On the hustings the wily politician had told the new citizen that brawn and bone were the bulwarks of the State, and that without regard to material or mental condition; that he was always called upon to do the labor of the State, and to fight the battles of the State; and that his voice should be heard in shaping the destiny of the State, especially when destiny called for the elevation of said politician to a place of honor or profit.

Under the new regime the monetary and municipal matters of the city have undergone a marvelous change. One can scarcely realize it. The salaried officers of the city now are—mayor, $1,200; chief of police, $850; one lieutenant, $700; two sergeants, $600 each, and twenty-two privates at $50 per month each, a grand total of $15,950 per annum for 1900. Compare this with the mayor, or Squire Patterson, police justice, of no salary; and Billy Fenn and Billy Williams, policemen, of $500 per annum each in 1850!

Nor does the sum of $15,950 include the salaries of city attorney, judge of the Hustings Court, auditor of accounts, treasurer, and commissioner of the revenue. The total expenditures for the fiscal year ending June 30th, 1900, were $284,165, and total receipts were $264,762. Compare these figures with Mr. Gregory's estimate of $20,000 expenditures and $20,000 receipts in 1850, and then consider that the population of the city has only increased during that period of half a century about 8,000, and we must conclude that "the world do move," the Rev. John Jasper's opinion to the contrary notwithstanding.

The fear of the fathers, however, that the city's credit would suffer and that she would be forced into bankruptcy has not yet materialized. On her bonded debt she pays only an average of a little more than five per cent, and finds no difficulty in sellng new bonds at par carrying an interest of five per cent. She, therefore, is far from being insolvent yet. And she not only finds no difficulty in realizing a levy of $1.60 on the whole of the real and personal property of her citizens, but she has solved a difficulty which the United States Government has not been able to cope with, viz: she can find and tax the income of the citizen. There is but one fraud perpetrated on her revenue which I am told that she has never been able to prevent—a man can expend the whole of his cash and utilize all of his credit in the purchase of United States bonds on the day before he

gives in his list of taxables, and sell them again two
days afterwards, he never having seen the bonds in the
meantime, they never leaving the broker's hands, but
not being taxable he has listed no taxable property.
If no one of my many readers has ever been guilty of
this little cheat, then him have I not offended.

The churches of the city have increased in the number of their edifices 50 per cent since 1850; but whether
pari passu in the number of the communicants, I have
no means of knowing.* I think it certain that there
has been a decided change in their regular denominational numbers. The Baptists were then a feeble folk,
worshiping in only one small church, at the corner of
Market and High Streets, Rev. J. R. Reynoldson, pastor. In 1854 he was succeeded by Rev. H. S. Keen,
an estimable gentleman and an able preacher. Mr.
Keen remained pastor until 1863. In the meantime the
old church had been given up and congregation and
pastor transferred to the church on Washington Street
now known as First Baptist, the building of which was
begun in 1853, but was not completed for perhaps several years. In 1863 Mr. Keen resigned.

In June, after Lee's surrender, this church was
struck by lightning and burned to the ground. It was
an exceedingly dark night, and the large ball near the
summit of the steeple, burning slowly at first, seemed
to those in the distance a great globe of fire in the firmament. I had lately returned to the city from my wanderings after the war, and occupied a rented room in
the third story of a house on Bank Street. It was about
11 or 12 o'clock at night when I was aroused by my
landlady rattling my bolt very vehemently and calling

---

*The aggregate membership of the Baptist churches of Peters-
burg was reported to the Portsmouth Association in 1850 at 318; in
1900 to the same Association 1244. And other denominations can
show the same increase.

to me in the most excited manner, "Get up, Doctor, get up! The planet Mars is on fire, and Judgment Day has come!" With such a startling announcement I lost no time in getting up and rushing to the window to satisfy myself in reference to the great catastrophe. And forsooth nothing could be seen from my position but an immense globe of fire, seemingly in the heavens, and nothing visible near it. I really could form no idea of what the phenomena meant, but thought it best to put on my clothes and make myself presentable and ready for any event. By the time I was dressed, however, the fire had made such headway that the roof of the church had caught and the illumination made the true condition of things apparent.

The city was filled, not only with Confederate soldiers returned from fields and prison, but with Federal soldiers, a number of whose regiments had been detained here, and some effort was made, the Federals assisting, to extinguish the flames, but with no regular fire organization—the city had not yet settled down to municipal order—nothing could be done, and the edifice was soon in ashes. But the planet Mars was saved.

The congregation worshiped in Mechanics' Hall until the present beautiful church was completed, having successively as pastors Rev. Mr. Keene, Rev. T. H. Prichard, Rev. W. G. Hatcher, Rev. T. T. Eaton, Rev. Mr. Dargan, all faithful and fearless, yet exceptionally beloved and popular, and at the present time the distinguished divine and eloquent pulpit orator Dr. H. W. Battle, under whose administration the church grows and flourishes.

There were two Methodist churches in Petersburg in 1851, one the Washington Street Church and the other the High Street Church, both standing yet in the same locality. The former was the outcome or overflow of the old Union Street Church, now occupied by one of the colored Methodist congregations in the city. Washington Street Church* might probably be called the mother church of the Methodist churches of Petersburg, as from it went out the other Methodist congregations, now numbering some four or five. The membership at that time was 666, and the church was probably the largest and the wealthiest, and the most influential in the city. Mr. D'Arcy Paul was the leader of the choir and the leader of the church. Tall, erect, dignified, commanding in figure, he was noted in manner, not only in the church, but upon 'Change, and more noted for his great generosity, his liberal charity, and a character so pure that the Evil One himself would have been ashamed of an attempt to smirch it. He lived long, a useful, public-spirited citizen, successful in business, amassing a fortune which he did not reserve to be distributed amongst others, as so many do, when he could no longer enjoy it for his own pleasure; but acting as his own almoner and executor, he placed it in his lifetime where vain folly could not garner it, nor moths corrupt, nor thieves break through and steal it.

The T. C. Paul's Female Orphan Asylum, founded by himself, cared for by himself when living, and dependent mostly upon his endowment for its present support, is a monument to his name and an inscription to his memory which time cannot destroy or efface. This institution was in its infancy in January, 1851, and

---

*At the close of the conference year 1850 the membership of the Washington Street Church was reported as 666, and at the close of the conference year 1900 the membership was reported as 575. Of the 666 reported in 1850, 230 were males, and of this number nine only are alive. For this information I am indebted to one of the nine, Mr. J. W. Bradbury, who can be relied upon for his figures, or for anything else which he endorses. Eight years afterwards, in 1858, 133 members of the church were transferred to Market Street Church, forming the nucleus of that congregation; of that number we can trace only some six or eight living at this time.

had been erected and endowed by Mr. Paul in memory of a promising young son whom he had lost, and who requested of his father before his death that the portion of his patrimony coming to him might be devoted to the erection of a home for homeless young girls. Hundreds of young girls have been housed and reared there, and many of them are worthy, respected mothers and grandmothers, filling honorable and useful places in life, who would otherwise have grown up in ignorance and vice. And their example and influence have gone out with them from that Home and have led others who were astray into paths of virtue and peace. I am personally cognizant of these facts, and I am sure that only eternity can reveal the wide-spreading, far-reaching power for good which the pious request of that dying boy has accomplished.

The Rev. Nelson Head was the pastor of the church at the time referred to, a plain, practical, godly man, and a preacher of sound doctrine as he saw it—a man "who never placed a flower of earthly sort about the sacred text." And after him, Anthony Dibrell, a Boanerges, catching his inspiration from Sinai, and with impassioned eloquence "persuading men" with the "terrors of the law." Transferred to Norfolk a few years after, he fell at his post, serving his people faithfully during the terrible scourge of yellow fever which swept over that devoted city in the summer of 1855.

After him came Jno. E. Edwards, polished, brilliant, versatile, eloquent, attracting large congregations to his church, and gathering great numbers of friends at his fireside. And then—but the rotating pastorate, the law and the genius of the Methodist people is such that it is difficult to trace from memory the successive ministers who filled the pulpit. I can recall, however, the Duncans, James and David, brothers—the former possessing powers of oratory which commanded and

kindled any audience, whether he spoke from the pulpit
or the rostrum; the latter, a loving, pious man, a good
preacher and a good pastor, whom the church elected
to the bishopric a few years subsequently; and Charles
H. Hall, who died in 1872 whilst serving a pastorate
term for that church, and whose death is commemorated by a tablet on its walls near the pulpit from which
he so often preached to the people. His life is commemorated in the hearts of hundreds of all classes and
of all religious associations, who loved to linger and
listen to the choice language in which he propounded
the law or plead mercy, and feeling in his soul the momentous import of his message, besought them as an
ambassador of God to be reconciled to Him. The
highest and the humblest waited equally upon his
words, and I have recently heard one of his humble
auditors say that "Charley Hall could preach all around
any preacher of the day."

Many men—good, true, faithful, learned, and earnest
—have followed him in the same pulpit and in other
pulpits of the city, but it is a matter of remark that they
do not draw now as they did some years ago.

Perhaps the pew is as much to blame as the pulpit;
the forward impetuous rush of the time for riches, the
great reward of wealth which awaits the zealous work-
er, and the astute speculator, have left men but little
leisure to look after interests eternal, it is true, but too
far off, and with no present prospect of yielding any
good.

The churches were, most of them, at Sabbath service, both morning and night, filled. This was especially true of St. Paul's Episcopal Church on Sycamore Street, and of the Methodist church on Washington Street, of which we are writing. It was no uncom-
mon thing for chairs and benches to be brought into
the aisles of the latter church, even on ordinary occa-

sions, to accommodate the people. This was often true in reference to Market Street Church, which, in 1857-'58, had been built as an overflow from Washington Street. This was a pewed church for some years, and was called the church of the Methodist aristocracy. Dr. J. E. Edwards, before referred to, was the first pastor, and indeed its founder, as is attested by a mural tablet near the pulpit. Some able men followed him in the revolving pastorate, among them Revs. Sledd, Langhorn, Judkins, Garland, Granbery, and others. Rev. Granbery, now an eminent prelate and bishop of the church, was a classmate of mine at college. After a three-years curriculum we took the graduating degree A. B., and curiously enough our record summed to the same number and entitled us both to the first honor. The faculty, in determining between us, resorted to the old device of drawing straws. Granbery got the long straw, and, forsooth, has kept it through life. This I have referred to before.

There were only two Episcopal churches in Petersburg in January, 1851. One, St. Paul's, on Sycamore Street, some forty or fifty feet back from the street, on the west side, and located where Russell's confectionery and Reinach's shoe store now stand. This church was the outcome of the congregation of the old Blandford Church, the congregation having removed to Petersburg in 1802, and worshiped in a small brick building situated on what is known now as the Court-House Hill. This church was enlarged and rebuilt in 1806, and answered the purpose, according to Bishop Meade, "until 1839, when a larger and more expensive one was erected in a more convenient place." This refers to the church on Sycamore Street, we presume, as we find that it was consecrated by Bishop Moore on the 5th of April, 1839.

This congregation was under the pastorate of Rev.
Andrew Syme from 1794 to 1839, forty-five years. "Old
Parson Syme," as I have so often heard my mother
speak of him, must have been a man of varied accomplishments, of rare grace, and of great good sense to
have retained his hold upon the people for so long a
time.

The church was under the charge of Rev. Horace
Stringfellow at the time to which I have referred, January, 1851. He was a grave and godly man of patri-
archial appearance, without any of the arts of oratory,
but sound in doctrine, and "rightly dividing the word
of truth" as he saw the truth. He resigned in 1855,
since which time the church has had in the forty-five
years intervening, eight successive pastors, all of whom,
excepting Rev. W. H. Platt, from 1856 to 1865, the
Rev. Bishop Winfield, from 1865 to 1875, and Rev. C.
R. Hains, from 1875 to 1895, have served but brief pas-
torates. As Dr. Platt and Dr. Winfield have both
passed beyond the reach of praise or censure, and as
the personal friend and trusted physician of both, I
had especial opportunity of knowing them, not only as
clergymen, but outside of the sacred desk; it pleases
me to write of them as I knew them, and to render such
witness to their worth as my humble words can carry.

Dr. Platt was a man of versatile genius, and had led
quite a checkered life—a lawyer in its beginning, a soldier in its prime, and in his maturer and better years, a
minister of the gospel of peace. In all these offices, and
in the duties incident to them, he measured up to the
full standard of manhood. He came to the church in
this city in troublous times, his pastorate covering the
eventful period of 1853 to 1865. His influence for
good, not only as a clergyman, but as a citizen and as
a patriot was marked. In the dark days of 1864-'65,
when the merciless and barbarous shelling of the city

from the enemy's lines, which encircled it, made it perilous for the congregations to gather in the churches, and public religious services had been well-nigh abandoned, he addressed a letter of protest to General Meade against such vandalism, and an appeal to him as a Christian soldier to stop the war, at least against worship and against women and children, of whom the worshipers mostly consisted; and to leave to them the sanctity of the Sabbath, one day's respite of the seven, from the unnecessary cruelties of the siege. This letter had the desired effect; from that day to the end of the siege there was no more firing on Sunday, and from that day there was peace in the city on the Sabbath.

As a preacher, Dr. Platt was graceful, classic, and eloquent; as a pastor he was gentle, sympathizing, and loving. His mind was cultivated, vigorous, and grasping, and its versatility wonderful.* From the deepest problems in philosophy and in the subtlest metaphysics, in which he delighted and of which he was no ordinary master, he could drift into poetry of the most perfect measure and of the sweetest minstrelsy. Indeed, it may be said of him that he was preacher, poet, and philosopher. In his intercourse with his fellow-men he had a charm of manner that was almost magnetic; and though pronounced in his own views, he trespassed upon no man's opinion, his theology, or his politics. Hence he was always popular.

The pastorate of Rev. Dr. Winfield extended from 1868 to 1875, when he was made Bishop of California. Dr. Winfield was a man of deep piety, dignified in manner, not easily approachable by any one, of most pronounced opinion, which he held, and was capable of

---

*In the above sketch of Dr. Platt I am plagiarizing from an humble record which I have heretofore made in another place.

holding, against any odds; a bold and aggressive advocate, and a most fearless and uncompromising defender of the doctrines of the church as he construed them. Those who attended his services might expect to hear the truth as he saw it expounded with vigor and with eloquence; with no waste of words of amity, and regardless where his scimeter fell, or whose harness it pierced to the dividing asunder of soul and marrow.* But he was very popular, he filled his church, and people went to hear him, not only because the purity of his life attested his professional honesty, but because he preached to them without the froth or foam of rhetorical display, in words worthy of the gravity of his theme, and in language commensurate in its force with the immense interests which he set before them. "Life or death, spiritual and eternal."

Dr. Hain's pastorate continued from 1875 to 1895, when from some affection of the vocal chords he lost the power of speech to such an extent that he was unable to preach, and felt compelled to resign. Whilst in the pulpit, he preached the pure word of God with plainness and with love, and has ever since to the present day, living amongst his old parishioners, commended in walk and conversation that religion which teaches one to suffer and to wait when one can no longer serve. The church increased in numbers and in favor with God and man during his pastorate; and the present active, energetic, earnest and spiritual man who was called to

---

*Probably some members of the present congregation of St. Paul's Church can remember an incident at a certain Sunday morning's service, showing Dr. Winfield's boldness in discussing a subject of some delicacy—that of dancing, that even now is considered difficult to handle, though the church and the world have made a compromise in the matter, a compromise in which some good people suppose that the world got the best of the church. I will guarantee that Dr. Winfield did not sign the paper.

fill his place, Rev. O. S. Bunting, promises, not only to keep the heritage, but to enlarge its borders.

Grace Episcopal Church, in 1850, was situated on Old Street, just opposite Snyder's drug store, but it was not completed till August, 1853. The brick building still stands, but given over to commercial purposes, and, though consecrated to God, is consigned to the keeping of peanut factors.

This may all be very well, but it always seemed to me to be a sort of desecration to divert a temple, reared to the most High God, to the baser purposes of trade. This congregation some eight years before had worshiped in a small wooden building immediately on the Appomattox, just about where Williams' Mill now stands, under the pastorate of Rev. J. C. Gibson. This house was so near the water that one could easily step from the side door or window into the river, forming at this point an admirable and natural baptistry. When the congregation grew so large that it had to seek an outlet, it was supposed that, "being much water there," another congregation, the administration of whose peculiar rites required such a convenience, might be induced to locate in the abandoned building. But if such suggestion was ever made it failed to materialize, and this house, also consecrated to holiest purposes, was turned over to the common uses of an ordinary tenement house.

Under the pious, zealous, and indefatigable labors of "Parson Gibson," as he was then called by many of his people, the congregation at the church on Old Street in less than ten years again outgrew the capacity of the building, and a lot was bought on High Street, and the corner-stone of the present edifice was laid December, 1859. The basement was finished sufficiently for worship in July, 1861; but the war and its incidents prevented its completion before 1870, and in April of that year Grace Church was consecrated by Bishop Johns for the third time. Let us hope that this building, at least, "erected for the public worship of God, and separated from all unhallowed, worldly and common uses," in order to fill men's minds with greater reverence for His Glorious Majesty, may never become a house of merchandise, but remain, as it was set apart in the offices of consecration, as a house where "His holy name may be worshiped in all generations."

In more than half a century Grace Church had only one pastor, Rev. J. C. Gibson. In that time he built up the church from a few straggling communicants to one of the largest and most influential in the city. It is difficult to give a correct portraiture of the character of this remarkable man, for remarkable he must have been to have gone in and out before one congregation for so long a time, not only without offense, but beloved and honored by all. As a preacher he had none of the graces of oratory, "hanging no flowers of earthly sort upon the sacred text"; plain, pungent, and practical, "he spake as one having authority," "and the people heard him gladly." In private he not only reproved sin wherever he found it, but he gave such a lustrous example in himself of a godly walk and of a pure life, that neither malice nor scandal ever dared to touch the hem of his garment; "wise as a serpent, yet harmless as a dove," he had learned of his great prototype, Paul, "to be all things to all men, if perchance he might save some." At the semi-centennial celebration of his pastorate, the ministers of all denominations assembled at his church to join in the services, and to express by their presence their great appreciation of his work, and by their prayers their earnest wish that God would yet retain him for many years as an ambassador of His cause and kingdom.

Petersburg in the Fifties

A purse of gold was presented him by his friends, but this gift was as nothing to the noble tribute paid him by the presence and congratulations of the clergy of other churches of the city, many of whom had differed from him in doctrine and opposed him in form, with a force and vigor characteristic of ecclesiastical discussion.

He lived several years after his semi-centennial, and was succeeded by his youthful curate—a young gentleman gifted, popular, and attractive, but who will need to keep his armor burnished if he is to succeed in maintaining the prestige of his predecessor.

The Presbyterians in January, 1851, consisted of two congregations, one worshiping in the Tabb Street Church (not the present building) and one on High Street, in a building which stood in the place now built up and known as Baltimore Row. Though the Hanover Presbytery was organized as far back as 1755, it seems there was no Presbyterian church, or even any stated Presbyterian worship, prevailing in Petersburg prior to 1812 or 1813.

About this time the Rev. B. H. Rice, a native Virginian, but who had been preaching in Pennsylvania, came South with a commission from the General Assembly as a missionary, and commenced to preach in an unfinished store on Bank Street. There were but two members of the church in his congregation, but in a twelve-month the membership had increased from two to twenty, and the church was regularly organized, and Mr. Rice chosen as pastor, and was regularly installed by the Presbytery of Hanover at the spring session of 1814. This was the humble beginning of the present prosperous, large, and influential denomination in Petersburg. In 1822 the congregation had so increased that more enlarged and more comfortable quarters were sought, and a church was built on Tabb Street, on a locality on the opposite side of the street from that occupied by the present building, and in 1824, in this building, known as Tabb Street Church, was held a session of the Synod. In November, 1841, this building was destroyed by a disastrous fire, which also burned Powell's Hotel, then standing where the Iron Front stores recently stood, and with it many valuable houses in the vicinity. The large stables belonging to Powell's Hotel were also burned, with many fine horses. I was in the city at the time, and, witnessing this accident, I was more impressed as a boy with the loss of those stables, I suspect, than I was with the loss of the church. In less than four years the present beautiful and substantial structure was rebuilt on the north side of the street, and was dedicated to God by Rev. W. T. Plummer in January, 1844, Dr. John Leyburn being at that time pastor. The pastor of Tabb Street Church in January, 1851, was Rev. A. B. Vanzant, a scholarly man and a good preacher, acceptable to the people, and successful in building up the church, it was said. I never had the pleasure of knowing him, and heard him preach only a few times, though he was the pastor until 1856. During the same year, 1851, the Second Presbyterian Church was organized, November 14, by twenty-two members dismissed from Tabb Street Church for that purpose. This colony settled in the old church building on High Street, which I think had been occupied at one time by a different branch of the Presbyterian Church, and before that time had been once utilized as a shot tower, a base usage, one would think—a manufactory of ammunition, but only on advanced lines, as the Christian nations had not then carried the Bible upon the bayonet, or sought to augment the teachings of the New Testament with shrapnel and grape. The Prince of the House of David was yet on His way to Jerusalem, hailed with hosannas by his exultant worshipers, and the warrior and the war-horse, with sabres of artillery and with the bugle's martial call, were awaiting the centuries of the promise of "peace and good will to men."

Is it a coincidence that of the three eminent gentlemen who served this church in the line of pastorate for the first ten years of its work, one was a Boanerges, a preacher of, and a believer in, muscular Christianity, a sterling and true minister of the Church Militant—and another commanded a battery of Confederate artillery, and fought with the same zeal and distinguished ability that characterized his subsequent services in the pulpit —that shot were moulded only a few years in advance of the occasion?

From the date of its organization in 1813 to 1900, Tabb Street Church was served by seventeen different pastors, one on an average of every five years. Of the ten who served the church during the last half century, I had the pleasure of knowing only four of them, the Revs. Rutherford, Witherspoon, Kerr, and Rosebro. These gentlemen were all noted for their polished manners, their unaffected piety, and for their scholarly, but earnest and eloquent presentation of the truth. Circumstances made me more intimately acquainted with Drs. Witherspoon and Rosebro; and few ministers have impressed me more forcibly with the idea that, unconscious of self or forgetful of self, they were going about their Master's business, ready in all things to do and to abide His holy will. To one who sat on the outskirts of the congregation and watched them in their daily walk amongst men, they seemed to "glory only in the Cross of Christ," and to commend not themselves, but only the Crucified One.

The Second Presbyterian congregation worshiped in the building on High Street before referred to, until 1863, when the present church was erected on Wash-

ington Street. Its first pastor, the Rev. Mr. Wilson,
was inaugurated the year of my arrival in Petersburg,
and served only a few years. He was succeeded by
Rev. Dr. Theo. Pryor; he by Rev. Dr. Miller, who for
a few years had served the Tabb Street congregation;
he by Rev. Mr. Petrie, and he by the present solid, conservative, and consecrated man of God, Mr. Wynn.
The average pastorate was ten years.

  Dr. Pryor, after a few years' service at this church,
removed to Nottoway County, and in the church at
Nottoway Court House preached with great vigor and
eloquence, even to an advanced old age. Dr. Pryor
was a man cast in the mould of which martyrs were
made in the olden time, and whether roasted, broiled,
or boiled, he would never have yielded one iota in the
confession of that faith which he so long held and so
strongly defended.*

---

  *Dr. Theo Pryor was one of four young gentlemen who com-
menced the practice of law in the county of Dinwiddie about 1820,
each one of whom on professing religion some few years afterwards,
left the law and entered the ministry. The others were the two At-
kinsons of that county, one of whom became a Bishop in the Protestant Episcopal Church, and the other a distinguished divine in
the Presbyterian Church and professor at Hampden-Sidney College,
and the fourth was my honored father, who left the law after he had
attained distinction, and became a local preacher in the Methodist
Church. I have lately unearthed his license to practise law, dated
the 14th day of February, 1820, and append the full text:
Virginia, to wit:
  Whereas, John Gregory Claiborne, gentleman, hath produced to us
the requisite certificate from the county court of Dinwiddie, touching
his honesty, probity, and good demeanor, and hath applied to us for
a license to practise Law, and having examined him as to his knowledge of the Law and found him duly qualified, therefore, we license
him, the said John Gregory Claiborne, to practise the Law in the
Supreme and Inferior Courts of this commonwealth. Given under
our hands and seals this 14th day of February, 1820.
                    SPENCER ROANE (*Seal*),
                    WM. H. CABELL, (*Seal*),
                    WM. BROCKENBOROUGH (*Seal*).

Petersburg in the Fifties

The Catholic congregation of Petersburg was organized about 1820 with about fifty members, and mass was said for the first time, and for twenty-one years afterwards, in a house at the corner of Short Market and High Streets. There was no regular pastor of this people during all that period, but in 1841 the church at the corner of Washington and Long Market Streets was built, and was dedicated in January, 1842, by Bishop Whalan as St. Joseph's Catholic Church of Petersburg, the Rev. S. A. Bernier the first resident priest.

In 1851, when I came to Petersburg, the resident priest was the Rev. Joseph Dixon. I do not remember to have met him. In 1853 the Rev. Father Hitzelberger was transferred from Norfolk to Petersburg and remained as pastor of the church for three years. In our mutual ministrations to the sick, especially in one family of prominence at that time, we became well acquainted. He was a man of great learning and research, and a most genial and agreeable companion. He resigned his pastorate in 1856 to become a Jesuit, and Rev. Father Mulvey, D. D., took his place, and continued in office for sixteen years.

During this eventful period, the most eventful and the most unhappy in the history of Petersburg, when for four years a cruel and relentless war was waged even to her doors, and the blood of father and son shed by a merciless foe stained the very lintels of the homesteads they were called to save from violence and rapine, and in the four successive years of the so-called peace, worse than the peace which reigned at Warsaw,—the years of oppression and humiliation of a gallant but unarmed people, when the foot of the slave was placed by the conqueror upon the neck of his master, and the grasp of the carpet-bagger, less pitiful and less respectable than the slave, was gathering up the little that was left to feed the hungry and to support the helpless,—Father Mulvey walked amongst us brave, cheerful, cheering, helping where help was possible, and dispensing to all, friend and foe alike, the consolations of his holy office. During the fearful assault of the siege, when shot and shell rained devastation upon this devoted city, he seemed as unaffected by danger as though devoid of fear. During the last day of the siege, when the fighting was almost continuous charge and repulse, a young captain, not yet of age, in leading a forlorn hope, was shot through the body, and brought back to the rear by the ambulance corps. I was called to him, but saw at once that his hurt was beyond human help. Recognizing him, and knowing that he was a Catholic, I directed a soldier to summon Father Mulvey. He must have been somewhere near, for in a few minutes he was at my side. I pointed out the young officer, and told the Father that he had but a little time left, as the death damp had already gathered on his brow, when the good man spoke up, "Oh, he is all right, he is all right, I saw him before you." But he came to us, and kneeling down administered the last offices of the church, the gallant young fellow receiving them with perfect faith, and passing away with a smile from the boundary line of battle to the borders of that land where the nations learn war no more.

Father Mulvey remained in charge of the church in Petersburg until 1872. He died in December of that year, and was buried on the 15th, followed to the cemetery by great crowds of people, irrespective of denominational association—people who gathered at his funeral to testify their appreciation of his worth and of his loss to a community in which he had lived to dispense so many deeds of mercy and of charity. Bishop, now Cardinal Gibbons, preached a most able and eloquent sermon; but nothing of the many good words in which he referred to the departed priest bore so telling a significance, built up so beautiful an eulogium, as when he said: "Father Mulvey lived and died poor, and his superflous means he distributed to the poor. At his death there was perhaps as much as $10 found in his house."

Father Mulvey was a man of ripe learning, an English, Greek, and Latin scholar of such accepted merit that the propaganda of Rome conferred on him the title of D. D., an honor which with characteristic modesty he declined. As a man he was most companionable, his conversation abounding in anecdote, and enriched with the brightest of Irish humor. It was my privilege to have held his confidence and to have enjoyed his friendship; and standing by his bed at the last to have witnessed his final fearless fight and victory over death. Gently in his bereft senses, cheerily, even playfully, he rallied a kind old parishioner who was weeping bitterly beside his bed—then simply closed his eyes and slept.

During a short interregnum of Father Mulvey's pastorate, whilst he was temporarily called to fill the place of Bishop Gibbons during a visit to Rome, Father Van der Plas, a talented and bright young priest from Holland, was assigned to St. Joseph's Church; but, poor fellow, he succumbed to an attack of fever and died after only a few months of service. After the death of Father Mulvey, the Rev. T. J. Wilson was appointed to the rectorship of St. Joseph's Church. Father Wilson was a generous, big-hearted, genial Irishman, who soon made his way to the hearts, not only of his own congregation, but of the people of all denominations, and those of no denomination. His charities were great and bestowed without regard to church affiliation. He was exceedingly active and zealous in his work, and during his pastorate St.

Joseph's Parochial School was opened, St. Joseph's new Catholic cemetery was purchased and dedicated, and St. Francis' Church at Jarratt's, in Sussex County, was built and dedicated. In 1884 he was transferred to Harpers Ferry, carrying with him the love and the prayers of the people, especially of the poor, to whom he was endeared by his many benefactions.

He was followed by Rev. W. B. Henley, of Richmond, who only remained until September, 1885, when he was transferred to Portsmouth, Virginia, and the present incumbent, Rev. J. T. O'Farrell, installed in his place. In the sixteen years of service of Father O'Farrell the congregation has increased manifold, and by his zeal and indomitable energy he has erected a monument to himself in the present beautiful church building, which will testify of his work as long as it shall stand. His people, and all the people, hope that he may be left with them for many years to illustrate in his life the doctrines of the Divine Master in whose footsteps he follows.

There were three colored churches in Petersburg in 1851. One of these was a Methodist church, the old Union Street Methodist Church as it now stands, and which had been turned over to the colored Methodists after the occupation of the Washington Street Methodist Church. Of the two Baptist churches, one was what is known as the Third Baptist Church, now the same building; and the other the Gillfield Baptist Church, which was then a wooden structure, and which, since the war, has been replaced by the present handsome and commodious edifice.

The colored congregations, especially that at the Gilfield Church, were large, but a great many slaves worshiped in the white churches, where a place was always reserved for them in the gallery. On communion Sundays the colored members were invited down into the body of the church, and, after the whites, partook of the elements at the same altar. There were some colored preachers of great gift in uncultured eloquence; one of them, whom I heard at the Gillfield Baptist Church some fifty years ago, still lives and preaches in Richmond, Virginia, the Rev. John Jasper, who has acquired some eminence as a disputant of the generally accepted theory of the solar system, and who still proclaims with dogmatic pertinacity that the "sun do move," not the earth.

After the tragic events of the Southampton Insurrection, twenty years before, in August, 1831, the assembly of slaves in church, or elsewhere, without the presence of some reputable white man or men, was forbidden by law. Often, or generally, the white man himself was a preacher and in charge of the congregation. Night service was impracticable, as the curfew rang at nine o'clock, and no slave was allowed to leave the premises known as his home without a pass from his owner or employer.

This vigor of requirement was made necessary, or supposed to be necessary, from the fact that Nat Turner, a fanatical negro preacher in the county of Southampton, had hatched a diabolical plot, known as the "Insurrection," in his nightly religious meetings, whereby he, with some hundred of his deluded followers, was enabled in one day and night to murder in cold blood, without regard to age or sex, but mostly women and children, nearly an hundred whites, before an armed resistance could be organized to repel and capture the insurgents. And though hundreds of slaves rallied to defend their masters and to show their fidelity, yet the possible recurrence of such a tragedy created a widespread alarm, and weakened the confidence of the master in the slave in many instances, and disturbed the kindly relations which had always existed between them. The kindness of their relations may be better appreciated when Nat Turner himself refused to murder his own master and mistress, "who," he said, "had been too kind to him," and when one of his chief aids made it a point in joining the insurgents, "that he should not be required to murder his own white people."

Ignorance, fanaticism, brandy, and the instigation of Northern emissaries evidently moved the misguided blacks more than the love or the desire of their own freedom.*

There was no Jewish Church in Petersburg in 1851. The congregation of the Rod of Sholem was organized in October, 1858, and worshiped in a building on Sycamore Street. In 1866 it removed to the basement of the Masonic Hall on Tabb Street. The first Hazan, or reader, was Mr. M. Oppenheimer, who served for four years. He was succeeded by Mr. Gross, who served for two years, and resigned, being subsequently recalled, however, and serving several years longer. In 1874 the congregation bought the old Baptist Church at the corner of High and Market Streets, but not liking the situation, afterwards bought a lot on Union Street and erected the present handsome and convenient synagogue. This church is now under the care of Dr. Tyre, a learned and eloquent German scholar, and numbers amongst its members nearly all of the Israelitish citizens of Petersburg.

---

* Those who wish to read a detailed account of this horrible massacre, with the accompanying circumstances, and of the capture and execution of the ring-leader, will find it, with much other matter of great historic interest bearing upon the subject of slavery, in an exhaustive and most interesting volume, "The Southampton Insurrection," by William Sydney Drewry, Ph. B., M. A. (University of Virginia), Honorary Scholar in History (Johns Hopkins University), 1900. Washington: The Neale Publishing Company.

Petersburg in the Fifties 91

Having noted the pulpit, perhaps I should speak next of the press of Petersburg in 1850. The leading papers, neither dailies, were *The Intelligencer*, founded in 1789 by William Prentiss, and edited by John W. Syme, and *The Southside Democrat*, founded in 1849, and edited by Roger A. Pryor. The former was, and had been for years, the mouthpiece and exponent of the Whig Party, which at that time represented the majority in politics, not only in Petersburg, but generally in the surrounding counties. Mr. Syme was a son of Parson Syme, so long rector of St. Paul's Church, and was a good representative of the dignity, intelligence, and conservatism of the class to which he was born, and whose opinions he boldly and faithfully upheld. He was a spirited, incisive writer, abounding in humor, quick at repartee, and bitter when provoked. He was a most genial, companionable man, fond of good cheer and exceedingly popular with his party. He represented the city in the General Assembly of Virginia for years; and owing to his influence, mostly, the Southside Railroad was incorporated, with its terminus in Petersburg, instead of Richmond.

Just before the beginning of the Civil War, Mr. Syme removed to Raleigh, North Carolina, and bought and edited the *Raleigh Register*, I think; and *The Intelligencer* passed into the hands of Bingham and Moore, but its course was short-lived and it did not survive the war.

The Southside Democrat was founded in 1849, owned and edited by Roger A. Pryor, now a distinguished jurist of New York City. Pryor was, as was Syme, the son of a clergyman, an eminent divine of the Presbyterian Church, and was talented, studious, ambitious, bold to contempt of consequences, and a fitting leader of the young Democracy which was springing up in the decadence of the Whig Party, tainted at that time with free-soilism and abolition at the North, and ready on that account for dissolution at the South.

For the first few years of his editorial life Pryor confined himself closely to his office, evidently studying the highest standards in his reading, and his editorials were a revelation of strength and purity in classic English. It was impossible, however, for a man of his tastes and force not to drift into politics outside of the sanctum of his paper, and the public soon recognized him as one of the ablest and most eloquent speakers upon the hustings and in the bitter dissensions that marked the proceedings of every gathering of the people in those years.

In the mutterings and threatenings of the storm that was soon to break in fury upon a hitherto peaceful and peace-loving land, he found abundant opportunity for the cultivation and display of those rare powers of oratory in debate which subsequently forced him to the front of the forum.

In 1863 he was called to edit the *Enquirer*, the paper which for years, under the venerable Thomas Ritchie, had been the mouthpiece of the Democratic Party in Virginia, and the ablest exponent of Democratic doctrine. Whilst filling the office of editor, Pryor was principal in several affairs of honor, as the duel was then called, but he came out of all unhurt. The duello was the fashionable mode of settling differences between gentlemen at that day; and though indefensible from some points of view, was less reprehensible and less barbarous than the present system, which places a revolver in the hip pocket of the aggrieved citizen and bids him open battle upon the street or elsewhere, as much to the danger of the innocent bystander as to his opponent.

After taking charge of the *Enquirer*, Pryor did not remain in the editorial chair very long, and from the tripod he stepped to the floor of Congress. Mr. Wm. O. Goode, who had been elected to the House of Representatives from the Fourth District of Virginia, died before taking his seat, and Pryor was elected to fill his place, his opponent in the canvass being Col. Thomas F. Goode. His career in Congress was short and he had only time to work up his reputation as an impassioned speaker and a fearless defender of the rights of the States. Before two sessions passed the dominant party dissolved the Union, broke the compact of the Constitution, and drove the South into secession.

He came home with the Virginia delegates, and as private in cavalry, as colonel of infantry, and as brigadier-general he drew his trenchant blade in defense of his native State in a cause as hopeless as it was just and righteous.

After the war, true to his combative and courageous instincts, he sought the fields of the enemy for forage, and though handicapped by poverty and regarded as an alien, and by many as a traitor to the old flag, he forged his way again to the front, and attained the ermine of a judge in a profession crowded with the wisest, the ablest, and the most astute men of the greatest city of the country.

The *Southside Democrat*, after Pryor left it, passed into the hands of A. D. Banks in 1863; then Banks and Keiley, then Banks and Thackston. Keiley I will note hereafter. Thackston was editor only a short time before the final collapse of the paper in the events of 1861-'65; but Banks was a character who is worthy of recollection. He was fat, genial, jovial, of imperturbable good humor, even in the exciting scenes and times of the last days of the old regime. He knew everybody and made friends with everybody. He loved play better than work, and found it difficult to confine himself to the routine drudgery of the editor's office, hence often absented himself therefrom on little trips of pleasure, and nowhere found so much to entertain and amuse him as in Washington, where he seemed to know intuitively and intimately the leading men of his party. A striking picture of Banks strolling about the Capitol with his arm around the neck of Stephen A. Douglas still remains in my memory. Douglas was at that time a great figure and a dominant character in the political arena; but no man could resist the genial and artless assurance of Banks. He seemed to know all of the big men, and to enjoy their confidence and their companionship. I perpetrated a little piece of mischief on him once, which his friends enjoyed more than he, I suspect. He was in the habit, when the fever came on him to go to Washington, of sending his exchanges by the printer's devil to my office, with the polite request that I would get out the paper for him until his return, which was always an unknown quantity as to time. I frequently did this with pleasure, and loved, as everybody else did, to oblige him; but it occurred to me on the last occasion of such a request that it would add some piquancy to the paper if I changed its politics, which I did, pitching into the administration with all the mad zeal of a new convert. The next day a telegram, more emphatic than elegant, came to the office from Pryor, then in Congress, inquiring who was "running the *Southside Democrat.*" Banks followed the telegram at his very early convenience, but he took the joke in good part, and it did not interrupt our kindly relations.

Poor, kindly, genial, generous, happy fellow, his paper perished in the general immolation of the rights of the States. I lost sight of him after I went into the army, in April, 1861, but I heard that he lived only a short time, fortunately dying without knowledge of the bitterness of the defeat of the cause which he had so enthusiastically championed.

But neither the *Petersburg Intelligencer* nor the *Southside Democrat* was published at the commencement of the war or during the war. The only paper which managed to live through those tempestuous times was the *Petersburg Express*. This was the first daily paper ever published in the city, and was founded in 1853 by Mr. Samuel B. Paul, then a resident of Petersburg, but now an eminent lawyer in New York. He sold it after a few months to Crutchfield and Campbell, under whose management it was a great success, financially and otherwise. It was independent in politics, yet boldly an upholder of the Southern cause; but on the entrance of the Federal troops into the city it was taken possession of by some Northern soldiers, and for the short time in which they published it it was aggressively and offensively a Yankee sheet. After its restoration to its rightful owners it was thought by some people to lean too much toward the North, and its popularity waned. It was then sold to O. P. Hains and William Campbell. In turn they sold it to T. J. Clark & Co., and they to Smith, Camp & Co., who changed its name to the *Courier*, and then it was sold to Charles Peebles, and then to E. B. Branch & Co., who christened it the *Progress*, and then in 1872 to Messrs. Venable, Gregory & Patteson, who rechristened it the *Appeal*.

In the meantime, soon after the war, in 1865, the Hon. A. M. Keiley, now Judge of the International Court in Egypt, and Major E. B. Branch, who is yet living, established a paper which they called the *News*.

Mr. Keiley had been distinguished as an ultra Union man, even voting against the ordinance of secession, though with a musket on his shoulder as a soldier of the Confederacy, yet so radically had his views been changed by four years of war and the reckless violations of all constitutional obligations by the Washington Government, that he attacked the authorities in power with a vigor and bitterness which soon drew upon himself their indignant interference. He was arrested and cast into prison by General Gibbon, then the military commandant of the district, and the *News* suppressed.

Having been released in a short time by intervention of friends and on the promise of better behavior, the name of the *News* was changed to the *Index*. It was then sold to Cameron, Sykes & Co., and then to Chamberlaine, Sykes & Co., and finally, in 1873, was consolidated with the *Appeal*, and published by a company under the name of *Index-Appeal*.

Soon after this Mr. R. P. Barham, from manager, became publisher and proprietor. Since that time it has been uninterruptedly published by Mr. Barham, and whilst independent of party, it is essentially Democratic, loyal to the South, conservative in sentiment, and withal one of the most prosperous and best-paying papers in this section of the country.

There were several other papers published between 1850 and 1860 in Petersburg—as the *Daily Star*, by Rev. A. J. Leavenworth; the *Press*, by S. B. Paul; the *Constitution*, by J. R. Lewellyn, in 1859; the *Bulletin*, 1860, by W. H. Ianson; *Prices Current*, 1858, by T. J. Clark; but all were short lived except the last. Mr. Clark, who is the veteran of the press in this city, still publishes the latter, a sheet of interest to the mercantile community.

Though there was no lack of educational facilities in Petersburg in 1850, and no lack of interest in the subject, yet, and especially in the matter of public schools, there was no comparison between the opportunity afforded for getting even a common-school education then and at the present time. The system of public schools provided for in the constitution of 1869, and as carried out in the city, at least, leaves no excuse for any parent to say that his child has had no opportunity for securing an education and a liberal one. The efficient Superintendent of Public Schools for Petersburg, Dr. Duncan Brown, reports for the year ending June, 1900: Whites—males, 741; females, 822; total, 1,563. Colored—males, 682; females, 1,012; total 1,694. With twenty-nine white teachers and twenty-four colored teachers, including two special teachers for stenography and cooking.

The present status of the public schools seems a miraculous evolution of the Anderson Seminary, the only institution of the kind a half century ago. David Anderson, a Scotchman by birth, but a citizen of Petersburg, died in 1819, and after providing in his will for his negro servant Jingo, bequeathed the balance of his estate to the city, the property to be sold and invested in bank stock, and the interest or dividends on the same to be "applied to the education of poor children, in reading, writing, and primary arithmetic."

A suit was instituted by the executors of the will against the City of Petersburg, but the defendants won the case, and the Common Hall appointed Lewis Mabry, Jabez Smith, and Edward Powell, a committee to mature a plan of instruction. The monitorial, or Lancasterian system, was adopted, and on January 1st, 1821, the plan was put in execution. During the first ten years of the school "upwards of four hundred children were educated in whole or in part," and there was a continued and uninterrupted success of the same until the adoption of the present system.

One of the public schools of the city is still conducted in the old Anderson building, which yet stands as a monument to the munificent charity of the generous old Scotchman, who really "inaugurated the cause of the education of the poor in Petersburg." In 1851 this school was in a most flourishing condition, filled to its capacity. The teacher at that time and for many years afterwards was the Rev. J. D. Keiley. He was an Irishman, educated, it was said, for the church, though at that time he was not a Catholic. He was a man of great learning, always a student, and of many eccentricities, but of rare qualifications for the management and instruction of boys. He was an exemplar in this respect, not only as a school teacher, but in the training and rearing of his own sons, of which there were four. One, the Hon. A. M. Keiley, not only attained to distinction early in his career, as a soldier, and as a representative of his city in the General Assembly of Virginia, but was appointed, by the President of the United States, Judge of the International Court at Alexandria, Egypt, a position of great honor and responsibility, and which he has held for nearly twenty years. Another is a distinguished prelate in the Catholic Church, and Bishop of Savannah; and the two others, men of mark and position in Greater New York.

Mr. Keiley had a special fondness for the old classics, and as our tastes in that respect were similar, we sometimes met and interchanged views on subjects that were of mutual interest. On one occasion, whilst walking out with some young ladies, I met the old gentleman, who accosted me with the Greek aphorism, "they that would be wise must walk with the wise." I did not consider it entirely necessary to translate this salutation to my light-hearted companions, but I noted afterwards that the old gentleman never took the same interest in my studies. We were good friends, however, to the last of his long life. After discontinuing teaching he gave himself up, soul and body, to works of charity. I never knew a man who exhibited in his life such utter self-abnegation. "What shall we eat and wherewithal shall we be clothed" did not enter into any of his calculations so far as he was personally concerned. Indeed, I fear that he did not have always in his last days that which he should have had to eat, or that which he should have had to wear, to render him comfortable—not than an hundred hands, besides filial ones, were not ready to contribute to his necessities; but he did not seem to recognize the fact that in his body he had any necessities. All that he could get he would spend for others, and as long as his strength enabled him to go, he went daily seeking the poor, the sick, the miserable, in hovel and in jail, carrying such comforts as he could command, and the consolations of that religion which he construed to mean "visiting the widows and orphans in their affliction and keeping himself unspotted from the world." There is many a one left living yet who could testify to his faithful and unfaltering efforts to help them in trouble, and who will testify when called before the Grand Assize that when they were "hungry or sick or in prison, he came to them and ministered to them."

No pupils were allowed to enter this public school except on tickets, and no tickets were issued to any child under seven years of age, or whose parents were considered "able to pay for their tuition in some other school." As significant of the estimation in which this school was held about the middle of the last century, we find appointed as trustees and visitors such men as John Bragg, Daniel Lyon, Thomas J. Gholson, G. W. Bolling, Lewis Mabry, Thomas N. Lee, Hugh Nelson, Thomas Branch, Francis Major, Robert Ritchie, D'Arcy Paul, and A. G. McIlwaine. The names of these men will be recognized as representing the highest class of the best citizens of the best days of Petersburg.

There were some other minor public schools, supported partly from the Literary Fund of the State and partly by city appropriation.

Of the private schools, there were three for boys. One, the Petersburg Classical Institute, at the present High School Building. This had been incorporated as far back as 1838, with a capital of $9,500, in shares of five hundred dollars each, and had had a long and distinguished career. "Its curriculum embraced, amongst others things, Latin, Greek, Hebrew, French, Spanish, and Italian," and had had in its corps of instructors some of the most noted educators of the day, such as the Rev. E. D. Saunders, Rev. Mr. Leavenworth, Mons. Armad Preot, and others. Mr. Thomas Davidson was the principal in 1850. After the war Mr. Davidson opened a large and flourishing female school on Market Street, in the house now owned by the Catholic Church, and occupied by the Sisters of Charity, who conduct a most excellent mixed school for girls and boys, known as St. Joseph's School.

Besides the Classical Institute, there was a male school at the head of Harrison Street, taught by Mr. Magee at the old Harrison homestead, in the yard of which was the mammoth white oak tree for so many years a landmark of the city, and which fell only a few years ago under the vandalism of business enterprise. Mr. Magee was a faithful and conscientious teacher, and had a good school for many years.

Another male school was taught by Mr. Charles Campbell, the noted author of the "History of Virginia." This school was located on Halifax Street, just opposite the New Market, on the old Campbell lot, which extended through from Market Street to Halifax. Mr. Campbell was a most scholarly and companionable gentleman, but he was a representative of the old regime, in which the rod reigned. He believed in the doctrine enunciated by Squire Jones in the "Hoosier Schoolmaster," "no lickin', no l'arnin'." Only a few days ago I met with one of his old pupils, who still cherishes lively recollections of a lively birch switch which adorned the master's desk. Indeed, the rod was the right-hand assistant in every male school of that day, and was recognized even down to the days of McCabe as a powerful help to the master and a most persuasive incitement to the pupil. Of late, flogging has been put away from the schools as a relic of barbarism, and it is now held that it serves to degrade the boy, to break his spirit, and moral suasion has usurped the fasces. Of course it is not politic, if pertinent, to inquire if the boys of this generation are any better, braver, more high strung, or more studious than were their fathers; but one cannot fail of recalling the struggles, the trials, the courage, the manhood of the latter, and asking if in the heritage they have handed down to their children they have shown the marks of men whose spirit had been whipped out of them at school?

Another male school was taught in the brick house, now the parsonage, in the rear of the Union Street Methodist Church on Union Street, by Mr. Williams T. Davis. Mr. Davis was a native of Gloucester County, but when I was a student at Randolph-Macon College, then located at Boydton, from the years 1845 to 1848, he was principal of the Preparatory Department. It was there that I first met him, and it was then that I recognized the rugged honesty of character and the unpretentious but unswerving truthfulness of life that made me his friend. From that time until I stood at his bedside, forty-three years afterwards, and closed his eyes, my regard for him was unabated and unbroken.

In 1851, after the loss of his first wife, a Miss Beale, a sister of an old friend and comrade of mine in the Senate of Virginia and in the Confederate Army, General Beale, he removed to Petersburg and opened the school to which I have referred. He continued to teach this male school until 1856, when he was elected President of the Female College in the house now occupied by Mr. Robert Gilliam at the corner of Sycamore Street and College Avenue.

This college had been erected and chartered by eighteen prominent gentlemen of the city in 1856—not one of whom now remains save the author of these memoirs. Amongst these incorporators we find the names of D'Arcy Paul, E. P. Nash, William Lee, Thomas Branch, B. P. Harrison, J. M. Shepherd, John Kerr, and others. How many of them are remembered by the present generation?

In 1862 Mr. Davis married Miss C. V. Robinson, a friend of mine and a frequent inmate of my house; and in 1863 became President of the Southern Female College, which position he held until his lamented death in July, 1888. True to the instincts of his sturdy manhood, Mr. Davis took his place as one of the defenders of the city when the day of danger came, and with that immortal handful of militia, 150 in all, who met Kautz's Brigade in sight of the city gates, helped to delay the attacking column of that command until reinforcements could be brought up. And not only that, but he had already given three sons to the Confederate service, one dying at Chancellorsville, too ill to do more than cheer on his comrades to that victory which he did not live to see; and another, a participant with Mahone's Brigade in the Crater fight, was wounded in that magnificent but merciless assault, "where none asked and none gave quarter," until thirteen Federal battle flags and Federal regiments went down before one brigade of Confederate bayonets, numbering 800!

At the death of Mr. Davis his eldest son by his second marriage, Mr. Arthur Kyle Davis, succeeded to the presidency of the school, and, adding to his father's inflexible tenacity of purpose the zeal of young blood and young ambition, has built up in a few years a school

Petersburg in the Fifties 103

which to-day has a corps of fourteen members of the faculty and numbers 137 students, representing five States of the Union.

There were three female schools in Petersburg in 1851. One at the corner of Marshall and Jefferson Streets, taught by Miss Simpson, an English lady who had long lived in Petersburg—a lady of refinement and of culture, who had a good school as long as she continued teaching and who is doubtless gratefully and affectionately remembered by some of the mothers and grandmothers of the present generation. Another was located at the corner of Market and Washington Streets, and was taught by the Rev. Mr. Leavenworth, a ripe scholar and a conscientious and painstaking instructor. The grade of scholarship in his school was always high, and the course thorough, especially in mathematics. Another school at the corner of Adams and Wythe Streets was taught by Mrs. Indiana Pannill. Mrs. Pannill was the daughter of the Hon. R. K. Meade, the representative from this district in Congress at that time, and, subsequently, Minister to Brazil. She was a woman of great beauty and vivacity, and a great belle, but, rejecting many suitors, she gave her hand to Mr. William Pannill, a young lawyer of fine attainments and of brilliant promise, but of very limited means. They opened a school at Dr. Worsham's, in Dinwiddie County, Virginia, immediately after marriage, but in about two years Mr. Pannill unfortunately died. Mrs. Pannill then returned to the city and opened a school herself, withdrawing entirely from the society which her personal attractions and accomplishments so well fitted her to adorn. She gave her whole time and life to the honorable profession that she adopted, and for twelve or fifteen years had a most successful career as a teacher. She then married the Rev. Dr. Platt, to whom we have referred before in these memoirs, and left Petersburg with him for Louisville, Kentucky, where he had charge of a large and fashionable church. After some years of pastorate in Louisville, Dr. Platt was called to San Francisco, California, and then some years later to New York, and finally back to Petersburg, where not long afterwards his wife ended her eventful and useful career amongst the scenes of her youth, and with the renewed love of her friends who had survived with her a quarter of a century of Death's inexorable calls.

These were the only schools of promise, but my story would be incomplete and unjust if I failed to note a mixed school for boys and girls kept by Mrs. Richard Weeks on Dunlop Street, and afterwards on Washington Street, the house now occupied by Mr. William Weeks, her son. Mrs. Weeks was most popular and beloved as a teacher, and had rare qualifications for winning the affection of her little pupils and training them in the rudiments of learning. I am sure that amongst those pupils who may be still living to-day there is not one who would not lovingly testify to her faithfulness as a teacher and a friend.

The professions of law and medicine were well represented in Petersburg in 1850, as they had been for half a century before. Amongst the lawyers whose brilliant talents and solid learning and distinguished services in the State and in the Union had thrown a halo around the bar, and made an inspiration for the men about to take their places upon the arena where honor and wealth awaited worth and genius, were the names of Bolling Robertson, who afterwards became Governor of Louisiana and U. S. Senator; and David Robertson, a Scotchman, who must have been a man of great energy and endurance, for it is said that he did not hesitate to drive in his old gig in one day between Boydton and Petersburg, a distance of eighty miles. (This

Mr. Robertson reported the debates in the State Convention in which the Federal Constitution was adopted.) Then there were Winfield Scott, afterwards the Commander-in-Chief of the United States Army; Jack Baker, a great wit, a distinguished advocate, and one of the counsel who defended Aaron Burr in his famous trial for treason in the beginning of nineteenth century—the trial in which Wirt won his unfading laurels; George Keith Taylor, whose name and whose fame are imperishable; Benjamin Watkins Leigh, second to no one as a representative man in those days of giants. Mr. Leigh was United States Senator from 1834 to 1838, and he was also a member of the convention which formed the Constitution of Virginia of 1829. In this connection Dr. Atkinson, in the Morstock Papers, says that to Leigh the "State was indebted for the modicum of conservatism retained in the constitution of that day." (To whom is the State indebted for the modicum of conservatism retained in the constitution of 1902? The modicum is too small to measure.)

Besides the names of the eminent lawyers of the Petersburg bar just recited, were Thomas A. Dunn, an eccentric man, but said to have been a brilliant orator; and John Allison, also a man of great eccentricity, but of reputation in the profession. Mr. Allison lived on Market Street, in the house now occupied by Mr. Beckwith, I think. He lived to some year in the fifties, and was the only one of the worthies mentioned with whom I had any acquaintance.

The members of the bar in 1851 were F. H. Archer, Judge John F. May, David May, James Alfred Jones, Thomas S. Gholson, W. L. Watkins, Alexander Donnan, James M. Donnan, John P. May, R. G. Pegram, Wm. Robertson, Wm. Robertson, Jr., R. R. Collier, Charles F. Collier, A. B. Spooner, Thomas Dunn, James E. Watson, Charles J. Cabaniss, Thomas Wallace, R. K. Meade, W. T. Joynes, Marcus Gaines, and John Lyon.

Of these only two are living at this date, Col. F. H. Archer and Mr. Charles J. Cabaniss.* The former, old, "full of years and full of honors," still lives in Petersburg, but has retired from the active practise of his profession. He commanded a company of the Petersburg Volunteers in the First Virginia Regiment during the Mexican War, and was the hero of the fight at Rives' Farm, on the 9th of June, 1864, commanding the handful of reserves of old men and boys who withstood for so many hours the assaults of Kautz's Brigade and saved the city from pillage and rapine. On casual acquaintance with Colonel Archer no one would imagine what manner of man was hidden under that quiet, gentle and dignified composure which characterized his personality, yet we doubt if he ever felt the emotion of fear. An earnest Christian gentleman, he would not court danger; but if duty called to any course, he would never recognize danger, but simply and unostentatiously obey the call, to the death, if need be, without reserve or hesitation. With a cultured and well stored mind, and long association with the best men of three decades, together with a graceful and ready pen, it is a pity that he has not put down on paper reminiscences of his eventful life for the pleasure and for the profit of the generation now watching the soft sunset of his closing career.

Mr. Cabaniss, the only other survivor, has long since retired from the practice of law, I believe, and is spending his remaining days on his estate in a neighboring county, illustrating, as only the old Virginia gentleman can illustrate, *otium cum dignitate*, and exhibiting to the *novi homines* the last living exemplar of the old regime.

---

*Both of these gentlemen have passed away, 1903.

He is the only man left in his vicinage, I am told, that has successfully resisted the covetous greed of modern commerce essaying to enter his paternal grounds, where neither the sound of axe nor saw has yet been heard in its forests.

I think I knew personally every member of the bar at the period spoken of, and I can testify that amongst them were men of note and mark who well measured up to the high standard set them by their illustrious predecessors.

Amongst the lawyers prominent at the bar were the Mays—Judge John F. May and Mr. David May. Judge May was the Nestor of the bar. Indeed, he had retired from practise and must have been quite old, as my father had studied law under him more than thirty years before. He was a man of sterling character, and learned in the law, and commanded both respect and reverence from all classes. His brother, Mr. David May, many years his junior, was also a man of the highest character personally and professionally. Neither he nor the Judge were eloquent advocates, but counsellors—safe, just, and conscientious. Judge May lived on High Street in the house now owned and occupied by Mrs. Spotswood. Mr. David May also lived on High Street in the house now occupied by Mr. R. R. Meacham.

The most noted lawyers were probably Messrs. Thomas Gholson, William T. Joynes, and James Alfred Jones. Mr. Jones had reputation for great legal research, industry, and acumen. He was a bachelor until somewhat late in life, when he removed to Richmond and married a lady of Mobile. He maintained and enlarged his reputation in Richmond, and attained to a large and lucrative practise.

Mr. Joynes was a great student, both learned and wise; an able counsellor and an eloquent advocate. He attained to the ermine in middle life and was a member of the Court of Appeals until his death. Though of excellent means and of lucrative practise while at the bar, he cared little for show, and lived on the alley distinguished as the place of the Police Department, and in the brick house adjoining the present Police Station. Here he dispensed an elegant hospitality to his friends, and those fortunate enough to be enrolled as his guests were sure of a treat of Attic salt—as a seasoning.

Mr. Gholson was a man of pleasing address, debonair and popular; an able lawyer and a brilliant and eloquent speaker. He also attained to the ermine and was Judge of the Circuit Court of this district for some years. He lived on Bollingbrook Street at one time in the house next to Wheaden's, or Dr. Robinson's stables, and also dispensed a most generous and elegant hospitality. Not long before the war he purchased the house on Friend Street now occupied by Mr. Dunlop, a more commodious and finer residence. But it must not be supposed that his house on Bollingbrook Street had its present surroundings. Lower Bollingbrook Street at that time was the home of the bon-ton of the city. Mr Gholson had only one daughter, a charming young lady, a beauty and a belle, who made his home not only happy to her parents but to her many young friends; and at her entertainments, refined and recherche, you might be confident of meeting the grace and chivalry of Virginia in her palmiest days. Miss Gholson married Mr. Norman Walker, of Richmond, and after the war went to England to live, followed soon after by the Judge and his excellent wife. He declined to take up the thread of the law, tangled and stained and broken by the miserable tinkers of legislation gathered under the curse of reconstruction, and left his profession to engage in more congenial pursuits. I recall very vividly my first visit to Judge Gholson's mansion. It was in the month of July, 1859, when returning from the University of Virginia, in company with Judge Gholson's son John, afterwards the Rev. John Y. Gholson. I stopped over in Petersburg with several others of the University students. Mr. Gholson gave us a dinner, and at that dinner I met a young Mr. Farrar, also a University student, whom, in some way, I had not met before. Mr. Farrar had with him a banjo, an original Virginia musical instrument, not as common then as now, and entertained the company greatly with his wonderful gift of music. Mr. Gholson was also greatly taken with his genius. He went to Farrar after he had ceased playing, and laying his hand upon his shoulder said, "My young friend, I would give a good deal for your talent now, but I am glad that I did not have it at your age," intimating that it would prove a dangerous distraction to a man who sought to engage in sterner pursuits. Farrar kept it up, however, through a moderately long life; was a lawyer of respectability, a County Court Judge, but was finally better known by the soubriquet of "Johnnie Reb," and with his banjo and old Virginia tales and melodies made many a company happy. He was a good man and a genial companion, and left many friends when called to his last account.

Another striking figure at the bar was the Hon. R. K. Meade, though at that time he gave but little attention to the law. He had been elected two years before to fill the vacancy in the House of Representatives from this Congressional District, left vacant by the death of the Hon. George C. Dromgoole, defeating George W. Bolling, Esq., who ran on the Whig ticket for the same office. Mr. Meade was a man of commanding presence, dignified, but courteous and accessible, and a perfect exemplar of the Virginia gentleman. He was therefore a most fitting representative of the wealthy, cultivated, and aristocratic constituency which sent him to Congress. He was intensely Southern in his feelings, and impetuous and sensitive to any affront, implied or expressed, offered to himself or his section. It was not unexpected, therefore, to his friends, when Joshua Giddings, of Ohio, made some offensive reference to the South in a heated debate in the House of Representatives, that Mr. Meade should have arisen and assailed and punished him where he stood. The affair was subsequently made the subject of an amusing cartoon, "Meade choking Giddings," which went the rounds of the comic papers, very much to the disgust of at least the party of the first part.

Mr. Meade was made Minister to Brazil during Mr. Buchanan's administration, but asked to be recalled, of course, as soon as Mr. Lincoln was elected President. He returned home in the spring of 1861 and was offered a commission as brigadier in the Confederate Army, but he was taken with an acute attack of the gout, and died before he had the opportunity of accepting the honor.

Mr. Meade had a son in the United States Army, a graduate of distinction of West Point, and a captain of engineers, R. K. Meade, Jr. He was highly esteemed by Gen. Winfield Scott, Commander-in-Chief of the Federal Army, and by Colonel, afterwards Gen. R. E. Lee, of the Confederate forces. Young Meade was probably the only officer who literally fought, and with honor, on both sides in the war between the States. He was with Maj. Robert Anderson in Fort Sumter when his State seceded, and could not get out to offer his resignation to the President; and when, owing to the duplicity of Mr. Seward and Mr. Lincoln, the Confederate Government was compelled to reduce the fort, young Meade took his part gallantly, with the gallant Anderson, in defending his flag.

Beauregard, in command of the Southern forces at Charleston, was desirous of saving the garrison of Sumter from the mortification of defeat, and proposed not to attack the fort if the Federal Government would promise not to attempt to reinforce or to revictual it; which promise Mr. Seward gave to Judge Campbell, of Georgia, and then perfidiously broke. After the garrison surrendered, which they only did after the fort had been knocked to pieces by the Confederate guns, and were sent North, young Meade lost no time in handing in his resignation, and as soon as it was accepted he came South and was commissioned in the Confederate Army. He had just distinguished himself in the fights around Richmond in June, 1862, when he was taken with the Chickahominy fever, and died, with thousands of other gallant young fellows, who had the good fortune to go down when our sun was in its zenith. I have made this diversion in memory of as brave a gentleman and as pure a spirit as ever left earth for Heaven.

The Donnans—Alexander and James M.—were counsellors attending mostly to office practise, had a large clientele, and were noted for their energy, their promptness, and her conscientious devotion to the interests of their clients.

Mr. James Donnan, after the war, was appointed Consul to Glasgow, and on returning to the United States, some eight or ten years afterwards, removed to Richmond.

Mr. Alexander Donnan lived for many years after the war, and accumulated a handsome estate, which he left, with the better heritage of a good name, to his family. His widow and children all survive him save one, the first wife of the Hon. Alexander Hamilton.

Mr. Thomas Wallace belonged to the old guard at the bar—steady, reliable, learned in his profession, and did good work; but, placed by fortune beyond the necessity of work, like many other men under similar easy circumstances, did not achieve the high results of which he was capable.

Mr. R. R. Collier was also prominent at that time, both as counsellor and advocate, active, energetic, pressing the interests of a client as he saw them, with a zeal and courage that neither quailed at difficulties nor feared danger.

Mr. James E. Watson—Dr. Watson in 1850, an eclectic physician, an Englishman who had made Petersburg his home for some years—left medicine and studied law, and in two years, by his earnest and assidious devotion to his business, had acquired a reputation that made him Commonwealth's Attorney for the city, the first, I think, that was elected by the popular vote. His career was short-lived, and he died in 1865, leaving two children, who are still living, with warmest recollection of his filial love and care.

Mr. A. B. Spooner was an old gentleman of high character and social position, but belonged rather to a generation that was passing away. I had but a limited acquaintance with him. He lived in the large white house on Adams Street recently occupied by Dr. R. M. Anderson.

Messrs. Charles F. Collier, J. C. May, John Lyon, R. G. Pegram, W. L. Watkins, and Marcus Gaines were all young men, companions of mine, just setting out for the race of life. With varied fortunes they followed the road, dropping out one by one, until I am left the last lone contestant for the rich guerdon that ambition held out at the goal, and which seemed then just within our grasp. What they attained, what I shall hold when the end comes, is beyond mortal ken. It may not be a marble shaft or a cenotaph of stone, but this we know—there shall be a prize to each one that did run the best that he was able.

Marcus Gaines was made Consul to Tripoli. I never knew his end, but he probably sleeps in the sands of a foreign shore.

John P. May, brave, peerless, fearless gentleman, fell at the front of the hotly-contested field of Second Manassas.

Charles F. Collier, John Lyon, and W. L. Watkins, after surviving the perils of war, await the final assize in old Blandford Cemetery.

Though not a lawyer, I was for some reason thrown very much amongst the men of that guild for many years, and in their bright, genial, and cultivated company were passed some of the happiest hours of my life.

When I came to this city on the first of January, 1851, I found the physicians organized in a body known as the "Petersburg Medical Faculty." This organization had been formed on the 28th of August, 1846, and proclaimed as its object, "First. The advancement of medical science; Second. The promotion of the legitimate interest of the practitioners of medicine, and the elevation of professional character amongst the people and amongst ourselves; Third. The establishment of harmony, good feeling, and amity of action amongst all engaged in the honorable practice of our art."

To the furtherance of these commendable objects, a certain code of laws and regulations were adopted to which every member was expected and required to subscribe. A physician failing to connect himself with this association would fail of the benefits of contact and consultation with his fellows. Every physician on coming to the city was waited on by the secretary of the faculty and given opportunity to avail himself of these benefits. Dr. S. A. Hinton, then secretary, waited on me and I subscribed to the laws. A meeting of the faculty could be called at any time by order of the president or on request of five members, but the regular meetings were ordered for the first Wednesday in May, and any member failing to attend a regular meeting of the faculty, and being unable to give a satisfactory excuse, was fined five dollars.

In 1848 the regular meeting was fixed for the 3d of November, and subsequently changed to the third Wednesday in November, and the fine of five dollars reduced to one and finally omitted altogether. This law abides to this date.

The first regular meeting after my connection with the faculty was on the third Wednesday, the 19th of November, 1851. Present: Dr. P. C. Spencer, President; Drs. B. H. May, James May, Luke White, J. E. Cox, J. J. Thweatt, J. Branch, J. P. Woodson, N. F. Rives, R. L. Madison, John H. Claiborne, C. F. Couch, W. A. Dudley, Andrew Field, and S. A. Hinton—fifteen; absent: J. F. Peebles, W. F. Jones, A. H. Christian, Thomas Withers, J. W. Whitmore, R. E. Robinson, J. Mettauer, William Durkin, eight—twenty-three in all, of whom only two have survived the half century, Dr. Dudley* and myself. Besides these, thirty others, with one exception, who have joined the faculty since that time have passed away, indicating a mortality difficult to account for.

Not all of these gentlemen died in Petersburg. Some who joined the faculty while refugeeing here during the war, and some who, broken up at their homes in other portions of the State, gravitated here soon after the war, moved away to different sections of the country; but the news of their deaths which reached us seemed authentic in every instance. I know of only one of these physicians—the exception noted above—who is yet living, Dr. Robert Page, of Berryville, Virginia. He

---

*Dr. Dudley has since died, 1903.

was a surgeon in the army, stationed here during the last two years of the war, and an able and efficient officer. He married Miss Patty Hardee, a beauty and a belle, and a daughter of one of the gallant defenders of the city who was killed in the ever memorable militia fight of the 9th of June, 1864. Dr. Page remained in Petersburg for one or two years after the war, and then returned to his former home in Berryville, where he is still engaged in active and successful practise.

By order and regulation, the first annual meeting of the faculty was held at the house of the senior member, and each subsequent annual meeting at the house of the next senior, in rotation; and it was an unwritten law that the member at whose house the meeting was held should give a supper, and these annual suppers were veritable symposia, where rich viands and generous wines conspired to create and cement good fellowship, and to preserve an honorable esprit de corps.

With relaxed strain upon the sober and arduous duties of a doctors daily life, and with story and song and jest, old scores were forgotten, old sores were healed, old friendships sealed, and we parted, as the night waned, none the worse for a little revelry that came but once a year. Oh! the memories of those evenings come as soft and balmy as the gentle south winds, which sweep the quiet resting places of the brave and noble gentlemen "who made the banquet so fine."

Changed times, changed circumstances, changed associations, and changed men came with the new regime. The new faculty of Petersburg preserves its organizations, its municipal and mandatory rules remain in letter, but one who knew it half a century ago misses the pervasive spirit of liberality and brotherhood which filled it then.

The new times early infected the professional relations, consultations between members of the faculty became less frequent and less confidential; the unwritten law, requiring of the president an acknowledgment of the honor conferred upon him, by giving a hospitable reception, was ignored or broken, and finally it was resolved that every man must pay for his own supper if that element of the annual gathering was considered essential to the good and perpetuity of the association; and at the regular meeting on the 15th of November, 1871, on motion of Dr. Lassiter, a resolution was adopted that "henceforth the refreshments at the annual supper should be furnished by the faculty," the secretary collecting from each member his quota of the cost. Drs. Leigh and Steel were appointed by the president as supper committee for one year. A new committee was appointed annually, and the honor of service thereon made an object of generous rivalry.

But we must note something of the material of the body politic of the Medical Society of Petersburg at the time when we were inducted into its honorable membership.

The profession of medicine, like the profession of law in Petersburg, had in the past history of the city men of the highest mark; men whose deeds might serve to awaken in their successors a noble ambition to be worthy of their sires.

The names of Dr. John Shore, Dr. Richard Field, Dr. John Strachan, Dr. James Gilliam, Dr. Thomas Robinson, and Dr. Richard Batte, all of whom had passed away before I joined the faculty, had left each the savor of a good name, and each a reputation whose glamour lighted the lives of the after men who then received me in their honored ranks. Few people now living know anything of these worthies, personally, and we find few records beyond tradition of their lives given so generously and often gratuitously to the good of their fellowmen.

Dr. James Gilliam was the owner of "Violet Bank," and planned the beautiful grounds and buildings which made it for years the most desirable suburban residence in Virginia. I had it from the lips of a Northern gentleman who visited the place some fifteen years ago, and who had traveled extensively abroad, that in some respects it was the prettiest place he ever saw. Dr. Gilliam must have been a man of great good taste. Some years ago I incidentally saw a copy of his will, and one provision of the document struck me very forcibly—a clause directing that no man unable to pay his bill should be annoyed by the executor, that the estate should lose it. This indicated the humanitarian spirit of the doctors of the olden time.

Dr. Thomas Robinson left perhaps the largest reputation of any of the old worthies of that day. He was an Irish patriot who was compelled to flee his country for political reasons, and who came to Petersburg about the beginning of the last century. He was a graduate of Dublin College, and a man of great learning and versatile talents, and like most Irish gentlemen, a genial and companionable person. He taught school for a few years after coming to this country, in Amelia County, and then determined to study medicine, going to Philadelphia and taking his degree. After returning he married a Miss Murray, of Amelia, and located in Petersburg. He attained, as before remarked, to the highest place in his profession, and left a record for skill and success in practise not excelled by any of his compeers. He was also noted for his open-hearted generosity and his kindness to the poor. It is reported of him on one occasion that, being without any money at the time, he borrowed from his wife the only few dollars she had, and spent it in furnishing supplies and medicine to a poor family, whilst for some days his own family were compelled to forego the luxuries to which they were accustomed. His practise partook of the heroic. I have heard some of his oldest patients say that his invariable directions were that before being sent for, the sick person, if an adult, should be given eight grains of calomel and four grains of Dover's powders. He would then pay his visit, without haste, and take charge, allowing no further self medication or domestic prescribing. He believed in and pursued the anti-phlogistic treatment in full, and as the diseases of that day all partook more or less of the sthenic type, and his clientele were a full-blooded, vigorous people, he had remarkable success. One especial peculiarity of his practise was the freedom with which he exhibited mercury. He tested to the last degree its alterative and antiseptic effects. Ptyalism, a sore mouth, he looked for daily in the patient, and was rarely satisfied until he saw it. He regarded that as an indication of the surrender of the enemy, which, forsooth, he fought with most phenomenal and fortuitous results, and he left the impress of this therapy both upon the laity and profession of his day, to an extent that thirty years or more only served to moderate. To the majority of the medical men of this vicinage to within a comparatively recent period, mercury was known, if not regarded, as the "Samson" of the materia medica. Had he known at that day of the theory of the microbic origin of all diseases, he would have been strengthened even in his faith in the great phagocyte, if such a thing were possible.

Of the doctors living and in practise when I joined the faculty—and a most able and honorable body of men they were, as a rule—I can speak particularly of those with whom I came mostly in contact. One of them was Dr. John F. Peebles. He was then about thirty-four years old, handsome, accomplished, debonair, popular—especially amongst the ladies—a student, and advanced in his ideas of medicine beyond the routine practise of the day. He died at the early age of thirty-nine, but two years before his death he published two essays, one on Intermittent Fever and the other on Prolapsus Uteri, both of which took the prize for which he competed, and attracted marked attention in the profession. With the exception of Dr. R. L. Madison, to whom I refer elsewhere, he was my most intimate friend amongst the faculty, and I felt his loss very keenly. He was gentle and tender-hearted, and, as such men always are, was cheerful and courageous. When dying, a friend standing by said to him, "Doctor, are you going to sleep?" "Yes," he replied, smiling, "my left lung is filling fast; the right will soon follow. I am going to sleep and I shall awaken no more." In a little while sleep had come, and as he was the first of my friends and compeers to die, the scene impressed me with a vividness that yet remains, and which time and change and many experiences of many years with death, at the bedside or on the battlefield, have never dimmed. His patients loved Dr. Peebles with a love that such a man would naturally inspire, and after his death erected in the old Blandford Cemetery a granite shaft to his memory, with the simple but touching inscription, "I was sick, and ye visited me."

Another member of the faculty with whom I was mostly thrown was Dr. J. J. Thweatt, a man personally the opposite of Dr. Peebles; maimed by gout and by the accident of a badly-broken leg, he was awkward in his gait, uncouth—sometimes to rudeness—in manner, and would impress a stranger unfavorably. He, though born in the vicinage of the city, had lived abroad many years engaged in the study of physic in the schools and hospitals of Europe, and was a master in his profession, both as a physician and surgeon. It was owing to this fact, probably, in his long absence from home and home people, that he was so seemingly indifferent to the most of those with whom he came in contact. But his professional brethren early recognized his worth, and he was more sought in consultation than any other member of the faculty. He possessed the rare qualification for a doctor—a combination of scientific knowledge and practical common sense; and though seemingly indifferent, apparently to coldness, he loved his profession, especially the humanity of it, and never considered himself in the service of his fellows. Indeed, he lost his life in waiting on a poor worthless waif who had nothing to compensate him for his attention, and no claim upon the doctor, except that he was sick and in pain and peril. It was my fortune for many years before Dr. Thweatt's death to be his partner and share his office, and to enter perhaps more fully than any other man into his confidence, and to know more of his inner life, and I am glad to have an opportunity of recording here that I never knew a better physician, a truer friend, or a more warm-hearted and honorable gentleman.

Another of the old physicians who received me in the faculty, and to whom I was often indebted for kindnesses which I had no right to expect, was Dr. Luke White. Dr. White was a native of New Hampshire, but came South in early life to Portsmouth, Virginia, first, I believe, but commenced the practise of medicine in Petersburg in the young years of the last century. He died a short time before the commencement of the war between the States—died, after he had passed his three score and ten, of a rapidly-maturing attack of pulmonary phthisis, the oldest person whom I have ever known to die of that disease. He was an excellent physician, thoroughly trained in every branch of medicine, but especially adept in the art of obstetrics. I cannot recall any physician whom I thought more skilful in that particular department of practise. As a man he was gentle, unassuming, modest as a woman, charitable in word and in deed. "Speaking no evil, and thinking no evil" of anybody. He was a model of the true man in all of his measurements.

Another man of note amongst the faculty of Petersburg in 1850 was Dr. P. C. Spencer. Dr. Spencer was an old bachelor on the shady side of the marrying line, but he was a great beau, gallant, and assiduous in his attentions to ladies, especially young ladies. He often said to me that he should "be married in ninety days," and when I would ask "who was the happy recipient of his favor," he would bravely answer that he "had not quite made up his mind as to the especial young lady." Poor fellow! He died in 1859 or 1860, well advanced in years, indeed an old man, but he never realized his bright anticipations—he died a bachelor. In speaking of his professional character I would say that he was a born surgeon. It is true there was no such thing as a specialist in his day. Doctors had not then divided the body amongst themselves, and taken, one the arm, and one the leg, and one the eye, and one the ears, and one the mouth, and one the stomach, etc. They had studied the anatomy of the whole body, the position of organs in place, and their relations, local and physiological; and they had studied medicine in every branch of it, and they were capable of practising every branch of it. But some physician would occasionally show himself more adept in one branch than another, or he would show more fondness for one branch than another, and so far, and thus far only, he was a specialist. After this manner was Dr. Spencer a surgeon. He had especially good opportunity for the study of surgery for several years under Dupuytren in Paris, and he availed himself of the opportunity. But he cared more for the art than the science of surgery. He was bold to recklessness in his operations, but his success was marvelous. At the time of his death he had operated for stone in the bladder as often as any man in this country, except perhaps Dudley, of Kentucky, and with as good results. He did not trouble himself apparently about the anatomy of the parts on which he was to use the knife, and occasionally severed a blood vessel, which gave no little annoyance to his assistant. For instance, in operating for stone he always used Dupuytren's doubled, concealed lithotome, and made a light matter of dividing the pubic artery. But his success, as I have remarked, was phenomenal. This was attributable to three things: 1st, the great care with which he prepared his patients for an operation; 2d, to a freedom in the use of soap and water, rendering both himself and his patients as nearly aseptic as possible; and, 3d, to his care and watchfulness of his patients after an operation. He also used in his operations a solution of creosote in alcohol, a most excellent antiseptic, though such a term was not in use at that time, and the doctor had never heard of microbes, and believed in pus—"laudable pus." The use of the antiseptic at that day must have been instinctive, or one of those curious coincidences often seen in the practise of physic, where the experienced use of a remedy was eventually sustained by scientific knowledge. A case often seen in other departments of life, where art precedes science.

Amongst the older and noted members of the faculty at the time were the two Mays—Drs. Ben. and James May. The former of these gentlemen was blind —had been blind almost from the commencement of his practise, soon after his graduation, some forty years before. But by force of intellect, shrewd, hard sense, courage and will, he had forged his way to the front amongst men who were no pigmies, and he stood easily *unus inter pares*. As is often the case amongst the blind, nature seemed to have supplemented his loss of sight by rendering his other senses so acute that he really did not appear to need any vision. He had a good practise and was much sought in consultation. He was the only doctor in the city at that time who practised in a buggy or gig. Physicians at that time rode on horseback or did their practise on foot.

Dr. James May, his brother and partner in practise, was a younger man, though not young. He was plain of dress, plain of speech, careless of his person to a fault, but professionally shrewd of diagnosis, hard of sense, accurate of judgment, conservative in conduct, and skilful in treatment of a case. I was indebted to him for much personal kindness and for much professional help. An incident in the life of the Doctor is so striking, and so illustrative of the customs and ways of a certain class of the country people of that day, that I am constrained to record it. It was not unusual when the doctor called, after a patient was convalescent and needed no further attention, for the master of the family to bring out a roll of bank notes, or more commonly a bag of specie, Spanish or American silver dollars, and, opening the mouth, dump it down on the table and say, "Doctor, pay yourself," and modestly and trustingly look away for a minute. On the occasion to which I refer, we had been attending a negro slave, very valuable, worth perhaps twelve or fifteen hundred dollars, and as he was sufficiently well to require no further medical service, the Doctor announced the fact to his master, a plain old country farmer, who only owned a few slaves. The old man, as the Doctor anticipated, brought out his bag of specie, and placing it on the table spread the mouth open wide, with the usual remark, "Doctors, pay yourselves." The Doctor had a remarkably large hand, and as he went for the "pay," it really looked much larger than usual. The old man noticed it, and his confidence failed him, and just as the

Doctor was about to "pay himself," he touched him on the shoulder and said, "Doctor, before you put your hand in that bag, remember there is a God in Heaven looking at you." The arrest was so sudden and unexpected that the Doctor's face was a study, but it did not stop him entirely, and he helped himself. After getting away, however, he asked me if I heard what "that old devil said to him," adding, "he scared me so that I did not get half my pay," and he often recalled the incident afterwards, and enjoyed the recital of it, but he did not enjoy it at the time.

Two other representative men of the faculty at that time were Drs. Walter Jones and Joseph Cox. They had each been residents and practitioners of physic in Petersburg for many years. Dr. Jones had an office and residence at the corner of Union and West Tabb Streets, the location of the present Post Office Building. He sold this property to the United States Government for a handsome sum, and shortly afterwards, having inherited a fine estate in Gloucester county, removed there. He was a man of great eccentricity, but always had a large practise, and was a good physician and a genial, generous gentleman.

Dr. Cox bore the reputation of being an excellent physician, and had a good practise, especially in the county of Chesterfield, of which he was a native. But he was fond of excitement, drifted into politics, represented the city in the State Legislature, and paid not much attention to his profession for several years before his death, which was tragic and untimely. On the 17th and 18th of January, 1857, occurred the worst storm of snow and the most intense cold that had ever been known in this section. For several days trade and travel were almost entirely suspended in the city and the surrounding country. In the most intense fury of the storm, Dr. Cox, taking a young friend with him,

Mr. Traylor, in a spirit of daring and against the protest of his friends, undertook to visit, in an open buggy, his brother, Judge Cox, who lived about eighteen or twenty miles from the city. Before reaching his destination he was overtaken by night, and frozen to death. The young man with him lost both of his legs from freezing, but survived a few weeks, never, of course, recovering from the shock.

Of the other members of the faculty of 1850-'57, who received me, and with whom I was perhaps not so intimately acquainted, I have to record of them that they were gentlemen of probity, of honor, and of repute—good physicians and good citizens. My intercourse with all of them was agreeable and kindly, with but one exception, and that was perhaps more my fault than his. I would recall, if I could, my part in the difficulty which occurred between us. Mutual friends probably were responsible for the trouble, but I have no apology to make for myself nor desire to inculpate others. I prefer to suffer the pain of the consciousness of the unnecessary hurt which I did him. Years ago he rendered his account—mine must soon follow.

One other gentleman besides myself is left whose name is found on the roster of the medical faculty at the annual meeting of November, 1851—Dr. W. A. Dudley.* The Doctor at that time was a young man of fine address, fine means and fine associations. He was connected with some of the best and wealthiest people of this section, who were loyal to the relationship, and who employed him freely and I think compensated him generously. In addition he had the good fortune to draw a prize of $20,000 in a lottery which was kept on Bank Street by Mr. Fred. Anthony. There were two or three lotteries in Petersburg at that time,

---

*Since deceased, 1903.

licensed by the city and State, and prizes were not infrequently drawn by adventurous investing in chance. I remember another chance that the Doctor drew, a beautiful Kentucky bride, and I recall one of the most elegant repasts, at the old mansion house on Market Street, which I ever attended.

Thus I have written of the men of Petersburg—business and professional men—whom I met and knew fifty years ago, and whose lives and characters maintained the name and reputation of the city as they received it from their fathers, and whose virtues their sons have illustrated in the courage and fortitude with which they met the convulsive upheaval of a civilization and the destruction of institutions which had meant in the past honor, and peace, and safety; sons who, when surpassed by numbers, and disarmed, and beaten down under the foot of the hireling soldier and the slave, accepted, with a patience and dignity that commanded the admiration even of their foes, the oppression of tyranny and the insolence of office, until malice exhausted itself, and the sentiment of the nation and of the world demanded that opportunity be given them to rise.

How they accepted that opportunity, with what vigor and spirit they arose, how they despised the miserable travesty of the government of carpet-baggers and scalawags, and placed municipal authority again in the hands of honest citizenship, let the present prosperity of the city attest.

Let her bonds, her banks, her credit, her schools—public and private, her merchants, her foundries, her factories, her busy streets, her railroads, her commerce—extending to the ends of the earth—attest. And to her magnanimity let her colored schools, in numbers and in excellence, surpassed by none in this country; and let the Normal School or College, just outside of her borders, for colored students, male and female, an institution with appointments and regime unsurpassed by any similar institution anywhere; and let the beautiful Asylum for Colored Insane, just outside of her limits, where more than a thousand of this unfortunate class receive the most humane and scientific care and treatment—let all these attest. And to her fealty to the new or Federal Government, and to her proud and patriotic spirit, let the fact attest that when the call was made five years ago for troops to uphold the flag and to defend the institutions of the country, two companies responded at once, and hastened to the front. This the present generation can know and can attest; but it seems difficult for them to know, and more difficult to appreciate, the fearful ravages of war, and the more fearful humiliation of reconstruction, when might made right a quarter of a century ago.

CHAPTER III

Politics of the Ante-Bellum Period.

Politics in the Past—The Two Parties of the Day—The Alliance of the Whig and Know-Nothing Parties to Fight the Democratic Party—The Wreck of the Whig Party—My First Vote Cast With the Democratic Party—Nominated by the Democratic Party for the House of Delegates—An Unwilling and Unexpected Launch Upon the Sea of Politics—Everything Goes Democratic—Some Account of Events in the Exciting Sectional Drama Leading to the Outbreak of Hostilities—A Nefarious Mission—The John Brown Raid the First Gun of the Fight—I Decline Re-election, But Am Renominated Against My Wish and Elected—Serve in 1857-'58 and Again in 1859-'60—An Account of Events and Measures Immediately Preceding the War—My Position Made Clear—Speeches in the Senate and Elsewhere—The Nominations of the National Conventions—The Secession Convention—The Peace Conference—The Call for Troops From Virginia by the Government, the Last Straw—The Union Men of Virginia—A Visit to Washington and Some Things Heard and Seen—Opinions of Eminent Men North and South—Governor Letcher's Proclamation.

And now, having recalled the institutions of Petersburg in 1850, its business, its banks, its commerce, its manufactures, and its men, we naturally turn to its politics. In accordance with the people of Virginia at large, so the people of Petersburg loved political excitement, and the eloquence and ardor and badinage of the political speakers, candidates, and contestants for office themselves, or representing such nominees of their relative parties.

The two parties of that day were the Whig and Democratic. All citizens were arrayed under the banner of one or the other. The term Whig had been used as far back as 1649, in Scotland, as distinguishing those who were opposed to the Crown, but in this country just came into use in 1776, designating those who, in contradistinction from Tories, favored the independence of the colonies, then subject to Great Britain. As a party it first came into life in 1828, or rather during the administration of Jackson. The party supporting Jackson for the presidency, against Adams, his opponent, was called the Democratic Republican Party; the party supporting Adams was called the National Republican. When, in 1833, Jackson removed the deposits from the United States Bank, this was considered a violent and tyrannical usurpation of power, and the party which had opposed his election now bitterly denounced him, and took upon themselves the name of Whigs, and the Democratic Republicans were called Democrats. To be a Whig meant bitter hostility to Jackson; to be a Democrat meant to be a vigorous upholder of Jackson. This feeling was intensified in both parties by the enunciation of President Jackson that "to the victors belong the spoils," that "our enemies must be punished, our friends rewarded." Under this rancor the parties were more bitterly divided than ever, and on the termination of Jackson's administration the Whigs brought out Harrison and Tyler, evidently in view of the availability of the candidates, and without any logical or definite declaration of principles. They elected their candidate, and on the death of Harrison, soon after his inauguration, Mr. Tyler became President. Disclaiming any obligation to carry out measures not defined in the political programme on which he was elected, he at once went over to the Democratic Party, and though an honest, able, and faithful executor, called down upon himself a storm of wrath and objurgation that would have crushed a man less fearless and conscientious.

At the expiration of Tyler's administration, the Whigs rallied again under the leadership of Mr. Clay, one of the ablest statesmen whom the country ever produced, and on this occasion adopted and promulgated a programme "pledging a well-regulated national currency; a tariff for revenue to defray the expenses of the government, discriminating in form of protecting the products of home industry and home labor; sales of the public lands and distribution amongst the States; single term for the Presidency and reform in executive usurpation." They went before the country on the asseveration of these principles, and Mr. Clay was defeated. In 1848 they again rallied under the leadership of General Taylor, who had won distinction in the Mexican War, and was deservedly popular with the people, and were successful, again getting possession of the Executive branch of the Government. But they were soon handicapped by dissensions in the ranks. Sectional feeling was becoming more and more intense. It was increased by the introduction in Congress of the Wilmot Proviso preventing the introduction of slavery into the common territories of the country. The Southern Whigs gradually failed to co-operate with their Northern brethren, many of them drifted into the Democratic Party (General Jackson, whom they so hated, was now dead), and the Northern Whigs, half-hearted, began to look for other combinations. The Whig Party was virtually disbanded in 1852, splitting into Northern and Southern wings on the slavery question; but in the desperate effort to dispute the supremacy of the Democratic Party, it formed an alliance with the American or Know-Nothing Party, a party having for its avowed object the restriction of the right of suffrage to foreigners, and the partial political ostracism of Catholics. It got as far South as Virginia in 1854-'55—a secret organization with its "grips," pass-word "Sam," and its battle-cry "Put none on guard to-night," two Americanisms attributing these words to an order of Washington whilst in his sorest peril on the Delaware, but not at all in conformity with the counsel of his Farewell Address, in which he warned his countrymen of the danger of secret political societies.

Whether by accident or by order this fight in the last ditch was made on the soil of Virginia, we do not know; but in the struggle for the ascendency, in the campaign of 1855, Henry A. Wise, leading the Democracy as candidate for Governor, a struggle, marked by great excitement and punctuated by great personal bitterness, the Whig Party met its final defeat, the State going Democratic by 10,000 majority.

The Whig Party to that date had undoubtedly represented the conservative element of Virginia. It was the party that had always represented the culture and the wealth of the State. It was the party of the cities and of the older and eastern sections of the State, the party of the low grounds on the big rivers, and the party of the owners of the old colonial mansions. It had become an old saw that "Whigs knew each other by the instincts of gentlemen." With its wreck, therefore, there went down many of the best, the purest, the strongest, and the most patriotic representatives of a time-honored policy. Some of the younger men, scions of the old Whig families, had commenced to withdraw from the party under the strong presentation of Democratic doctrine, as taught by Wayland in the text-book of Political Economy used in the colleges and schools of that day. The extension of the right of suffrage to the unwashed suffragans, in Virginia, occurring about the same period, made it apparent also to the young man ambitious of office that he would have to court popular favor under the guise of the popular party. The old men left their old lines and old associates slowly and haltingly, and some felt it proper that they should turn back and give a reason to their fellow-citizens for the radical change in their opinions and followings. Judge Thomas S. Gholson published a pamphlet entitled "Why Old Line Whigs Should Attach Themselves to the Democratic Party," an able and lucid exposition of the existing conditions in politics, a paper which, strong in itself, bore additional weight from the fact that it emanated from one of the oldest and most honored and trustworthy of the old Whigs.

The young Whig who came into citizenship at this juncture, say from 1850 to 1855, found a hard problem to solve, a problem more difficult than any he had encountered in Euclid or in the Calculi, just left behind him at college—the problem of how he should shape his course, true to himself, true to his State, and true to the heritage and traditions of his fathers. It so happened that I was one of those young Virginians. My ancestry all the way down from the American Revolution to the gates of my father's house were Whigs. I had drunk deeply from boyhood of the traditions which had elevated the name of "Whig" as the shibboleth of gentleman and patriot; and "Democrat," as I received it, was a synonym of Demagogue.

But as my views became enlarged by study and my vision extended by observation, I became convinced that the true policy of our Government consisted in carrying out the principles promulgated by Democratic formula—sovereignty of the States, restriction of the power of the President, economic administration of the finances, a tariff for revenue only, no sales or absorption of the public lands for public improvement, a sound currency based upon silver and gold, and banks disconnected with, and independent of, the Government. I cast my first vote in 1852 or 1853, and voted with the Democratic Party, giving pain and surprise to my friends, followed by greater pain and greater surprise in 1855, when I accepted the nomination of the

Politics of the Ante-Bellum Period

Democratic Party for the House of Delegates of the General Assembly of Virginia. I say accepted—I neither courted, expected, nor wished for the nomination. I was not present in the convention which nominated me. I was very young—comparatively a stranger to the great majority of the people of Petersburg, with no political affiliation and no political aspirations. I was fond of quiet, loved general literature, and had marked out my course as a student and practitioner of the science and the art of medicine, and to that I was devoting my best energies, with good prospect of early and pronounced success. I was flattered by the unanimity and urgency of a call which I could not understand, but the honor of which was unmistakable and well appreciated. It invited me to contend for a position which up to that period had been sought by the highest type of the citizen, and which had been filled only by men representative of that class. I could not afford to ignore it. I saw that it would break in for a time certainly, and perhaps permanently, upon the plans and purposes of life as I had laid them, but there were duties which a man owed to the State as binding and as imperative as those which he owed to himself.

These seemed to me the duties of the hour, and, without consultation or conference with any one, I accepted the nomination. It was a sudden transition, as if from the cloister of the student to the stormy harangue of the Hustings. Of course it was an interruption of professional work and a draft upon new resources of mind and person, but how great the change of life and pursuit this demanded can only be appreciated by those who remember the exciting scenes and who participated in the embittered disputes of the political campaign of 1855. After all, however, it proved but the prelude to a play of greater tragedy which, placed upon the boards five years subsequently, startled the world by the immensity of its ghastly horrors—a play in which a million and a half of actors went down in blood.

I was on the Hustings more or less continuously from the commencement of the campaign in the spring to the final vote in the fall. In companionship with, and sustained by, such men as Henry A. Wise, Roger Pryor, Timothy Rives, and some others, all men of force and unsurpassed for fiery invective, for thrilling eloquence, for immovable logic, my position was not difficult to hold; and I must confess that as my blood warmed in the combat, I enjoyed the melee. I refused, however, to mingle amongst the people, never asked a vote, never contributed to a "treating fund," nor expended a dollar except for the legitimate purpose of hiring and lighting halls or paying the expenses of visiting speakers, and I thereby incurred the displeasure of some one or two leaders. One of these did not hesitate to say that I was "an aristocrat—above the people," and bet and voted against me. But I proved the good sense of the people and their appreciation of honest manhood by coming out in the end ahead of my party vote.

The city went Democratic, the State went Democratic, the United States went Democratic. Buchanan, the Democratic candidate, receiving 174 electoral votes; Fremont, the Black Republican candidate (they were called Black Republicans at that day), received 104; and Fillmore, the American candidate, 8. The National Democratic triumph, however, was short-lived. Defections became more and more common in the Democratic ranks, as one and another, yielding to sectional feeling or sectional demand, went over to the enemy—not the Whig Party, but the Republican. When Congress assembled on the 1st of December,

1855, the Republicans were strong enough to dispute for the ascendency, and after 133 ballots, elected N. P. Banks, of Massachusetts, speaker, and so got control of the House. This was the beginning of the end of both of the old, time-honored, patriotic parties—Whig and Democratic, which, however bitterly they had fought each other for more than thirty years, had fought upon honest differences in the construction of the Constitution, and upon the wisdom or unwisdom of policies dictated; not by sectional hate, sectional jealousy, nor by a partisanship born of personal avarice and personal fanaticism. Another four years saw both of them swept from the political arena, though the fights in the National House of Representatives seemed contests between giants and pigmies. Eloquence, argument, invective was wasted upon ambitious leaders or their gibbering followers; and before another President took his seat, State after State in the South withdrew from the arena, and recalled their Congressmen, whose voices and whose votes counted as nothing in the councils of a nation which foreshadowed the death of organic law by elevating to its priesthood a citizen who denounced the Constitution as a "League with hell, and a covenant with the Devil."

But to return to Virginia. The Legislature elected during the stormy canvass of 1855 convened on the 1st of December of that year, and in the following January Henry A. Wise was inaugurated Governor.

Whilst the Know-Nothing Party had met its defeat and its death, the two parties, Whig and Democratic, still maintained to some extent their separate organization. There was but little occasion to draw the division of party lines. The Legislature was busied mostly in railroad building and in finance. John B. Floyd, formerly a Governor of the State and subsequently Secretary of War under Buchanan, Chairman of the Committee of Roads and Internal Navigation, championed the cause of the railroads. The unwise, extravagant, and destructive policy of net-working the State with roads running parallel with each other, and competing for the patronage of the same sections, and the worse policy of starting a road from the confines of the State, directing it to the sea, and to the cities and ports of the State, and then tapping it at every point where travel or trade could be diverted to communities outside of and inimical to the Commonwealth, had just been inaugurated, and was being developed under what was known as the system of "log-rolling," viz: you support my measure and I will support yours—never mind your oath to make the law for the good of the whole. In 1859 the State had up to that date expended between twenty-nine and thirty millions of dollars in this so-called system of internal improvements, the State holding three-fifths interest and private individuals two-fifths. The clamor ceased after that session for more money to "develop the resources of the State." What proportion of this thirty millions was ever returned to State or citizen it would be difficult to estimate. It would be safe probably to say—to the State nothing, to the citizen less.

Alien corporations own the railroads, and one of their presidents naively said in a public meeting, "the roads will be run in the interest of the owners"—and the owners are not citizens.

When the General Assembly of 1859-'60 convened, a graver problem was presented, viz: How shall the autonomy of the State itself be preserved? How shall the liberty of the citizen and his property be secured? The right of a citizen of Virginia to carry his property, his slaves, to Massachusetts, as guaranteed by the fugitive-slave law, or into the common territory of the United States, as provided for in the Kansas-Nebraska

Act, was not denied; but the liberty and life of the citizen who attempted to do so were endangered and assailed with riot and bloodshed. Not only so, but emissaries were sent from Northern States to entice and steal the slave of the Southerner, and to incite them to arms and murder.

On the 30th of May, 1858, a barque, the *Kesiah*, from Brandywine, Delaware, tied up at the wharf of Petersburg on this nefarious mission, and before exciting any suspicion, had gotten away with five runaway slaves. She was followed down the river, however, by a steamer, on which were several policemen and several citizens, and overhauled and searched. The negroes were found stowed away in the hold of the vessel. Her captain, Bayliss, was arrested and brought back to the city and tried on five indictments for kidnapping, found guilty on each, and sentenced to eight years in the penitentiary on each, forty years in all, though he was ably defended by two of the most prominent lawyers of the city, Messrs. Jones and May. It was said that he remained in the penitentiary until released by the Federals on the capture of Richmond in 1865. This incident not only served to awaken our citizens to a sense of the insecurity of their property, with secret emissaries plotting crime on their streets, but it also aroused resentment toward a people who, under the guise of friends, could arm and employ such emissaries as robbers and assassins to do their own dirty work. But let us suppose, as many of our people did suppose, that this was but the work of a few fanatics, and that our Northern brethren did not all endorse the injustice and wrong perpetrated upon a people who had done them no evil, and who had a right to claim, and to expect, equal rights and equal protection under the law and the Constitution of the whole country.

This episode fades into nothing beside another, the tragic scenes of which were enacted a year afterwards, when Virginia was invaded by John Brown. This man had not only been notorious for his lawlessness in participating in the troubles in Kansas in 1857-'58, but as a murderer and assassin had forfeited his life to justice, though he had been allowed to go free, even after having been captured by a detachment of United States troops under Colonel Sumner, sent to suppress his violence.

Collecting a number of young men in that territory, with several of his sons, he came East, went to Canada in the spring of 1858, and assembled what he called a convention, and formed a constitution. This convention, after appointing a committee with full power to fill all executive, legislative, judicial, and military offices named in the constitution adopted, adjourned *sine die*. Brown then took his party to Ohio and disbanded them, subject to recall, but sent one of the number, Captain John E. Cook, of Connecticut, to Virginia, who, under the guise of a book-agent, teacher, or something of that sort, made himself familiar with the country about Harpers Ferry, the location of the United States armory, and furnished such information to his leader as he thought advisable. In July, 1859, Brown himself, under the assumed name of Isaac Smith, appeared in the neighborhood of Harpers Ferry, with two of his sons and a son-in-law, giving out that he was a farmer from New York wishing to rent or purchase lands. Further to conceal his real purposes he rented a small farm some four miles from Harpers Ferry, where he did a little farming, prospecting, etc. In the meantime he kept several of his men at Chambersburg, Pennsylvania, who forwarded arms and ammunition to him at his habitation. On the 10th of October he issued "General Order No. 1," from "Headquarters War

Department, Provisional Army, Harpers Ferry," organizing his command, line and staff; and soon after moved to a school-house near Harpers Ferry, where hundreds of carbines, pikes, pistols, etc., were stored for the purpose of arming the negro slaves when they should rise in insurrection against the whites. On Sunday night following October 16th, Brown, with fourteen white men and five negroes, all fully armed and all from Northern States, crossed over the Potomac into Virginia, overpowered the watchmen at the Baltimore and Ohio Railroad bridge, and at the United States armory and arsenal, and established himself in a thick-walled brick building at the armory gate. He then sent out Cook, his spy, and Stevens, one of his so-called captains, and six of his men to the residence of Colonel L. W. Washington, whom they captured, and forced him and four of his servants to accompany them; next they captured on their way back Mr. Alstadt and six of his servants, placing arms in the hands of the latter; then captured some forty citizens of Harpers Ferry, and confined them all in one room of the brick house which he had selected as his quarters or fort, keeping them, as he said, for hostages.

The first person slain by the insurgents was a negro porter at the railroad, then Mr. Beckham, the mayor of Harpers Ferry, and then Mr. B. W. Turner, a prominent citizen of Jefferson County, all unarmed. News of these occurrences spread rapidly and by noon of the 17th, volunteer troops from Charles Town, from Shepherdstown, and Martinsburg, had hurried to the scene; and Colonel Baylor, taking charge of them, forced the insurgents into the armory enclosure, and surrounded it by a cordon of pickets. Brown then withdrew his men into the gate-house, which he proceeded to loophole, and from these openings fired upon all white men who came in sight. By the night of the 17th other companies of volunteer troops arrived from Winchester, from Frederick City, and from Maryland, and a company of United States marines, who had been sent by the Secretary of War, accompanied by Lieut.-Col. R. E. Lee, of the Second Cavalry, who happened to be at his home at Arlington on a furlough, and Lieut. J. E. B. Stuart, his aide. Colonel Lee was ordered to take command, recapture the United States property, and restore order. On the morning of the 18th Colonel Lee disposed of the volunteer troops around the grounds so as to prevent escape of the insurgents and sent Lieutenant Stuart, under flag of truce, to the brick house with a summons to Brown to surrender. This summons Brown indignantly refused, and Lee ordered forward the marines, under Lieutenant Green, with orders to break down the doors with a ladder used as a battering-ram. This quickly ended the contest, and the troops, fearing to fire lest they should injure the citizen hostages, bayoneted the insurgents that resisted, Lieutenant Green cutting Brown down with his sword. Brown's fire must have been very ineffective, as only one marine was killed. Ten of the white men, and two of the negroes with Brown, were killed during the fight. Brown and two white men and two negroes were captured, and turned over, by order of J. B. Floyd, Secretary of War, to the sheriff of Jefferson County. Cook escaped, but was afterwards captured and hung. Brown recovered from his wound, and with his accomplices was indicted and tried at the regular fall term of the Circuit Court of the county for treason and murder. His prosecution was conducted by Hon. Andrew Hunter, and he was defended by Hon. D. W. Voorhees, of Indiana, and other counsel of his selection, but, with his accomplices, found guilty, condemned, and executed. The trial lasted nearly a month, and as Brown admitted himself, was fair and

Politics of the Ante-Bellum Period   141

impartial. During the trial so many threats of rescue were made by the Northern people, and papers, that several hundred troops were kept under arms at Charles Town, costing the State of Virginia a heavy sum.

This episode not only created great excitement in Virginia, but aroused the indignation of the whole Southern people against the North. It opened the eyes of the Southern people to the great gulf which separated them from the North, a gulf not wide enough nor deep enough to insure them safety nor to secure them from rapine and murder.

It was vain to say that these were the acts of a fanatic and a madman. Unhappily, this was not true, or, if true, there were thousands of madmen and assassins and traitors at his back, proclaiming a higher law than the law of their country, and a law calling for "pikes for the slave-holder, fire for his dwelling, and poison for his water!"

Instead of receiving sympathy and support from her Northern brethren in capturing and executing with form of law a notorious murderer, who even the semi-civilized settlers of Kansas drove from their State, Virginia was denounced throughout the North, her Governor threatened with death, and John Brown received the honor of an apotheosis. Let us recall some of the current events and the publications of the day. In many churches of the North services of humiliation and prayer were held on the day of his execution. Minute guns were fired, an immense meeting was held in Fremont Temple, Boston, and amongst other bitter speeches, Mr. J. I. A. Griffin declared that "The heinous offense of Pilate in crucifying Jesus whitened into virtue when compared with that of Governor Wise in his conduct toward John Brown." Church bells were tolled, and similar meetings held in different portions of the North, and resolutions passed in honor of the "martyr"; and Southern people were given to understand if they continued to contend for their constitutional right to hold slaves, which their fathers had bought from New England or Northern slaveholders, that, in the future, they must expect to be subject to rapine and slaughter. Wendell Philips said in Beecher's Church in Brooklyn that John Brown had as much right to hang Governor Wise as he had to hang John Brown, and that "On the banks of the Potomac history will visit that river more kindly because John Brown has gilded it with the eternal brightness of his glorious deed, than because the dust of Washington rested upon one side of it."

These sentiments were endorsed by a great many papers. More than this, it was proven that Brown's purposes were known beforehand to such men as Seward, Sumner, Chase, and others high in authority, who, if they did not approve, took no steps to thwart them. Governor Andrews, of Massachusetts, said that John Brown was right.

But let us return to the political condition of the country, and especially of Virginia, during these evil times. Recurring to my personal narrative, when my term of service of two years expired, for which I had been elected to the lower house of the General Assembly of Virginia, I declined to stand for re-election. But when the convention was called to nominate a candidate for the upper house, the Senate, for the City of Petersburg and the County of Prince George, which were then in one district, my name was presented to that body by Dr. Harrison, of Prince George, and my nomination urged. This was wholly without my knowledge or consent, and as I was present in the convention, I not only declined, but nominated in my place a young friend of mine, Mr. John Y. Gholson, a lawyer of the city, who desired to enter politics, and who was the worthy son of the distinguished lawyer before referred to in these pages, Mr. Thomas Gholson. I not only declined the nomination, but pressed my friend's claims honestly and vigorously. I did not wish to remain on the political arena. I had passed through one stormy and bitter campaign successfully, and I thought I saw before me in the near future events calculated to arouse the passions of men and to separate chief friends; events of a gravity never weighed before in any recent time, and upon which good men and good citizens would certainly be divided. I was willing for some one else, more fond than I of contention, and an abler advocate, to leap to the front, and to hold the standard of the party. But my efforts for my friend, and my persistent declination of the honor of the nomination were drowned in the "No—noes" of the Convention, and it adjourned, and forced me upon the people, an unwilling candidate. However, there was honor in such a call that no man, and especially no young man, could afford to despise; and both personal pride and a sense of duty as a citizen impelled me to accept the situation and to enter upon the canvass. The opposition, as much of it as had been left after the demolition of the Know-Nothing Party, nominated Col. Williamson Simmons, of the County of Prince George, a wealthy planter, a man of large connections, and of great popularity, an Old Line Whig; but there were only few men willing to rally to what was esteemed a broken standard, and I had an easy victory. This, however, was but a prelude to another play, the calm before the coming storm; and when the legislature met on the December following, no public man with any sense of the responsibility of his position, or any appreciation of the gravity of the political situation, slept on a bed of roses. The question was not now one of Whig or Democratic doctrine, but of the autonomy of the State; how its sacred rights, guaranteed by organic law, could be preserved; whether it were better to withdraw from a Union, the compact under which it had been formed having been ignored or broken by sundry States, or to remain and escape the ills which would follow a severance of our Federal relations. In other words, union or disunion, secession or revolution, were the exciting topics discussed and disturbing the public mind. There were three parties —first, the Unionists, under any circumstances, ready and willing to bear the evils of an unjust and sectional government rather than to rush to other evils which they knew not of; second, Unionists, provided equal rights, equal protection, and State autonomy could be secured by further guarantees of national compact; and third, Secessionists, who, disgusted with the sectional animosities displayed by the North, and the nullification in some fourteen States of laws passed to protect the citizen and to secure his property, recognized and proposed, as the only remedy, separation from the Union, and the setting up of a new federation amongst the Southern States. But soon party lines were drawn more closely, and men were known either as Unionists or Secessionists. This was most unfortunate. The former were regarded as ready to accept the situation, holding the Union as it was more sacred than the Constitution, which was set aside and trampled under foot by the dominant party, and which guaranteed nothing of safety or of rights to the South; and three-fifths of the people of Virginia were arrayed upon this side— were Unionists. This was a fatal mistake, as was shown when the day for decision came, when Virginia was called on to say upon which side—North or South— she would stand. With a unanimity of sentiment beyond any calculation or conception, she arrayed herself upon the side of the South, though she well knew that her fair fields would be the fighting grounds of the opposing forces, and that desolation awaited her homes and destruction her every interest. But her halting, as we shall see—the misconception of her position as a Union State—gave encouragement to the North to believe that, if not an ally, she would at least prove to be a breakwater to the possible Secession movement which had swept the most of the Southern States.

And the Secessionist, or at least the Virginia Secessionist, was equally misjudged. He was regarded at home as a man ready for an idea—an abstract idea, if you please—that his section was endangered and his people defrauded of their constitutional rights, and denied equal protection before the law of the country, ready to plunge the State into revolution and throw a fire-brand into smouldering elements of discontent and destruction. Upon this side I was arrayed, and found myself at variance with my constituency, and denounced by some of my warmest friends and strongest supporters. But the position which I took, and which the Secessionists, one with me, assumed, seemed the only safe exit out of the difficulties which environed the State. It was reasonable and consonant with all experience to say that the time to oppose any difficulty was in its inception, and that a bold, determined front, and a readiness for the fray, was the surest road to safety. Had the people of Virginia shown this unity of purpose, instead of division and instead of tampering with compromise, occasion would never have arisen for the exercise of armed resistance.

On the 1st of January, 1860, John Letcher took his seat as Governor of Virginia, a Union Democrat, a strong Union man, and an exponent of the views of probably three-fifths of the people of Virginia, as the term Union man was then understood. How far these views extended, and how suddenly and radically they were revised will be seen in the sequel. But as the Union Governor of Virginia, his election gave countenance and encouragement to the people of the North, who believed that Virginia, with her powerful resources, her commanding position, and her prestige in the past would prove an able ally in case of trouble with the more southern States.

On taking his seat, Mr. Letcher sent in a message to the General Assembly directing their attention to the excited condition of the public mind, and suggesting the calling of a Convention of the States for the purpose of recommending the adoption of some method for the preservation of the Union, "consistent with honor, patriotism, and duty"; but at the same time urging a "re-organization of the militia of the State, an enlargement of the Virginia Military Institute, and purchase of munitions of war." On this recommendation a bill was introduced in the legislature appropriating "$500,000 for the purpose of arming the State." The State had already expended some $200,000 during the autumn of 1859 in the John Brown War, as it was facetiously designated by many people in and out of the State, who failed to recognize the gravity of that seemingly insignificant affair; and Governor Wise had been severely criticized for what they assumed was an unnecessary collection of troops at Charles Town, and their retention, during the trial, and until the execution of the condemned prisoners. To all such persons this "bill for arming the State" seemed still more unnecessary and uncalled for, and it met with strong and determined opposition. As I have stated, I was not now in consonance with the majority of my constituents, who doubtless would not endorse my course, but I was thoroughly convinced both of the wisdom and the urgency of the objects commended in that bill, and I felt it my duty to press it, and to vote for it; and that my views at that time may be certainly and accurately understood, I introduce here a part of a speech which I delivered in the Senate on the 19th of January, 1860, the bill being before that body on its passage. The reader can judge how nearly my words amounted to prophecy subsequently, and soon, fulfilled:

Mr. Claiborne said:

Mr. President, I offer no apology, sir, for urging upon the Senate, at this late hour, the reasons which induce me to think that this bill should receive its prompt attention and its cordial support. I confess that I have been wearied with the delay which has attended its progress. I am aware that, amongst so many men, all cannot be expected to entertain the same opinion upon scarcely any point of general legislation; but I had hoped that, upon a subject of so urgent importance, little difference of sentiment would have appeared, and that Senators would have been willing to have resigned, with readiness, any unessential matter of disagreement, and to have adopted with alacrity any feasible plan of compassing the ends proposed by the bill. Upon the main object of the bill, I am unwilling to believe that there is any disagreement. Of the necessity for the passage of the bill, so far as it contemplates the defense of the State, there cannot be two opinions. It requires no prophet to see and to predict the day of danger. It is not in the future, it is in the present. It is not foreshadowed in portentous but uncertain sign of trouble. It has been inaugurated in the bloody raid made upon our soil, and the tocsin was sounded in the summons of soldiery to assemble upon our borders. If Senators were asleep when these things happened, if they are yet unaware of what has occurred, I must remind them that some of their constituents have been awake, and that they are apprised of their danger. The people, sir, without respect of party, burying political differences, have met in primary assemblies throughout this excited Commonwealth and protested against this insult to our sovereignty, and demanded of their representatives that this indignity should be resented, and that our defenses for the future should be made secure and impregnable. One-half of the session has passed, and as yet no practical step has been taken to accomplish this object. * * *

The present bill has passed the House of Delegates, fresh from the people, with only two dissenting votes; it has been recommitted, it has been reported after days of delay; and now, when on its passage, we are asked to table it, to print it, and to postpone further action on it for the present. And we are rebuked by members of the Senate, who tell us that we are proceeding in hot haste— "in indecent haste," says the Senator from Albemarle (Mr. Rives), and cautioned not to crack the lash over Senators' heads, and force them to vote on so distasteful a measure. Sir, I would be one of the last to forget the courtesies of debate which ever characterize the proceedings of the Senate of Virginia, but I must tell Senators that if they hear the cracking of a lash, they hear it outside of this chamber.

Sir, the people of this State have set aside party prejudices and sectional disputes at home, and they will rebuke the kindling of old fires of discord here. They desire to stand before the world with united front, in unbroken lines; and they will not be distracted by the quarrels of jealous leaders. I protest, in their name, against the compromising of the speedy passage of this bill with amendments not germane to the object of its provisions. It is a bill appropriating a certain amount of money for the purchase of arms for the defense of the whole State, and for the establishment of an armory for their manufacture; and the Senator from Marion (Mr. Neeson) wishes to tack on an amendment providing for the erection of a Military Academy in the northwest; and another Senator proposes another amendment insuring a certain distribution of arms on the border. Sir, we do not propose to divide the defenses of this State; we will concentrate them where most effective. I am as jealous as any man on this floor of ever permitting one section to defend itself when assailed. We have a common inheritance in the material interests, as well as in the historical glory of Virginia; and we will share the proud office of protecting the one and perpetuating the other. When our late chivalric Governor Wise declined the offers of brave men from other States, who stepped forward last October at the invasion of the State, and begged to share our danger, and to shed their blood in defense of our homes, his answer met with a thrilling echo from every true heart in this Commonwealth, "that we could meet our own foes, and guard our own fires!"

Mr. President, I would that the facts of the late unfortunate foray into our territory justified any reasonable hope that no further defenses were necessary. I would that they were less solemn, less momentous than they are. I would that no blood had been shed, that no widowed woman, no orphaned child could look back to the 17th of October, 1859, and chronicle a sorrow not much to us perhaps, but very near to them; then I could palliate the indifference with which some Senators seem to regard this whole affair, and pardon the levity with which they refer to the "Harpers Ferry War." I can applaud the man who, speaking on this subject, allows his feelings to find utterance in impassioned declamation, but I have no sympathy, no more than I have for John Brown, with the man who can contemptuously point his finger at the graves of the gallant men who fell in opposing the first abolition invasion of Virginia.

But not to digress. These recent events have served to show us our exposed and defenceless condition. * * * In a day, in an hour, we were summoned, with limited resources, to repel an enemy on

Politics of the Ante-Bellum Period 149

our border, who, had his wisdom been commensurate with his daring, would have proved a terrible foe. With not two score men he seized and held for twenty-four hours the very Gibraltar of the State. And though he has paid the penalty of his crime with his worthless life, yet many of his compeers in villainly adventure still live, and his daring and sworn associates are scattered throughout the northern portion of this land; if haply some of them are not nearer home, surviving to embalm his martyred memory in their hearts, and to carry in their breasts fiendish purposes of revenge.

Sir, I am one of those who believe that John Brown is not yet done with. We all remember a very ridiculous letter which was received by Governor Wise, after the body of the old reprobate had been sent to its own place amongst the howling dervishes of abolitiondom—a letter stating that he was not dead, but that by the introduction of a silver tube into his larynx before hanging, and a sort of artificial respiration, his life had been saved, and the gallows been cheated of its dues. Sir, that letter was absurdly false, but it was prophetically true. It was symbolical of the resurrection, not of the carcass of the vile old murderer, who has nothing in reserve but a fearful looking for of the second death; but of the rising of men clothed in his bloody garments, who have caught his mantle, and who wrap with it around them hatred to the South, and who cover with it machinations of treason and revenge. But, sir, it is useless to conceal the fact that we are threatened with an eruption, and with danger more serious than that which such marauding may contemplate. In spite of Union and conservative meetings in the cities of the North, it is impossible to conceal the significant grumblings of the rural population of that section.

The dogged stubbornness with which their immediate representatives resist the organization of the Congress of the United States is a better exponent of that abolition, agrarian, and socialistic faction in reference to the South. [The House of Representatives spent two months, from December 1st, 1859, to February 1st, 1860, wrangling over slavery, secession, etc., the Republicans refusing to permit an organization, until one of their own number, Pennington, of New Jersey, was elected Speaker.] The fiat of power, which is the fiat of doom, has gone forth from that party; the irrepressible conflict has begun, and we must submit gracefully or ungracefully. They are toying with us as the cat toys with its helpless victim before licking up the blood of its vitals. Let us show vacillation now, let us show irresolution, let us show division in our counsels and our fate will be sealed, and sure. Sir, I will not repress this plainness of speech, nor be deterred from urging the arming of the State, lest I be accused of kindling fires of discord, and disunion thereby. I repudiate the implication of being a disunionist, but I cannot shut my eyes to the imminent danger of disunion; and I should be a false sentinel upon the watch-tower if I failed to raise the voice of warning in the ears of my people. Disunion is not coming through State legislatures; it is not coming through the Federal Congress; it is not coming through conventions, State or National—it is coming through the people, when it comes. It is coming as the taking of the Bastile came upon the quiet and slumber of Louis XIV; it is coming as all revolutions come, in a moment, in the twinkling of an eye. It is coming when some bold man for selfish purpose, or smarting under sense of sectional wrong, shall throw a fire-brand suddenly into elements always smouldering here in the South. It is coming when another John Brown comes. It is coming when any one State, having borne the last straw upon its breaking back, shall throw off the load, and walk out of this confederation; and it is coming, in all of its horrors, when the General Government shall marshal its forces to coerce such a State into submission. It is coming, I had like to have said, beyond all the powers upon earth or in heaven to prevent, when it is announced that a Black Republican President is elected to the command of the Army and Navy of these United States.

Whether Senators will hear or whether they will forbear, this event will be precipitated upon them, and it becomes the wise to make ready. Mr. President, I love this Union, I acknowledge fealty to it second to none. I have a right to love it—it is a part of my heritage. It was bought by men whose blood runs in my own veins, and preserved to me by the sacrifices and suffering of my own fathers. I will never leave it until I am driven from it by the might of the oppressor. I will go with any man as far as he dare go to perpetuate to my children their inalienable and inestimable rights in this great structure of Constitutional freedom. But, sir, when it is to be prostituted into a Temple of Dagon, where, blinded, I am to be brought forth as the sport of my enemies, I pray for unshorn strength that I may put out my arms, and, grasping its pillars, bury friend and foe in one wreck of crumbling ruins.

I reproduce this speech, or parts of it, not to parade my offices, but to show how clearly some could foresee impending trouble, and how blindly some others followed the phantom of faith in a faithless and fanatical people. Eliminating from the common stock of the people of the Northern States some thousands of good, true, and patriotic men, who loved their whole country, and who stood for years a bulwark and a breakwater to stem the tide of abolition folly, and abolition fury, amongst the remaining we could constantly recognize the narrow-minded Puritan of Plymouth Rock, who, fleeing from his old home, sought another and a new one here, for the averred purpose of securing and

Politics of the Ante-Bellum Period   151

enjoying for himself freedom of opinion, civil and and religious. For himself truly. But when any other man claimed the same right, with a bigotry born of the Evil One, he immediately denied him such right, and visited upon him persecution and banishment. And when the banished brother grew in favor amongst the heretics to whom he had fled, he was followed with malediction and excommunication. And when the said Puritan had grown into bands, and spread over the whole of his cold and inhospitable section, carrying with him still the leaven of jealousy in despite of anything that was better and happier than his narrow religion allowed, he looked upon the South and hated her for her genial, generous spirit, and the gladness with which she enjoyed her prosperity. Surely one of his chroniclers has well said, "the Puritan hated and condemned bear-baiting, not because it gave the bear pain, but because it gave the people pleasure."

But to follow events. The General Assembly of Virginia adjourned *sine die* at the expiration of ninety days, having done but little so far as providing for the coming storm was concerned, except to invite Col. R. E. Lee, of the U. S. Army, who was on a furlough at Arlington, to come to Richmond and give some advice concerning the organization of the militia. When I saw him for the first time, trim, erect, soldierly, with clean-shaven cheeks and coal-black moustache, I thought him the embodiment of grace and manly beauty. After four years' campaign of hardship and of battle, which he bore and shared with his iron veterans, and which sprinkled his locks and beard with gray, and framed that faultless form into sturdier mould, I could not recognize one feature of Col. R. E. Lee. But as General R. E. Lee, if anything in that magnificent presence had ever been lacking, time had filled in the last touches of the picture that proclaimed him easily the most perfect specimen of man and soldier which the world has ever seen. The last time that I ever saw him during the war was just after the unfortunate affair at Sailor's Creek, when he had just lost some 5,000 of his best troops, captured or slain, and when the dense blue columns of the enemy were pressing his thin gray lines back—back, ever back, until the end was but too evidently near. Yet he sat upon "Traveler," erect, firmly, the light of battle still in his eye, and a face immobile, in which no soldier could read one thought of the sure disaster which he knew so well was impending. To me he seemed greater in defeat than I had ever seen him in his greatest victories.

The beginning of the year 1860, the year for the election of a President and a Vice-President to succeed Buchanan and Breckinridge, found the National House of Representatives engaged in contention over sectional issues, the Republicans holding the balance of power. The legislatures of the different States, which assembled at the same time, did little else than discuss slavery, secession, and disunion.

The Democratic Party of Virginia met in Richmond on the 16th of February, and appointed delegates to a National Convention. The Constitutional Union Party of Virginia, embracing the most of the Whigs and all of the Democrats who were opposed to disunion and secession, met in Richmond on the 28th of February and appointed delegates also to a National Convention. The Democratic Party met in National Convention in Charleston, South Carolina, and met their doom, split on the same sectional issues that had divided and destroyed the Whig Party, and after forty years of practical control of the Government from 1828 to 1860, went out of business. Instead of nominating candidates, this convention divided into two sections, one to meet in Baltimore on June 23rd, which met and

Politics of the Ante-Bellum Period 153

nominated Douglas, of Illinois, and Johnson of Georgia, and declared in favor of leaving slavery in the Territories to the voters of the Territories, or to the Supreme Court. The other wing of the party, called the Southern wing, met in Baltimore on June 28th, and nominated Breckinridge, of Kentucky, and Lane, of Oregon, and declared that neither Congress nor a Territorial legislature had a right to prohibit slavery in a Territory, and that it was the duty of the Federal Government to protect slavery in a Territory when necessary.

The Constitutional Union Party met in Baltimore on May 9th, and nominated John Bell, of Tennessee, and Edward Everett, of Massachusetts, announcing for its platform the "Constitution, the Union, and the enforcement of the laws."

The Republican Party met in Convention in Chicago on May 18th, and nominated Abraham Lincoln, of Illinois, and Hannibal Hamlin, of Maine, and declared in favor of the prohibition of slavery in the Territories. Bitter political excitement raged during the canvass throughout the country, only intensified after the announcement of the final vote on November 6th, when it was known that Abraham Lincoln had been elected President. He received 180 of the electoral votes from eighteen States, "all north of Mason and Dixon's line." Breckinridge received 72, all from the Southern States, even Maryland and Delaware voting for him. Bell and Everett received 39 votes from Virginia, Kentucky, and Tennessee, the border States. Douglas received 12 votes from the single State of Missouri. Thus for the first time a sectional President, from a sectional party, was elevated to the Chief Magistracy of the Nation, with a sectional Congress to back him, and the Army and Navy at his command. This sounded the knell of the Union. The Southern people felt that they were in the hands of their enemies, as was so early and so unhappily seen in the sequel. Some good men argued that the election of a sectional President was no reason why the Union should be dissolved, a fallacy that was made apparent even to the best, and wisest, and most patriotic before six months had elapsed. On the assembly of Congress on the 3rd of December, President Buchanan sent a message to Congress denying the right of secession, but doubting the right of Congress to coerce a State into obedience by military force. His Cabinet soon began to desert him. Howell Cobb, of Georgia, Secretary of the Treasury; Lewis Cass, of Michigan, Secretary of State; John B. Floyd, of Virginia, Secretary of War; and Jacob Thompson, of Mississippi, Secretary of the Interior, successively resigned within a month. On the 20th of December South Carolina passed an ordinance of secession; and on the 30th took possession of the United States arsenal at Charleston, Major Robert Anderson in the meantime having transferred the forces of the Federal Government from Fort Moultrie to Fort Sumter. And now the work of disintegration proceeded with an earnestness and rapidity which gave signal to the country that the rupture between the States and the Federal Government was complete.

From the 20th of December, 1860, to the 1st of February following, the States of South Carolina, Georgia, Florida, Alabama, Mississippi, Louisiana, and Texas, consecutively, had passed ordinances of secession, and seized the forts and arsenals of the United States within their borders.

But let us return to Virginia. Governor Letcher, by proclamation, called a convention of the General Assembly of Virginia in extra session on the 7th of January, 1861. The assembly ordered an election on the 4th of February proximo of delegates to a convention of the people, that they might determine in their sovereign capacity what relations they should sustain to their Southern brethren who had left the Union, and what relation to the Federal Government, of which they were still a constituent part—in other words, whether they should abide by the Union or adopt an ordinance setting up their own sovereignty. This was known as the Secession Convention. It met in Richmond on the 13th of February. On the 19th of February the General Assembly, anxious to avoid division, and to avert the calamitous results which would inevitably ensue, invited a Peace Conference of all the States to assemble in Washington, and appointed six of the ablest and most conservative citizens as delegates to that conference, viz: ex-President John Tyler, Hons. Wm. C. Rives, John W. Brockenbrough, George W. Sommers, and Jas. A. Seddon. These met in Washington on February 4th, with representatives from seven of the border slave States, and thirteen free States. This body of illustrious, patriotic citizens submitted a plan of reconciliation, which Congress rejected—and adjourned.

On the 4th of March Lincoln was inaugurated President. On the 6th the commissioners of Virginia from the Peace Conference of all the States reported to the Virginia Convention the failure to accomplish any satisfactory results. But the Virginia Convention, still anxious to secure peace and to preserve the Union, sent three of its most distinguished members, Messrs. A. H. H. Stuart, William Ballard Preston, and George W. Randolph, to visit Washington, and see President Lincoln, and to ask what course he proposed to pursue in reference to the seceding States. "He handed them a paper setting forth in writing his intentions to coerce the seceding States into obedience to the Federal authority." On the 15th of April he issued a call for

"75,000 troops apportioned amongst the States to suppress combinations against the laws of the United States in the States of South Carolina, Florida, Georgia, Alabama, Mississippi, Louisiana, and Texas." This call was communicated to Governor Letcher, on the same day, by Simon Cameron, Secretary of War, who also notified him that the quota of troops to be furnished by Virginia was "three regiments, containing 2,340 men, to rendezvous at Staunton, Wheeling, and Winchester." To this communication Governor Letcher promptly replied: "I have only to say that the militia of Virginia will not be furnished to the powers at Washington for any such use or purpose as they have in view. Your object is to subjugate the Southern States, and a requisition made upon me for such an object—an object in my judgment not within the purview of the Constitution or the Act of 1795—will not be complied with. You have chosen to inaugurate civil war; and having done so, we will meet it in a spirit as determined as the Administration has exhibited toward the South."

This call for troops from Virginia to coerce the Southern States fell as a bombshell upon the Union men of the convention, as it doubtless did also upon her Union Governor. The subject of coercion had evidently not been considered as one of the sequences of the election of a sectional President. They declared that the election of Mr. Lincoln did not imply any danger of interference with the rights and institutions of the States—an opinion which was fortified by the President's perfidious declaration in his inaugural address on the 4th of March, that "he had neither the right nor the intention of interfering with slavery in the States."

Up to the time of this call the people of Virginia, three-fifths of them at least, or those constituting the

Union Party, had expressed at the polls, in the election of delegates to the convention, their willingness and determination to abide the issue of a Republican President. This was not the view of the Secessionists, the remaining two-fifths. As the secession leader and exponent of the views of that two-fifths, in the district of the Senate which I represented, after a bitter political campaign, in which a man met upon the hustings foes as implacable as if they had never held his hand in friendship, and where the pistol and the rope were the unconcealed pledges of what awaited the traitor to his country, I felt it my duty to publish an address or manifesto to my constituents, which I introduce here, in my defense and in defense of the gallant minority which stood by me in those perilous times; and I ask of the reader now to remember that the address was published some six weeks before the inauguration of Mr. Lincoln and his call for troops for coercion. If the Secessionists were not patriots they were pretty good prophets:

Address (in part) of Hon. John Herbert Claiborne, of Petersburg and Prince George, to his Constituents of the Sixth Senatorial District, January 20th, 1861:

I desire, fellow citizens, to say a few plain words to you on the all-engrossing subjects of public attention, and I know not how I can more conveniently reach you than through the public press. I have a sincere desire, as I believe it to be my solemn duty, to contribute something toward healing the breach which unfortunately divides many of our best citizens, and to pour mollifying oil, if possible, upon the stormy waters of the present political strife. Divisions amongst a people who are one in interest, one in honor, and who must be one in destiny, are unfortunate, often disastrous, especially at a time of public danger, when unity of thought and sympathy of feeling and concord of action are vitally essential to the preservation of those things which men hold sacred and dear.

We are, fellow-citizens, in the very presence of an enemy—an enemy uncompromising and implacable, an enemy in the flush of the first victory, an enemy united and resolved to push the results of their triumph to the end of the contest. And instead of uniting our broken forces and making one last stand upon the common ground of our hearths and homes, we are standing apart, distrusting one another, debating abstractions, divided as to whether there be any virtue in this mode of resistance, or necessity for that, whilst our watchful foe is deriding our indecision and strengthening himself for the final onset.

Is it possible that this unfortunate condition of things can longer exist? What are the sources of our differences? What are the grounds of our disagreement? Can they not be adjusted? Come, let us reason together. Let us banish all asperity of feeling, let us examine our hearts and cast out from them all pride of opinion, and all prejudice of party association, and bring ourselves, as men of one blood and one brotherhood, to the noble task of preserving this old Commonwealth in all the prestige of its past renown and in all the glory of its past history.

Who is the enemy who has endangered our peace and who has summoned us to be ready for war? A political party of the slow but progressive growth of forty years has at last obtained possession of the ballot box in this country of elective franchise, and is about to be inaugurated into power. It is consistent with its character, as with the character of all parties, to administer the Government in accordance with the policy it has heretofore exhibited, and the principles it has heretofore announced. This policy and these principles we consider as subversive of our interests and destructive of our property; our property in that peculiar institution which is a power in the State, and to which the State owes much of its prosperity and its wealth. But are these dangers which we contemplate real or imaginary? And if real, is the institution worth preserving? Is it worth contending for? Would a quarrel in its behalf be just and righteous?

> "For thrice armed is he who hath his quarrel just,
> And he but naked, though locked up in steel,
> Whose conscience with injustice is corrupted."

If we can agree upon these simple propositions, then we can consult and co-operate, and thus keep our domestic institutions secure, preserve our altars untouched, and, maybe, with heaven's help, perpetuate in its purity a Federal Union which has come down to us baptized in the blood of our fathers, and which has been our love and our song at home, and our pride and our shield abroad. Or if this boon be denied us, we can assert our own State sovereignty, dictate the terms of separation from a people who have betrayed us, and, throwing the sword in the balance with the right, proclaim our independence of all earthly power or potentate. But is it the purpose of the Black Republican Party to interfere with slavery in the States, or to prevent its extension into the Territories of the common country?

Let us examine its history—let us consult its oracles. None will dispute but that the negro has been its one idea for good or for evil. It was organized upon this idea, it has grown and matured upon its elaboration and development, and now it has enlarged its borders and spread its sable folds, until their sombre shadow is falling upon the fairest heritage of earth, and a sense of impending darkness is making the land to mourn.

It showed embryonic life at the adoption of the Federal Constitution, and manifested its falsehood and duplicity when its founders persisted, in spite of the protest of Virginia, upon a continuance of the African slave trade, and left it in pious injunction to their sons to deny the right of property in negroes which their fathers had sold to the South. It made its first unlawful seizure upon territory in the days of the Louisiana purchase, when it robbed us of more than half of that acquired from France. It followed up its unhallowed appropriation of the public domain when it admitted California into the Union by a *coup d'etat,* and forever debarred from the fatness of that new Canaan the very men whose valor had won it, and whose blood had sealed it as the heritage of their posterity. And to-day, in the thousands of millions of acres of land toward the setting sun, it has declared that the foot of the slaveholder shall never enter; and with the help of its emigrant aid societies has supplanted the son of the hardy pioneer, whose father's prowess wrested the soil from the red man, and has given his inheritance to the scums and outpourings of its redundant prisons and work-houses.

Nor has it been contented to invade and appropriate the common territory of this country. It has essayed to found a colony in our own State. Not eighteen months ago it opened a depot for arms and munitions of war in a frontier country, and sent an outlawed banditti to incite insurrection and to proclaim "alarm to the sleep, fire to the dwelling, and poison to the food and water of the slaveholder." And when, under the forms of law, and in the clemency of justice, a jury of freemen had found these marauders worthy of the gallows, a howl of indignation went up from the North, and John Brown was voted a crown of martyrdom and the honor of an apotheosis.

Such, fellow citizens, are some of the unlawful doings of this party. Under pretense of law, a law higher than the Constitution and holier in their eyes than the law of God, they have stolen from us our property, have refused to restore it, have built jails and penitentiaries for our incarceration if we pursue it, and have murdered our citizens and their own for endeavoring to secure us. They have shielded criminals and traitors when taking refuge in their midst, and have refused to surrender them to the just requirements of our authorities. Their leaders and founders have proclaimed an irrepressible conflict begun, and declared that it should not end until the States were all free or all slave, until Charleston and New Orleans should become legitimate marts of trade or New York and Boston markets for the souls and bodies of men. Their chief mouthpiece and expounder has announced that "all nations have their superstitions, and that the superstition of the American people is the Federal Constitution." In addition he has characterized this instrument of organic law, which we have always considered the palladium of our rights, as "a league with hell and a covenant with the Devil."

They have not left untouched our social character, but have invaded the sanctity of private life. Through the public press and upon the floor of the Congress of the United States, they have held us up to the scorn and contempt of the civilized world, have traduced the honor of our men and defamed the virtue of our women, and covered us with every epithet of spite and malignity.

Such in feeble portray is that party which, on the 4th of March next, will possess itself of the Executive and Legislative, if not of the Judiciary, Departments of the Federal Government. Will it scruple to use its power to the prejudice and hurt of the institution of slavery? What, but this, was the original object of its organization? What are the results in those States where it has already acquired control of the different departments of government? Let history answer. In eleven of them it has boldly nullified the fugitive-slave law and ignored the Constitution. In four of them it has denied the right of jails, court-houses, and all public buildings in aid of the master. In seven of them it has provided means of defense for the fugitive, and in three of them declared him absolutely free, whilst the penalties which master and officer incur in endeavoring to carry out the guarantees of the Constitution are onerous and oppressive, including fines and imprisonments, in some cases for fifteen years.

Is it reasonable to suppose that it will not inaugurate an analogous policy when it shall become possessed of the Federal Government? Can any man doubt it? Does the future ever so belie the past? Has it ever given the poor guarantee of a pledge that it will not? Its elected chief preserves a sullen silence, its premier promises no hope of better counsels, whilst its insolent minions in the hall of the National Congress defiantly reject all propositions of compromise.

Now, fellow citizens, shall we cravenly submit to the rule of this party? Let a Northern statesman, a true-hearted and consecrated patriot, speak. Said Mr. Fillmore, four years ago, "The South would not and ought not to submit to the election of a sectional candidate for the Presidency." The Republican President-elect, himself, has declared that this country must be all slave or all free. He will take care that it is not all slave, let us take care that it is not all free. Shall Virginia surrender three hundred millions of dollars worth of slave property at his dictum? And our present helpless and attached dependents, our family servants, the servants of our fathers and of our mothers, what of them? Shall we visit upon them the curse that freedom would entail, and cruelly cut them off from our providence and care? In the light of truth and conscience I cannot surrender these helpless dependents upon my intelligence and my protection to the tender mercies of a Beecher, a Stowe, or a

Garrison. No. When the hypocritical abolition preachers of the North shall have filled the mouths of the hungry paupers at their own doors, and clothed their nakedness, we will hear with more patience their sentimental sermons upon the sin of slavery. We will not be put upon the defense of slavery by such subsidized ranters. An institution sanctioned by all the ordinances of divine law, and sustained by constitutions of human enactment, I will do all in my power to perpetuate in my State, and to preserve to my posterity this institution so humanizing to an unfortunate race. As to myself, I can only part with it in the demolition of my household altar and the destruction of my household gods. But, fellow citizens, if our property in slaves cannot be protected, and equal rights be guaranteed to us under Republican rule, what course shall we adopt? Here I think that I hear throughout the length and breadth of this Commonwealth but one reply—the day of settlement has come, and we must have new quarters, and a confirmation of our rights, or a dissolution of partnership. But some may say, let us make resistance to this encroachment upon our rights in the Union. What Union? The Union that was? That has gone. Five States have already severed their connection with the Federal powers and resumed their sovereignty. Five stars have been blotted out from the firmament of the flag, and the marred escutcheon proclaims the glory of the Republic departed. As the pious Æneas, recounting the mournful story of Troy, so we record in sadness, *Ilium fuit que ingens gloria Dardanidum.*

Virginia, it is true, still keeps her representatives on the floor of Congress, but the withdrawal of their colleagues from the seceding States is daily leaving them in a greater minority, and very soon they, and the few patriotic Northern men who act with them, will be powerless for good in any of the ordinary or extraordinary devices of parliamentary strife. Through them you can demand nothing of your rights which will be accorded. With a Republican Executive and a Republican Congress, they will be little more than automatons for the amusement of the dominant party. Let there be no resistance by arms in the Union. Nothing but immediate miracle could save you from utter overthrow, and only the plea of insanity protect you from the doom of treason. Let me pray you, before you resort to the *ultima ratio regnum,* to withdraw your representatives from Washington, fly your own flag over you, and proclaim to the world your independence of all other government, and your equality with the nations of the earth. This can only be done by ordinance of secession, adopted in sovereign convention of the people, the holders and arbiters of all power in a democratic government. The General Assembly of Virginia, in extra session, in fulfillment of your wishes, and in obedience to your instructions, has summoned such convention at your Capitol in Richmond on the 13th of February next. With that convention, subject in its action to the final arbitrament of your ratification or rejection, will rest the inherent power to do or to withhold all that a people may do or

withhold in the exercise of the sovereign right of self government.
Whether the right of secession from the Federal Government ac-
crues to any State or every State, composing the present Union,
under the inherent rights of the self-governed, supported by the letter
and the spirit of the Constitution, I leave you to determine each for
himself. I trust, however, you will pardon me for saying that of
which none of you are ignorant, that I believe and uphold the doctrine of States Rights with all my soul and body and strength. In
my study of the Constitution and in reading the debates of the convention of 1788, which adopted it, I can make out no other meaning. And in the present dangers and developments of consolidation,
I see nothing which would lead me to distrust my own judgment or
to impeach the wisdom of the fathers. Some of them seemed to
have cast a prophetic eye along the vista of years and to have recognized in the hazy distance the very troubles which now becloud our
political sky.

But, fellow citizens, I will quarrel with no one on the abstract
right of secession. I am willing to leave every man to his own honest
convictions, conscious that the true patriot will find a salve for his
conscience in the indisputable rights of revolution when necessity
bids him draw the sword of a freeman.

The General Assembly of Virginia has taken other steps, in addition to calling a convention, to bring this matter to your final and
sovereign decision. It has appointed a comission of five gentlemen,
your fellow citizens, distinguished for their wisdom, their integrity,
and their eminent service to the State, to repair to Washington City,
holding in their hands a proposition assumed to be the ultimatum of
Virginia, which, while it claims nothing that is not justly due, as-
serts all that we can hopefully demand.

An invitation has been extended to all other States to appoint
similar commissions to assemble in Washington on the fourth of
February next, and to confer with our own, to hear mutual com-
plaints, and adjust mutual grievances, and, if possible, to devise
some plan of restoring peace and union to this distracted country.
If they fail in recommending any plan of adjustment of sectional
differences and report all prospect of an honorable compromise at
an end, with you will rest the responsibility of saying whether further effort shall be expended in attempt of solution of the question in the Union; or whether, out of the Union, you will open
other systems of negotiation, and assert before the world that which
is your right. The hope and the prayer of the patriot is that the
finger of God may point in the darkness, sealed to human vision,
some way of escape from the impending evil, some path of peace
and safety and honor, that this land of freedom may remain forever, in the fullness of its promise, the home of religion and the
asylum for the oppressed of all nations.

But, fellow citizens, as painful as it may be for me to do so, I
must warn you, as a sentinel whom you yourself have placed upon
the outpost, and who has used all of his watchfulness and all of his

sagacity in view of the tremendous interests at stake, that I see full reason to fear for the worst. It is my solemn conviction that the party in power will yield no principle, and relinquish no claim; that without the promise of indemnity for the past or security for the future, you will be called on to vote whether Virginia shall abide by the North or the South, whether she shall establish her own government and trust to new alliances, or whether she shall submit to Black Republican rule. In this unhappy event my ballot is already prepared. I trust we shall all cast our lots together. Let Virginia be our first care. Her interests, her honor, her safety our chief concern. For myself, I pledge my love, my life, my all. She is the land of my birth, the home of my fathers. The bones of my dead sleep in her bosom, and I would mingle my own dust with her hallowed soil. It was her sons who constructed this magnificent temple of human liberty, their wisdom strengthened it, their genius adorned it, their valor defended it—and now treachery and fanaticism would pull it tumbling about our ears. In a Southern Confederacy Virginia will find a sisterhood of States whose interests are her interests, whose people are her sons, and whose destiny must be her destiny. To this she will naturally look for sympathy and association and help; and from this I would be the last to turn her away. But broken covenants, misplaced confidence, and present revolution should teach lessons of prudence, and inculcate jealous care of all future union with other governments at home or abroad. Forget not that before this time Virginia surrendered voluntarily, and generously, an empire in the Northwest to a nation that peopled it with her enemies, and erected no barriers to prevent them from her coasts.

You hold in your hand to-day the return for this magnificent bequest, a dishonored flag, and a menace of subjugation. Weigh well the price before you make out the title deed to another purchaser, and heaven help you to a better bargain in the future. But dividing the loss and sharing your lot for better or for worse, I am
Respectfully and truly,
Your friend and servant,
JOHN HERBERT CLAIBORNE.

In reproducing this address I again call the reader's attention to the fact that it was made some three months before the actual dissolution of the Union and the inauguration of war by the President of the United States. It was made in hope of opening the eyes of my constituents to the dangers consequent upon the election of a sectional President, dangers to be averted only by a wise and prompt preparation for resistance to the encroachment of the Republican Party, upon rights guaranteed by the Constitution; but an instrument which they had denounced as the "superstition of the American people," and as a "league with hell and a covenant with the Devil." I could not see what else we had to expect from such a party in power than the denouement which so soon and so inevitably followed —war, subjugation, and destruction. But I failed to make my people see with my eyes. "No danger, no danger," it was said, that any men elected as President of this country by the free suffrage of the great American people would inaugurate a war between the States, would lay waste the heritage left us by our fathers, and which had been so dearly bought with their blood and treasure. They failed to see that Mr. Lincoln was not elected President by the great American people, but by a plurality of votes between three candidates, and votes from one section exclusively; a section which had repudiated the organic law of the land, and denied to the other section any right which faction, fanaticism, or hypocrisy could assail. They failed, also, to take cognizance of a most significant fact, viz: that the man elected President by the great American people could not reach the Capital of the country to take upon himself the oath of office except stealthily and under disguise, so great was the indignation of the public at the perpetration of so foul a wrong. The Union men, even then, failed to see anything more in this remarkable episode than the ebullition of a partisan, and perhaps a lawless element of an excited population. The last expiring, mistaken, but honorable effort of the Union men in Virginia was to call a Peace Convention of the border and Northern States, to assemble at Washington, in order to devise if possible some plan of perpetuating in its purity a government which had served for three-quarters of a century to secure to the citizen safety at home and protection abroad; a government which had been literally a palladium of rights of all the people. Every border State and nearly every Northern State sent commissioners to the convention, men mostly of mark and patriotic service to their States and to the country. The Convention did itself and Virginia the honor of electing John Tyler President of the Convention. Some of the Northern and Northwestern States declined to send delegates. The vicious and venomous old fanatic who filled the chair of Governor of Michigan recommended that commissioners be sent from all the States, out of courtesy, but that "only men of backbone" be sent; saying at the same time that the "Union would not be worth much without a little spilling of blood."

Mr. Tyler had served the people of Virginia in various offices of distinction and trust for nearly half a century. He had been a member of the General Assembly, of the Executive Council, had been Governor of the State, member of the House of Representatives of the Congress of the United States from Virginia, Senator in Congress from Virginia, Vice-President and President of the United States, President of the Peace Conference, member of the State Convention of 1828-'30, member of the Convention of 1861, member of the Provisional Congress of the Confederate States, and a member-elect of the permanent Congress of the Confederate States. At the Convention of the Peace Commissioners in Washington he was literally "an old man full of honor." But he as literally laid aside his years, and with all the vigor of manhood, and the thrilling eloquence which had so often electrified senates and swayed assemblies, he called the attention of the members of the convention to the monuments which their God-like fathers, through their wisdom and patriotism, had built up, and to the task of preserving them spotless—"a task equally grand, equally sublime and quite as full of glory and immortality." Mr. Tyler was a Union man and represented the Union men of Virginia as no other man could have done. In another address in Baltimore, speaking of the Union, he said: "I will not believe that a people so favored by Heaven will most wickedly and foolishly throw away a pearl richer than all their tribe. No, when I open the Book of Sybils there is unfolded to my sight, in characters bright and resplendent, glorious and revivifying, the American Confederacy in the distant future, shining with increased splendor, the paragon of governments, the example of the world. If I misinterpret these prophecies, let me live and die in my error. Let it rather be thus than to awaken me to the opposite reality, full of the horrid spectre of a strong government sustained by bristling fortifications, large standing armies, heavy burdens on the shoulders of industry, the sword never at rest in its scabbard, and the ear ever deafened by the roar of cannon. No! Leave me for the remnant of my days the belief that the government and institutions, handed down to us by our fathers, are to be the rich legacy of our children and our children's children to the latest generation. If this be a delusion, let me embrace it as a reality, keep at a distance from me that gaunt and horrible form which is engendered in folly and nurtured in faction, and which slakes its thirst in the tears of broken hearts and appeases its appetite on the blasted hopes of mankind."

Governor Wise, of Virginia, the lifelong friend of Mr. Tyler, quotes in his "Seven Decades of the Union" a great part of this eloquent address, and adds in his own fervid and loving words: "He did misinterpret the prophecies; the gods loved him too well to grant his prayer. He was taken away from the touch of subjugation. He never tasted the bitterness of its ashes.

His heart was not broken, he died in hope, and was never forced to see the 'gaunt and horrible form' of that despotism of Congress which destroyed the Constitution, States, laws and liberties of the people of the United States." The calling of the "Peace Conference of all the States" was the last effort of the Union men of Virginia to preserve the Union, and John Tyler was an ambassador worthy of them and worthy of the cause; like them, he was "too much for forbearance, peace and compromise."

Three-fifths of the leading men of Virginia were for the Union as the Union was construed and handed down to them from their fathers. That they had the right peaceably to secede from this Union; that this compact, which they had entered into with States, could be broken when the terms of the compact had been violated, they had never entertained a doubt. War waged upon them for the perpetuation of the Union was regarded as a delusion. Again quoting Mr. Wise: "Had they foreseen that war was inevitable upon their withdrawal from the Union, they would have prepared for it, and if at the very beginning they had prepared for it, and at first 'had drawn the sword instead of blowing the horn,' there would have been no war. The prompt, prepared attitude of war would have brought a peaceful adjustment which would have sheathed the drawn sword without a drop of blood. But the Union men could not see it in that light. Earnest, honest, patriotic, the best representatives of the best ideas of a conservative government, united for the best interests of all the people, their last struggle for the preservation of the Union was as noble as it was unfortunate. Until the assembly of the Convention of Virginia for the purpose of determining the relation of the State to the States which had already severed their connection with the Union, the Northern people never doubted but that the border States, and especially Virginia, would side with the South. They had regarded the Secessionists, the "fire-eaters," as called by some, the true exponents of the policy which would be pursued by Virginia in case of dissolution of the Union, and they had made up their minds to a peaceable separation.

Horace Greeley, the mouthpiece and Magnus Apollo of the Republican Party, said in his paper, in contemplation of disunion, which was then already *fait accompli*, as far as some half dozen States were concerned, that "If the Declaration of Independence justified the withdrawal or secession of three million of colonists from the British Empire, in 1776, he could not see why five million Southern men could not withdraw from the Federal Union in 1861. The *New York Herald*, an equally blatant and proscriptive Northern paper, said on the 23d of November, 1860, "that coercion in any event was out of the question, and that a Union held together by bayonets would be nothing better than a military despotism."

I have personal knowledge of the views and intentions of some of the leading men of the dominant party in Congress after the election of Mr. Lincoln, and I am sure that they decided on permitting a peaceful secession of the Southern States, and that the idea of coercion was not at all entertained.

After the adjournment of the Senate, and on the assembly of the Convention on the 13th of February, two members of the Virginia Senate besides myself, Honorable Benjamin Nash, of Chesterfield, the youngest Senator in the body except myself, and the Hon. Mr. Lynch, of Campbell, one of the oldest members of the body, but a genial, hearty, young old gentleman, visited Washington together, remaining a week for the purpose of studying the situation and watching the trend of matters. As members of the Virginia Senate we had access by courtesy to the floor of the House of Representatives, and by the politeness of some of our Virginia Congressmen made some pleasant acquaintances amongst the Republican members. We heard also two capital speeches, one by Mr. Sigourney, of New York, and one by Mr. Kellogg, of Illinois, both leaders and able parliamentarians, both of whom were for peace. We did not hear a speech advocating coercion in the lower house, and only one in the Senate, which was by Andy Johnson, as he was then called, the Senator from Tennessee, and subsequently Vice-President, and after the death of Lincoln, President of the United States. To this we will refer again.

Dissolution of the Union was undoubtedly contemplated, but a dissolution peaceably and without contest. The idea of dissolution of the Union was not of Southern birth or origin. The people of the South loved the Union, as was shown by the action of Virginia and of the border States, even to the last days of the Union. Not only the right of any State or States to secede from the Union, but the propriety of such action under certain circumstances, had been announced and had been endorsed as far back as 1814, when the States of Massachusetts, Rhode Island, Connecticut, and others, which were opposed to the war of 1812, called a convention at Hartford and published a manifesto, in which it was declared that "if the Union be destined to dissolution, wherever it shall appear that the causes are radical and permanent, a separation by equitable arrangement will be preferable to an alliance by constraint among nominal friends, but real enemies." In 1839 ex-President John Quincy Adams said in an address in New York that "it would be far better for the people of the disunited States to part in friendship with each other than to be held together by constraint."

Mr. William Rawles, a distinguished jurist of Pennsylvania, in his work on the Constitution, said "it depended on a State itself whether it would continue a member of the Union or not." Mr. Webster, "the great expounder of the Constitution," said ten years before this date of 1861 in a speech at Capon Springs, Virginia, and afterwards in Buffalo, New York, "that if the South were to violate any part of the Constitution intentionally and systematically, and persist in doing so year after year, would the North any longer be bound by it; and if the North, deliberately, habitually, and of fixed purpose were to disregard one part of it, would the South any longer be bound to observe its other obligations?" How absurd it is to suppose that when different parties enter into a compact for certain purposes, either can disregard any one provision, and expect, nevertheless, the other to observe the rest. A bargain cannot be broken on one side and still bind on the other.

And Senator Benjamin F. Wade, of Ohio, a bitter South-hater, said, from his seat in the United States Senate: "Who is the final arbiter (of this question of secession), the General Government or the States in their sovereignty? Why, sir, to yield that point is to yield up all the rights of the States to protect their own citizens, and to consolidate this Government into a military despotism." And later, on the 18th of December, 1864: "I do not blame the South so much, because they have been led to believe that we, to-day the dominant party, who are about to take the reins of government, are their mortal foes and stand ready to trample their institutions under foot" (which they immediately did). And so might we quote from other distinguished Northern men, Republicans—Williams, of Massachusetts, Cabot Lodge, of Massachusetts, Gen. John A. Logan, of the United States Senate, and afterwards major-general in the United States Army, who said, as late as the fifth of February, 1861, "that the abolitionists of the North have constantly warred upon Southern institutions by incessant abuse from the pulpit, from the press, on the stump, and in the Halls of Congress. By these denunciations and lawless acts on the part of abolition fanatics, such results have been produced as to drive the people of the Southern States to a sleepless vigilance for the protection of their property and the preservation of their rights." Even the subsequently notorious Edwin M. Stanton said "there was no power under the Constitution to coerce a seceding State." These authorities are not collected and quoted in defense of the right of secession. Were such defense necessary, arguments indisputable and irrefragable, and from higher authorities, could be produced and piled one upon another, until a structure would stand, as such a structure ever stands, impregnable and unassailable by sophism or logic.

What I wish to show is that representative men, men who voiced the opinions of the people of the North, not only yielded the question of the right, but sustained the right of a State to retire from the Union in virtue of its own sovereign power as expressed by the votes of its citizens. More than that. The trend of opinion of the party which had come into power with the election and inauguration of Mr. Lincoln, as shown by their speeches and their papers, was that a peaceable dissolution of the Union was not only possible, but desirable. The Union-loving people were of the South, and of that conservative, patriotic, and law-abiding party of the North which had no representative in the factious, fanatical, and revolutionary class that damned the Constitution and the laws, and elevated, by a plurality of votes, one of their own ilk to the Presidential chair.

What cared those people for a Union that stood as a menace to their machinations and as a bulwark against their mad assaults upon their neighbor's property and possessions? What had they or their fathers done to build up this Union, to adorn it, to enlarge its borders, and make it great at home and glorious abroad? They had gotten their hands upon the strong box of the Government, and were awaiting the division of the pelf. But they never meant to fight for it. That was not in their line, and but few of their company fell into line when the roll beat, and they found out that they had awakened the demon of war. Let their own chief answer. Ida M. Tarbell, in her "Life of Lincoln," says that she was told by the late Joseph Medill, editor of the *Chicago Tribune*, that he went on an occasion and as one of a committee, from Chicago to Washington, to intercede with the authorities to be relieved from sending more troops to the war, in accordance with a new draft just ordered, and which was giving trouble. The committee went to Mr. Stanton, and failing to get relief from him, went to Mr. Lincoln. Mr. Medill says: "I shall never forget how he (Mr. Lincoln) suddenly lifted his head and turned on us a black and frowning face. 'Gentlemen,' he said, 'after Boston, Chicago has been the chief instrument of bringing this war on the country. It is you who are largely responsible for making blood to flow as it has. You called for war and we had it, you called for emancipation and we have given it to you. Whatever you have asked for you have had. Now you came here begging to be let off. You ought to be ashamed of yourselves. I had a right to expect better things of you. Go home and raise your extra six thousand men.'" That is documentary proof of what I have said, taken from their own authorities.

Mr. Lincoln did not anticipate war in earnest. Had he done so his hard common sense would never have permitted him to perpetrate the absurd blunder of calling for 75,000 men to subjugate the four million of people South of Mason and Dixon's line. The persistent, patient dogging of the Union men of the border States, sending commission after commission to Washington to treat for, and to implore, a recognition of their rights, finally convinced the party in power that if the Union were dissolved they would find powerful allies, if not most influential friends, in the State governments of the border States.

After the assembly of the convention of Virginia in Richmond, the Hon. M. Carr, of North Carolina, came to my seat in the Senate with a letter from a mutual friend, and asked me if I would go with him to the Executive Office and introduce him to Governor Letcher, saying that his mission to Richmond was to see what Virginia intended to do; what her course was to be in reference to the seceding States; saying at the same time that his people were, the great majority of them, for the Union, but he felt that the interests and destinies of all the Southern States were one; and that his State was waiting anxiously to see what we would do. I took him to the Governor's office, where I found, not only the Governor, but several of the most prominent Union men of the Convention, and introduced him, intimating to the gentlemen present the object of Mr. Carr's visit. And as I was not one of the Governor's way of thinking, I was not sure that in the presence of the little group assembled there I was persona gratis. After a few minutes, therefore, I bowed myself out, not too late, however, to hear the Governor say: "Mr. Carr, whatever Virginia does she is not going to be dragged out of the Union at the tail of a Southern Confederacy." Mr.

Letcher undoubtedly voiced the sentiment of three-fifths of the Union men of Virginia at that day and hour. How different that ringing reply of the Governor a few days later to the call for Virginia's quota of troops to subjugate the Southern States; and how like a bomb it must have fallen into the Lincoln camp! Had a letter embodying these views been sent to Mr. Lincoln by the hands of the Hon. A. H. H. Stuart, William Ballard Preston, and George W. Randolph, on the final mission of the Virginia Convention to Washington to secure information, and to ask what course the President intended to pursue toward the seceding States, they would never have returned to Richmond with a message of war on the 12th of April, nor would Mr. Lincoln have issued his call for troops from Virginia on the 15th, nor would the Ordinance of Secession have been passed on the 17th. When the commission returned to the convention and reported the results of the final interview with the Washington authorities, it was asked what the Union men proposed to do. Hon. John Baldwin, of Staunton, one of the staunchest supporters of the Union cause, and one of its ablest advocates, arose from his seat and replied, "There are no Union men now." Thus, in one short week, event upon event of the most momentous import and issue crowded upon each other's trail, and history was made with almost indecent haste.

I was in Washington with several of my comrades of the Virginia Senate, as I have before said, and after the announcement of the first vote in the Virginia Convention, which determined seemingly its political character, and which made apparent that a large majority of that body was opposed to secession, I witnessed the most complete tergiversation of men and measures that I had conceived possible. The representatives of Virginia, and of the border States generally, were men who believed that their respective States would follow the fortunes of the cotton States, and had imbued the minds of the dominant party with that idea. Hence, as we said, a peaceable separation of North and South was not only contemplated, but mutually agreed upon. The constant and repeated efforts of the Union men of the South, by commissions and re-commissions, of men of the greatest prominence, and whose pure and patriotic motives none could question, had undoubtedly begun to weaken the minds of the Washington authorities in reference to the true position of the border States; but I could never have believed, had I not witnessed it, that so complete and so sudden a revulsion of feeling, that so complete and so sudden an announcement of a change of policy, could have pervaded any party or any people. It was no longer, as Greeley said, "let the erring sisters go in peace." Our Republican friends still received us socially, and with warmth, but guyed us, some of them unmercifully. "Why," said they, "you gentlemen could not have been well acquainted at home, or at least with public sentiment at home. You told us that your State would secede from the Union. Look at the announcement in the Richmond papers. Not one-fourth of your Convention are secessionists; your people are for the Union, and we will kick the cotton States back, and you will help us."

A representative from Massachusetts, the Hon. William Burlingame, who rose to a good deal of distinction afterwards as Minister to China, and who had been particularly genial and generous with us, sought us out at once and said, "I told you that Virginia could never leave the Union; that we would not let you have any more ice for your juleps, and you could not do without that." I confess that my own faith weakened in the stand which I thought Virginia would and ought to take, and we paid fewer visits to the Capital thereafter, and held fewer interviews with our radical friends.

Walking the streets of Washington one morning a few days after these incidents, we noticed armed and uniformed sentries in sections of the city where we had never noticed their presence before, and on asking what it meant were referred to a morning paper. On doing so we saw that General Winfield Scott, whose headquarters were in Washington, had assumed virtual control of the police department. This, in time of peace, seemed rather a departure from civic precedent, and to us prognosticated danger. We did not foresee the imminence of that danger, nor dream of a Bastile at the old Capitol, in whose black shadow so many citizens were soon to be shut out from light and liberty. Had we done so, we probably would not have lingered so long about the Holy City, but left more promptly, leaving our cards and excuses. As it was, moved perhaps more by a spirit of what the world's people style deviltry, than by any decent desire to pay our compliments to the President, and the Commander-in-Chief of the Army and Navy of the United States, we called on Mr. Buchanan, and sending in our cards as Senators from Virginia, they secured us I suppose an immediate hearing, and we were ushered into the private office of the Executive. Acting as master of ceremonies, I introduced, first myself, and then my confreres. One of the young gentlemen with us inaugurated proceedings by asking after the health of Miss Harriet Lane—the President's niece, and whilom mistress of the White House. I suppressed his politness by a wholesome pressure of the boot heel upon his toe, and improved the solemn occasion by saying with all the dignity that I could crowd into my manner, "Mr. President, as citizens of Virginia, a State without one stain upon her escutcheon, and as accredited representatives in the

Honorable Senate of the General Assembly of Virginia, we have been estopped this morning upon the streets of the city of Washington, the Capital of our common country—estopped by armed sentry, and informed that we cannot extend our walks in this direction or that direction; and had the reason assigned us, that General Winfield Scott has virtually assumed command of the civil police. In this time of peace, would it be asking too much, Mr. President, if we ventured to inquire, before leaving for our homes, what grave reasons of state have rendered these extraordinary measures necessary?" Mr. Buchanan disputed the statement, politely, but with some feeling, and I handed him the morning paper, and called his attention to the paragraph upon which my inquiry was founded. I do not think that he was really aware of the facts before. He did not say so, but retaining his seat, which he had not left to greet us, he commenced to speak with a tearful voice of the delicate and responsible position of his office; of the strict account to which he would be held as guardian of the muniments of state, of how he loved Virginia and Maryland, and of the disturbed and distressing condition of public affairs, etc., etc. As soon as we could politely adjourn the meeting we retired, convinced that we had not seen the President. Mr. Lincoln had not taken his seat, of course, in the latter part of February, 1861, but Mr. Buchanan was not President. Some of the party suggested that Jeremiah Black, and others that General Scott, was President, but we made no further presidential calls.

Strolling into the gallery of the Senate, we heard the final debate between Andy Johnson, the Senator from Tennessee, and Wigfall, Senator from Texas. His State had seceded, but Wigfall persisted in retaining his seat at his pleasure, and for the purpose, it is said, of scoring the Republican Senators as often as he could get opportunity. Senator Johnson was speaking upon the all-engrossing subject when we entered the Senate, and from his standpoint made an able effort. As soon as he took his seat, Wigfall obtained recognition from the Chair, and commenced a speech which for rugged eloquence, pathos, humor, satire, and crushing assault exceeded anything I have ever heard. He commenced by saying, as well as I can recall his words after forty years, that he proposed to direct his remarks to the Senator from Tennessee, and that, but for his respect for the decencies of debate and his regard for Senatorial courtesy, he would apply to him the well known remark of another gentleman on another occasion, "Lord Angus, thou hast lied." And then for fifteen minutes there followed such a hot strain of charges, and merciless assault, that S. A. Douglas took pity on Johnson, evidently, and putting his arm over his shoulder, led him into the cloak-room. In the meantime the gallery had caught up the furor, and with storms of applause made a temporary bedlam. The President of the Senate used his gavel vigorously, but without silencing the commotion, and he ordered the galleries to be cleared. I was sitting by the Hon. Alexander Rives, of Albemarle, one of my confreres in the Senate of Virginia, a grave and dignified gentleman, and when the Sergeant-at-Arms approached us, and commenced to hustle us out, as he did every one else, Mr. Rives protested strongly, saying with an expression that he often used when he wished to be emphatic, "God bless my soul, sir, I have not made any noise, nor have I sympathized in this disturbance." But the officer was inexorable, and turned us out with the others. We wended our way to our hotel. Mr. Rives, no little crestfallen at his treatment, said to me as we went to dinner, "My friend, if you have any Virginia bonds, sell them; great trouble is pending." I left Washington the next day, confident that disunion was at hand, but I really feared from the action of the Virginia Convention that the old State would either stand alone, or with the border States, fix up, or attempt to fix up, some defensive alliance with the Federal Government. The words of Mr. Burlingame in Congress to myself and my confreres, "We are going to kick the cotton States back into the Union and you are going to help us," rang in my ears, and knowing how far my own personal help would go in that direction, on reaching home commenced making my arrangements to remove my family to Mississippi. But events moved too rapidly to permit me to complete them, and in a day the revolution came, as I had predicted in the Senate of Virginia on the 19th of January, 1860, it would come—when some State, staggering under the burden of oppression, should walk out of the Union; and that it would come, in all of its horrors, and with no power upon earth or in Heaven to prevent, when a sectional President should be summoned to the command of the Army and Navy of the United States, and should marshal the Federal forces to coerce such a State into submission.

This prophecy did not amount to much with three-fifths of my own constituency—much less was such a sequence of events contemplated by any great number of the people of the border States, and by fewer of the people of the Northern States; that is, amongst those who loved the Union and desired to maintain it. The radicals of the Northern States, the Republican Party, which cared nothing for the Union except so far as it could be made subservient to their interests, and which was ready to dissolve the Federation when it failed to foster their fanatical designs, were not averse to a separation from the Southern States, as has been clearly shown by the authorities cited; but they did not anticipate war, certainly not a war of such magnitude as their

blind partisanship developed. Mr. Lincoln, then, when
he precipitated the culmination of these events by the
egregious folly of summoning 75,000 men to subdue
the Southern States,* was simply bluffing, but in a game
the most momentous, and with stakes the most stupendous of any game which was ever played on this or
any other continent. And when Mr. Letcher called
him and showed him the mailed hand of Virginia, he
threw down his cards. He had lost. Nothing was
left him then but to accept his own wager, the wager
of battle—war! Two years later, as before stated, he
said to the chairman of the committee from Chicago
who waited on him and protested against furnishing
more troops, "Gentlemen, next to Boston, you are responsible for all of this blood which has been shed.
You asked for war, and I gave it to you." Not wonderful that he should have wished to shift upon other
shoulders the responsibility of a war so unnecessary, so
cruel, so causeless, so costly in blood and treasure.
When, following Virginia, North Carolina, Tennessee,
and Arkansas fell into line in a day, and bared their
front to the Federal menace of subjugation of their
sister States; when the proud-spirited people of Kentucky, and their worthy scions who had wrested Missouri from the red man; and when liberty-loving Maryland, fired by the memory of the traditions of her past,
all essayed to join their fortunes with the men of the
South, until throttled by the hand of the despot at their
doors—Mr. Lincoln realized, perhaps for the first time,
speaking in his own homely vernacular, "the bigness of
the job which he had undertaken." He was aware,
moreover, that he was not the President, by choice,
of the people of the United States, but only of a faction
of them, not all of which even sustained him; and he

---

* See Appendix.

was aware that even if he were President, he had not the right to declare war, that such power was vested only in the Congress of the United States. The Senate, though radical, refused to ratify his course and to declare it legal, yet with the black brow of his imperturbable will, and with a heart steeled to do the Devil's bidding, he set section against section, State against State, until this fair land had been deluged with fratricidal blood and a million of yawning graves had received a million of ghastly dead. No wonder that he wished to shift the responsibility upon another, and that he shrank from the office of High Priest at the altar where this horrid holocaust was offered. He sought, of course, to throw this responsibility upon the South. Was not the South the aggressor? Did it not strike the first blow, and did it not fire the first gun? And dividing with his treacherous Secretary of State the honor of the duplicity, he made it appear for a time that he was the innocent and incorruptible patriot who had striven in vain to keep the peace and to preserve the integrity of the nation. Many people believe this yet. To those at the North who have not taken such interest in the subject as to lead them to examine into the truthfulness or falsity of the record, we make no address; but to the Southron, especially the young Southron, who can coolly and without contradiction listen to and accept such perversion of fact, we wish to remark that he is unworthy of the noble heritage of courage and of honor which he received from his fathers. He should know enough of the traditions of his Southern home to know that there was ever an unwritten law, but sustained by judge and justice, which made "the lie direct the first blow." Mr. Hallam ("Constitutional History of England") more elegantly, but not more forcibly, elaborates the law and refers to it as of universal application. He says that "the aggressor in a war, that is, he who begins it, is not the first who uses force but the first who renders force necessary." Who was the aggressor in the war between the States? We have seen that several of the States of the South, after repeated acts of contumely, aggression, and robbery on the part of certain States of the North, had, in the exercise of their constituted right, determined to leave a Union in which the compact creating it had been repeatedly and wickedly broken; and taking possession of the common property of such Union as lay within their borders, had sent commissioners to their Northern brethren to adjust the terms upon which such property should be divided. And we have quoted argument and sentiment, not from Southern, but from the highest Northern authorities, admitting and sustaining the legality and the propriety of this course of action in the South. Not one act of violence had been committed, nor any blow had been struck anywhere in the South by the Federal Government, and the Government had not attempted to reclaim or retake any of its so called property prior to May, 1861. But South Carolina, which had left the Union six months before, had, in the harbor of Charleston, a fort still in the occupation of the Federal troops, and which as long as it was held by such troops was not only a menace but a source of irritation and a seat of danger. She requested the evacuation of this fort, and sent commissioners to Washington to treat with the authorities in reference to the terms on which the garrison should leave. The Federal authorities refused to receive these commissioners, but treated with them through Judges Campbell and Nelson of the Supreme Court of the United States, two gentlemen of the greatest integrity and of the highest position in the land. It was agreed on between the commissioners of South Carolina and Mr.

Seward that Fort Sumter should not be fired upon unless attempts were made by the Government to revictual or reinforce it, and meanwhile Mr. Seward gave Judge Campbell to understand that Fort Sumter would be evacuated in a few days.

In the meantime an expedition, called the "Relief Squadron," of eleven ships, heavily armed, and twenty-four hundred men, was being gotten in readiness for reinforcing Sumter and revictualing the garrison—"peaceably if possible, forcibly if it must be." This occupied twenty-three days, during the whole of which time Mr. Seward kept Judge Campbell ignorant of the facts, and even notifying him in writing on the day the squadron was ordered to sail, May 7th, "Faith as to Sumter fully kept." Judge Campbell demanded of Mr. Seward what this deception meant, but no explanation was ever given. He simply took Mr. Lincoln into partnership in his base duplicity, and the words have passed into history, affixing to the joint names a stigma as damnatory as ineffaceable. Only at the last minute were Governor Pickens, of South Carolina, and the Confederate authorities made aware of the sailing and destination of this fleet; and then, without awaiting its appearance at their doors, they reduced Fort Sumter and saved Charleston from the horrors of a bombardment. By order of the Confederate authorities, General Beauregard fired the first shot. But who made the first shot necessary? Who was the aggressor? Let the South be silent if you please. Let the North speak.

Mr. S. S. Cox, of New York, for twenty-four years a prominent member of Congress, in his "Three Decades of the Federal Union," whilst discussing the subject of the "Republican Reprisals of Compromise" in that remarkable session of 1860-'61, says: "The real question which history would regard as of the first importance at this time was this, Could not this Union have been made permanent by a timely settlement, instead of being cemented by fraternal blood and military rule?" And answers, "Yes, by an equitable adjustment of the territory this was possible."

The Crittenden Compromise offered such an adjustment. This proposition the radicals denounced. Notwithstanding the President-elect was then in a minority of a million of votes, they were determined,—as Mr. Chase wrote to Portsmouth, Ohio, from the Peace Convention,—"they intended to use the power whilst they had it, and to prevent a settlement." "It had been stated," continues Mr. Cox, "that in order to rid the Republicans of the odium of not averting the war when it was possible, the Northern members tendered the South the Crittenden Compromise, and it was rejected. *This is not true.* It was tendered by Southern Senators and Northern Democrats to the Republicans, and they, in conjunction with some half a dozen extremist Southern Senators, rejected it. It was voted on only once in the House, and received only 80 votes against 113. These 80 votes were exclusively Democratic, or 'Southern Americans,' like Gilmore, Vance, and others. The Republican roll, beginning with Adams, and ending with Woodruff, was a unit against it. The climax is reached. One more earnest appeal is made to the Republicans. Senator Cameron answers it by moving a reconsideration. His motion is called up on the 18th of February. He votes against his own motion. On this occasion all the Democrats voted for, and all the Republicans against it. The truth is, there are nothing but sneers and skepticism from the Republicans at any settlement. If every Southern man and every Northern Democrat had voted for this proposition it would have required nine Republican votes then to have carried it by the requisite two-thirds vote. Where are they? Dreaming with Mr. Seward of a sixty-days struggle, or arranging for the division of the patronage of the Administration." (Congressional Globe, 1st Part, 36th Congress, page 270.)

Whether, therefore, the public records are consulted, or the inquirer goes within the veil and consults those who know the men then at work in the committee, and in social life, one leading fact will always stand stark and bold, viz: that with the help of a handful of secessionists *per se*, the whole body of the Republicans were, as Andrew Johnson described Senator Clark when the latter defeated the Crittenden Compromise by his amendment in the Senate, but "acting out their own policy." In the light of subsequent events that policy was developed. It was the destruction of slavery at the peril of war, and disunion, or, as Senator Douglas, of Illinois, expressed it, "a disruption of the Union, believing it would draw after it, as inevitable consequence, civil war, servile insurrection, and finally the extermination of slavery in the United States." Yet the leader and mouthpiece of this great faction declared a few days later, upon the most solemn oath that could be administered on the most momentous occasion, that "he had neither the right nor the desire to interfere with the existence of slavery in the States."

Once more, and from Northern testimony: Speaking of the "Relief Squadron" sent to Charleston Harbor to reinforce and revictual Fort Sumter, Mr. Lunt, of Massachusetts, says, "It was intended to draw the fire of the Confederates, and was a silent aggression, with the object of producing an active aggression from the other side." Again, Mr. Williams, of Massachusetts: "There was no need for war. The action of the Southern States was legal and constitutional." The South was invaded, and a war of subjugation, des-

tined to be the most gigantic which the world has
ever seen, was begun by the Federal Government
against the seceding States, in complete and amazing
disregard of the foundation principle of its own existence, as affirmed in the Declaration of Independence,
viz: that "governments derive their just powers from
the consent of the governed"; and, as established
by the War of the Revolution, for the people of the
States respectively. The South, with the eager and
resolute courage characteristic of her proud-spirited
people, accepted the contest thus forced upon her.

Who was the aggressor? The North has answered
through some of her truest and most patriotic sons.
The aggression had been a cumulative evil and wrong
for twenty years, and its culmination occurred when
the Republican President, by the menace of an armed
fleet at Charleston, compelled the Confederate author-
itites to fire the first shot for defense. It was said that
the first shot fired at the British troops in Lexington,
Massachusetts, by a continental militiaman on the 17th
of April, 1775, awakened an echo of constitutional liberty that went resounding through the whole world—
and the first shot fired from a Confederate battery at
Charleston, South Carolina, on the 12th of April,
1861, sounded the knell, not only of constitutional,
but of personal liberty, as far the power of the
United States Government extended. Mr. Lincoln
declared, in grim joke, that "he had the Constitution
locked up in his trunk in his room at the White
House"; and Mr. Seward said to Lord Lyons, the
British Minister: "My Lord, I can touch a bell on my
right hand and order the arrest of a citizen of Ohio;
I can touch a bell again, and order the imprisonment
of a citizen of New York; and no power on earth but
that of the President can release them. Can the Queen
of England do as much?" Nor was this idle gas-

conade. With a stroke of his pen he swept out those words, *nullus liber homo capeatur*, which, though written in a dead language, were "vital with liberty and worth," as Chatham's nervous eloquence declared, "all classic." The Magna Charta, wrested from King John at Runnymede, for more than six centuries the pride and glory of the Saxon and his descendants, was crumpled up as common paper and pigeon-holed in the secret drawers of the radical administrator.

The writ of *habeas corpus* was suspended in every State, and the summons of the civil courts ignored, and trial by jury abolished. Mr. Stanton became Military Dictator, with military satraps of his own appointment, in any number at his own discretion, and with authority to hold, arrest, and imprison at their own will. The consequences can scarcely be conceived of at this day. There was a Bastile in every State. Mr. John A. Marshall, in a book called the "American Bastile,"* gives the history of more than an hundred of the victims of the Bastile, from Col. Lambdin P. Melligan, of Illinois, to Francis Key Howard, of Maryland. But these were only a few of the hundreds that were arrested upon the merest trumpery of a charge, and imprisoned without trial and without appeal. "Nor was civil liberty restored to the citizen at the close of the war," says Mr. Cox, in the volume before quoted. "When secession died, as it did in the last ditch, then it was that the malign spirit which had hovered in the rear of the conflict came to the front to gloat over the prostrate Southern land. The gray picket was no longer at his post to challenge the spirit of hate and eternal discord. No right was now known but the right of spoliation and conquest."

---

*See Appendix.

A new executor (President Johnson) had come with
a "very small olive branch in his hand." What cared
the victorious conspirators for that? They spat upon
it with contempt. They impeached him for that small
tender. What cared they for executive clemency?
What cared they for constitutional guarantees or Supreme Court decisions? They would have no law but
martial law in the "conquered provinces." Then, after the war, began a contest for the restoration of civil
liberty, "a contest which was not finally settled until
the last year of Republican sway. It took almost a
quarter of a century to silence the guns of Moultrie
and Sumter." But there were brave men in the North
who, in the legislative halls and outside of them, denounced this tyrannical usurpation of authority, and
who fought with reckless courage for the maintenance
and the restoration of the right. Ganson, Voorhees,
Vallandigham, Cox, Winter Davis, Garfield (afterwards
President), were conspicuous in this struggle, and their
memories should be kept alive and honored by every
lover of liberty. But the immediate effect of the first
shot is the question. It "fired the Northern heart,"
as Mr. Lincoln, according to his garrulous chroniclers
Nicolay and Hay, intended that it should do, and for
which reason he held the fleet inactive in Charleston
Harbor until after the reduction of Sumter and the surrender of the garrison. The sacred flag had been assailed by the Rebels, and the "life of the country was
in danger." He had no difficulty in securing the 75,000
men at first called for, though the border States refused to send their quota; nor had he any difficulty in
securing any number of volunteer troops, as long as
the idea prevailed that the fight was for the flag and
for the Union. But after it became evident that the
fight was for the negro, for the emancipation of the
slave, and for the subjugation of the white man, then

troops were only raised by levy, by conscription—and conscription resisted by riot. But in vain! Personal liberty had been sacrificed to the Moloch of hate and fanaticism, and in four years the actual enlistment of Army and Navy was 2,780,000 men volunteered, recruited, or conscripted. Of these, 359,528 were killed in battle or died of wounds or disease.

On the 31st of March, 1865, there were on the rolls of the Union army 1,000,516 men; at the same time the cost of the war in treasure had been $3,400,000,000! Nearly two and a half millions a day whilst it lasted. The first shot had been effective at the North. But the firing of the first shot had an effect at the South which Lincoln perhaps did not contemplate, though he could not have felt the same shock of surprise which Governor Letcher's manly letter of refusal to furnish Virginia's quota of troops for the Federal Army gave him. It united the South. The people, as one man, said to the Federal authorities, in the words of Governor Letcher, "you have chosen to inaugurate war, and you shall have it." They but repeated Baldwin's reply on his return from Washington after the failure of the last effort for peace, "there are no Union men now." Such unity of sentiment, such unanimity of purpose never before existed, I suppose, in a population of some four million of souls. Men of all classes and conditions vied with each other in offer of self and substance to resist Federal invasion and secure Southern independence.

It is not the purpose or within the province of these papers to pursue the history of the protracted—the fearful—war which followed, a veritable battle of the giants, a shock to every instinct of humanity, and a shame to Christian civilization. More than once, when witnessing the bloody horrors of the field of carnage, I have asked myself the question, "Can Central Africa, with all the savage cruelty of the brutal nature of its people, exceed this show?" I only propose to recite briefly some account, a bird's-eye view, of the contest as it came within the scope of my observation.

Five days after the call of Simon Cameron, Secretary of War, for Virginia's quota of troops for Federal service, the Convention, then in session, passed an ordinance authorizing and requiring the Governor of the Commonwealth "to call into the service of the State as many volunteers as may be necessary to repel invasion, and protect the citizens of the State in the present emergency." These volunteers were to be received in companies and organized into regiments, brigades, and divisions, according to the force required.

On the 21st of April, 1861, the Governor issued the following proclamation: "By virtue of authority vested in the Executive by the Convention, I, John Letcher, Governor of the Commonwealth of Virginia, do hereby order that each volunteer company equipped and armed, whether infantry, artillery, or riflemen, in the counties lying west of the city of Richmond, between Richmond and the Blue Ridge, and in the Valley of Virginia, from the county of Rockbridge to the Tennessee line, establish forthwith, on the lines of speedy communication, a rendezvous, and hold themselves in readiness for immediate orders: telegraph or send by express to the Executive the names of the captains, number of men, and description of force." But before this, on the 18th, General Wm. B. Taliaferro was ordered to assemble troops at Norfolk for the purpose of capturing the Gosport Navy Yard. This was done secretly, in hope of getting possession of the valuable stores of ordnance, ammunition, etc., before they could be destroyed by the Federals.

CHAPTER IV

THE WAR.

The Fourth Virginia Battalion Receives Orders—Quartered in Norfolk—The Companies and Officers—I Accompany the Battalion as Captain and Assistant Surgeon—Am Again Elected to the Senate—Ordered to Take my Seat by the Secretary of War—Obey the Order and Resign, and Apply For Orders For the Army—An Interview—Ordered to Open Hospitals in Petersburg and Made Surgeon in Charge—Appointed Post Surgeon—How Some Supplies Were Acquired—Events Preceding Siege of Petersburg—Arrival of the Enemy—Incidents of the Siege—Ordered to Remove the Hospital Patients and Correspondence With General Lee—The "Fiasco of the War"—An Adventure Before the Lines of the Enemy—"In Vinculis"—The Crater—General Mahone's Part in the Crater Affair—I am Visited by a Shell at Night—More Incidents of Our Great Generals, and Another of Mahone in Particular—What Manner of Man Was. He? What Manner of Men Were They?—Five Forks—Evacuation and Events Immediately Following.

On the 19th of April, 1861, D. A. Weisinger, major of the Fourth Virginia Battalion, made up exclusively of Petersburg troops, was ordered to hold his command in readiness to move at a minute's notice. On the morning of the 20th the command was called out, and marched to the Norfolk and Western depot, where they found a train awaiting them, the engine fired up and puffing steam, as if awaiting, with the same impatience as the men, the order to start. The destination, of course, was "unknown to the rank and file," but it was an open secret that Norfolk was the destination and the taking of the Navy Yard the duty assigned. The troops got off about noon amidst the cheers and tears and prayers of the hundreds who had assembled to see them leave. This was war, suddenly and in earnest, and amongst a people who had known for a third of a century only the blessings

of peace, and who had seen only the martial parade
and heard only the fife and drum of a holiday soldiery.
The excitement incident to the scenes of that day cannot be described, as mother, wife, sister caught hold
of the soldier hurrying away to battle, and pressed the
last loving kiss to his lips, and as the soldier himself
gathered his loved ones in his arms and folded them to
his heart in one last embrace. Imagination may paint,
but no pen can depict the overwhelming emotions
which crowded that hour. Before the battalion em-
barked on the cars, the Rev. Dr. Platt, before referred
to in these memoirs, and who himself had been a soldier
in the Mexican War, made a short address, and offered
prayer that "God would cover the heads of the boys in
the day of battle." The companies were then drawn up
in double order, the rear rank confronting the first, and
the citizens passed through the line, bidding a final farewell, and begging such blessings upon the soldiers as
their tumultuous hearts would permit them to frame.
There was no element of humor on the occasion at the
time, but a recollection of some of the scenes afterwards made me smile in the days that followed. As
the days grew into years, those callow boys, scarred
and seamed into veterans by war's rough usage, could
recount by the bivouac fire, with a laugh, many a joke
upon each other which had its birth upon that solemn
morning. "Judgment day," it was yclept in soldier's
vernacular, as it was not believed that any day other
than the Judgment could ever be ushered in with such
overwhelming and stupendous excitement in any class
of people, high or low, white or colored.

Late in the afternoon we reached the South Branch
of the Elizabeth River, a few miles from Norfolk, and
the troops were ordered out of the train, a line was
formed parallel with the road, and for the first time the
ball cartridge was rammed home in the bright pieces

The War

which heretofore had only fired blank cartridges in salute. I do not know what were the feelings of any others, but for myself I confess that I realized, as I had not done before, that war was upon us, and that an unpleasant duty was ours. This feeling was intensified to some extent when Captain Dodson, commanding Co. E, the crack company of the battalion, in a few well-chosen words of encouragement cautioned the men to be "steady, to look along the line of their piece, and to fire low." We had expected to go into battle and to encounter resistance, either before getting to Gosport or in driving the Federals from the Navy Yard by assault—a desperate undertaking for some four hundred green troops, whatever their spirit and courage, against marines and trained soldiers of the Regular Army, of whose number we were ignorant, but presumably in force sufficient to hold and protect the valuable property which we coveted and were contending for. But there was to be no fight yet, thanks to a strategy of Mahone, then president of the Norfolk and Petersburg R. R. He had empty cars run to and fro all day for several miles outside of Norfolk, conveying to the Federals the idea of the frequent arrival of troops in numbers. They, ignorant of what these numbers were, and indisposed to try issue with an unknown foe, hurriedly fired the Navy Yard, spiked most of the guns, and left for the safe retreat of Fortress Monroe. This maneuver of Mahone showed the instinct of the soldier, into which he developed as soon as opportunity offered—and opportunities were many before the war was over. It is mild encomium to say that no opportunity was ever lost, and that he developed into one of Lee's most active and trusted lieutenants. We reached Norfolk about dark, to find the enemy gone on board the vessels which they had not burned or scuttled, and steaming down the river for Old Point Comfort. That night the battalion was quartered in a large empty building in the city, whilst the staff rested in quiet at the National Hotel. Indeed that was headquarters for a week or more, although on the next day the battalion was moved out in the neighborhood of the old Fair Grounds. A few days afterwards it was ordered into quarters at Berkley, then little more than a village of straggling houses, and located at the U. S. Marine Hospital, which, on the evacuation of Norfolk, the Federals had left comparatively empty. To this point headquarters were also transferred, where we made ourselves quite comfortable, though not in a style comparable to our first quarters of the first week of our first service in the war between the States. The Fourth Battalion as it left Petersburg consisted of four companies of infantry and one company of artillery, and numbered, rank and file, about four hundred men. The companies were—

The City Guards—Capt. John P. May and Lieuts. Chas. E. Waddell and F. M. Wright.

A Grays—Capt. Jno. Lyon and Lieuts. Robert Bowden and Thos. P. Pollard.

B Grays—Capt. Thos. A. Bond and Lieuts. L. L. Marks and S. G. White.

Petersburg Rifles—Capt. Daniel Dodson and Lieuts. R. R. Banks and Jno. R. Patterson.

The staff consisted of Maj. D. A. Weisiger, commanding; Lieut. W. F. Carter, quartermaster; Lieut. Samuel Stevens, commissary, and Capt. Jno. Herbert Claiborne, assistant surgeon.

Light Artillery attached to battalion—Capt. J. N. Nichols and Lieut. Edward Graham. This battery was detached from the Fourth Battalion on the day following our arrival at Norfolk, and I saw no more of it until the 9th day of June, 1864. The story of that day will be told later.

The War

The Fourth Battalion as it left Petersburg on the 20th of April, 1861, was made up of the flower of the manhood of the Cockade City. After four years of service it had been so decimated by disease, by death, by promotion, and by transfer that it showed scarcely more than a skeleton of the original body. It was the nucleus upon which was formed the famous Twelfth Virginia Regiment, whose banner bore the device of almost every field on which the Army of Northern Virginia grappled with the enemy, from Seven Pines to Appomattox, and whose flag, stained with the smoke of battle and shredded by ball and shell, was never surrendered, but torn into slips and buried in the bosoms, right over the hearts, of the veteran survivors. On being formed into a regiment, two other companies from Petersburg—the Lafayette Guards, Capt. D. N. Jarvis and Lieut. J. E. Tyler, and the Archer Rifles, Capt. F. H. Archer, Lieuts. J. R. Lewellyn, Douglas Chappell, and D. W. Paul—were attached to it, and also a company from Richmond, the Richmond Grays, and a company from Greenesville county, Capt. Everard Field.

Major Weisiger was raised to the rank of colonel, with F. A. Taylor, of Gloucester County, as lieutenant-colonel, and Maj. E. Brockett as major. Colonel Weisiger retained the same staff, which went up a grade with him, the lieutenants being raised to the rank of captain, and the surgeon to the rank of major. Dr. J. W. Claiborne, who was a private in Co. E, the Petersburg Rifles, was promoted to the rank of captain and made assistant surgeon. The regiment was then ordered to an entrenched camp, about two miles below Norfolk, which it held, with the Sixth Virginia Regiment, commanded by Col. Wm. Mahone, until the evacuation of Norfolk in the following spring.

The days spent at these quarters were gala days, and
soldiering an idle, and mostly a pleasant, pastime.
Guard mounting every morning and dress parade every
evening filled the role of duty. Secure and commodious tents, with plank floors, and chimneys during the
winter, made everything very cosy and comfortable
in quarters—and as for the menu, the regulation ration
was not considered. Located near the market of Norfolk, with its rich stores of fish, flesh, and fowl, with
products not yet depleted, and boxes from home sup-
plementing any possible want, the inner man did not
suffer; and with books, papers, and periodicals to while
away the idle moments, and the frequent visits of the
girls to the camps to enliven the scene, soldier life for
the first year of the war was very, very tolerable.
There was little sickness, and no casualty or death occurred in the whole command to mar its symmetry from
April, 1861, to December of the same year, when I was
ordered to another field.

The coming campaign of the following year attested
the travesty and the simulation of war of our first year
of service. From the opening of the campaign of 1862,
and from thenceforth to the tragic end at Appomattox,
the Twelfth Virginia knew nothing more of ease, of
rest, of comfort; saw no more holiday soldiering—
but WAR, WAR, in all of its terrible earnestness, its
privations, its sufferings, in cold and heat, in hunger
and sickness, in bivouac, in battle, in wounds, in death.
And when overpowered, and the last order from their
commander came, "surrender," the little handful left,
bereft of all but honor, threw down their arms, still
bright and burnished, and accepted the honorable
terms which the valor and endurance of the Confederate soldier had exacted from the victors, and returned
to their homes to exhibit the same courage and fortitude in peace in rebuilding their broken fortunes. Here

at Appomattox I met again, for the first time in three years, my old comrades, or those of them who had survived those bitter years, and as I had marched with them in all the pride and hope of their early days of soldiering, so I sat down with them at the last in the dust and ashes of final defeat.

But I anticipate my story. When I left Petersburg with the Fourth Virginia Battalion in April, 1861, my term of service as Senator in the District of Petersburg and Prince George had expired, and as I had not been in accord with my constituents on the question of secession and the necessity for early and aggressive action, I supposed that my political career was finished. But whilst in the field, and without offering myself for the place, I was again elected to the Senate, my constituents recognizing, though too late for the common good, the wisdom of the course which I had counseled, and wishing, I suppose, to compensate me by the compliment for the lack of confidence which they had shown in my teachings. In the meantime I was no longer a Virginia soldier nor subject to Virginia authorities. One week after the passage of the Ordinance of Secession the Convention of Virginia appointed commissioners to meet Vice-President A. H. Stevens, commissioner on the part of the Confederate Government, already set up in Alabama, and an agreement was made and ratified whereby the constitution of the Confederacy was adopted, and in May the seat of the Confederate Government was removed to Richmond and the troops of the State were transferred to the authorities of the Confederate States.

When the Legislature of Virginia assembled, therefore, in December, 1861, it was discovered that none of the soldiers in the field who had been elected to civil office by the people could leave their posts in the Army to take possession of such offices. An officer in the

Army could resign his commission and then take civil office, but as I did not choose to resign my commission, I was ordered by the Secretary of War, with other officers who occupied similar positions, to report to Richmond, and take my seat in the Senate of Virgina. I obeyed the order, took my seat in the Senate, wrote my resignation as Senator, and sent it to the President of the Senate. A new election was directed to be held, and on the appearance of my successor, Hon. R. R. Collier, I reported to the Secretary of War, Judah P. Benjamin, for reassignment to duty in the Army. When I called on Mr. Benjamin, and announced my name, he spoke up promptly, saying, "I ordered you a month ago to take your seat in the Senate of Virginia." How he could have recalled this fact amidst the many more important and urgent matters which demanded his attention, I could never imagine. However, I replied as promptly, that I had obeyed his order, taken my seat in the Senate, sent in my resignation, a new election had been held, and that my successor was in the city. He regarded me in rather a quizzical manner, as if he thought that I must be a little daft to wish to leave Richmond and to go back to the Army. However, he said nothing more, but wrote an order, and directed me to take it to the Surgeon-General, Dr. S. P. Moore. I obeyed this order also, but not so cheerfully. I had had one interview with General Moore, soon after I received my appointment from the Governor of Virginia as surgeon of the Twelfth Virginia Regiment, at which he treated me with such discourtesy that I had no wish to meet him again. I was in Richmond on business soon after General Moore had been appointed Surgeon-General, and in obedience to army regulations, called on the chief of my department, as was required, to pay my respects. He took my card when I handed it to him, and without giving me any sign of recognition, threw it away. I felt the rudeness keenly, but stood before him unmoved, intending to stand in my place all day, if necessary, until I received some notice. After a few minutes he lit a cigarette, which he made extemporaneously, and motioned to me to sit down. That drew my fire, and I said, "Dr. Moore, being in the city of Richmond on business, I have called at the headquarters of the chief of my department to pay my respects as required by army regulations. I have no favors to ask, and with your permission will retire," and without permission, and without saluting, retired. After this first interview, I was averse to a second. I presented my order, however, and on this occasion received prompt recognition. He asked to what command I belonged, and on noting the regiment, remarked on the exceptionally good report which had been returned from it, that there had been no death from disease in nine months, etc., and then asked me where I was from. He then told me he could not send me back to my old command, but to go home and await orders; that he wanted me for an especial purpose. I lost no time in withdrawing from his presence or in finding my home, but after six weeks of an unasked furlough, for I heard nothing from the Department in that time, I began to feel a decided curiosity to know what "especial purpose" I was wanted for and what was to be my destination, and thinking possibly I had been overlooked or forgotten, I reported by letter for duty. In a very short time I received a curt reply that I would be "called for when I was wanted." This did not satisfy my curiosity, but it silenced me. I made no further inquiry of General Moore as to my duty or destination. He was a man of great brusqueness of manner, and gave offense to many who called on him, whatever their business, and without any regard to their station or rank, though he was an able executive officer, and I believe an efficient and impartial one. After the war he remained in Richmond, and I am told was a useful and honored citizen.

Soon after the campaign of 1862 opened on the Peninsula, I received my orders to secure a suitable building in Petersburg and open a hospital with four hundred beds, and to purchase a large amount of ice, as much as could be had, and to house it. I rented a large and comparatively new tobacco factory, known as Ragland's, which stood at the corner of Jones Street and West Washington, just opposite the residence of Hon. W. B. McIlwaine. It was a three-story building, commodious and well ventilated, and furnished regulation space for about four hundred beds. This I soon fitted up and put in commission. It could not have been better fitted for hospital purposes if it had been built with that view, and had never before seen any hospital civil or military, which surpassed it in its appointments. I was made surgeon in charge, and Drs. R. E. Lewis, and G. W. Claiborne, my brother, were sent me as assistant surgeons. Dr. John Chappell was made apothecary and mustered in as hospital steward, and Mr. T. R. Moore chief ward master, and Mr. Jos. Todd commissary, both mustered in as hospital stewards. These gentlemen retained their places as long as I was surgeon in charge, for eighteen months or two years, and a more faithful and efficient corps of men could not have been secured. In about twelve months my brother was transferred to the Navy as assistant surgeon, but the other gentlemen held their places until the end of the war.

About six months prior to this a hospital after the pavilion order had been established at West End Park, then the Fair Grounds, known as the Confederate States Hospital, of which Dr. Blackwood Strachan was the first surgeon in charge. Some six months afterwards he was transferred to the field, and the surgeon and assistant surgeons in charge were often changed. During the winter of 1861-'62 the North Carolina Hospital was organized and commissioned in Cameron's Factory, and the South Carolina Hospital in Osborne and Chieves' Factory, now John H. Maclin & Son's, and the Virginia Hospital in Watson and McGill's Factory, then known as Robert Leslie's.

In 1862 Dr. Peter Hines, in charge of the North Carolina Hospital, being senior surgeon, was made Surgeon of the Post, and all the hospitals were under his care, and all reports and requisitions were made through him. In 1863 he was ordered to Raleigh and I was appointed Senior Surgeon, or Post Surgeon, a position which I held until the retreat of Lee's army in April, 1863, with the exception of three months of sickness, when Dr. Douglass, of Georgia, took my place.

My family, which had been refugeeing in Louisburg, North Carolina, during my absence from home early in the war, were now brought home, and my life was as comfortable as the privations and perils of war permitted. Rations were light, provisions of all sorts scarce, luxuries unknown, and clothing without suspicion of style or fashion. Cut off by the blockade from foreign supplies, we were dependent upon home resources, already overtaxed and imperfect, for almost everything. Only cornbread, peas, and sorghum were plentiful. The latter took the place of molasses, and at the same time was known as "long sweetening," in the place of sugar, for our coffee, which consisted of parched rye or dried sweet potatoes. It was also the saccharine element of the "pies" without which the soldier's menu was never complete, and for which his appetite seemed insatiable, they being the first investment from his meagre pay. Only the blockade runners, or their intimate friends, could indulge in the luxuries of eating and drinking, or in the display of fine clothes.

A great many adventures were made in shipping cotton and tobacco from this city and from Richmond through the blockade at Wilmington; and when a vessel successfully made the voyage to Nassau, the nearest British port, and more successfully returned, laden with articles of prime demand, the Government very properly was the first purchaser, and thus supplies for the Army, and especially for the hospitals, were often gotten. Hospital supplies were especially difficult to procure, and our refined and Christian enemies, who had made such articles as chloroform, morphine, quinine, and indeed everything which could solace human suffering or save human life,—whether of man, woman, or child,—contraband of war, gloated over the capture of a blockade-runner carrying such cargo, as ghouls ravishing the graves of the dead. However, we kept, during the last year of the war, and especially during the siege of Petersburg, fairly supplied with some of these essentials. I had men in my service whilst I was chief of all the Military General Hospitals, during the siege, who discovered that cupidity had not been eliminated from the Christian virtues of all of our enemies, and many a good trade was effected, nearer home than Nassau, of tobacco, snuff, and cotton yarns for quinine, morphine, and chloroform.

When in June, 1864, the Army of Northern Virginia filed into the trenches at Petersburg, and more than fifty thousand men were added to the population of the city, and the daily casualties called for more hospital service, the difficulties of meeting the exigencies entailed thereby were of course greatly increased. But with the help of a most efficient corps of assistants, I am sure I can say that the sick and wounded did not

The War

suffer for anything necessary to their comfort. I had one assistant especially, Sergeant Joseph Todd, who, as a forager, could ferret out any food to be found in the city or its vicinage. His genius in that direction amounted to instinct, and to the last day of the occupancy of the city by Lee's army he never failed to respond to any call. And when money—the money which we received from the Government for the purchase of supplies—failed to procure them, I made requisition for tobacco and cotton yarns, and in any quantity I thought necessary, the Department never failing to honor the requisition, and putting these articles in the hands of Mr. Todd, I never feared for results. After the war he went to Baltimore, and I heard obtained the place of purveyor or steward to the Maryland General Hospital, in which I am sure he illustrated his peculiar talents.

After the arrival of Lee's army my duties as senior or executive officer were greatly increased, and my position was neither safe nor a sinecure. From the first day of the occupation of the city to the last, I had no further opportunity of taking a knife in my hand or of administering a dose of physic. I received my first introduction to my new duties on the third or fourth day of General Lee's arrival.

The enemy had reached Petersburg on the afternoon or evening of the 15th of June, 22,000 infantry, under General Smith, and extending their lines parallel with our works from near the Appomattox River to the farm of Colonel Avery, about two miles southeast of the city, had opened their fire upon the few troops in our trenches—2,200 of all arms, including old men and boys—and had nearly swept them off the earth. They did not assault, however, nor even the next morning, when we had fewer still to oppose them; but according to their own historian, Swinton, and to General Grant's expressed disgust, awaited the arrival of General Lee, whose forces only entered the trenches at eleven or twelve o'clock, replacing the gallant men who for twenty-four hours held their position against such odds. Lee dismissed the boys and old men of the militia with cheers.

But still the enemy did not assault, but entrenching themselves, though outnumbering the besieged army five to one, they commenced the tactics of moving on the left flank which they had inaugurated at the Wilderness a month before. They reported in these movements, which they termed assault, a loss of 11,400 men in three days, and got another lesson in war which they had been slow to learn, besides the loss of 60,000 from the Wilderness to their present base, a loss of men greater in number than General Lee had in the whole army with which he had opposed them. They had made their last assault at Cold Harbor, a few days before reaching Petersburg, when with 80,000 men they rushed on our extemporized works, and in less than an hour lost 6,000 men killed and 12,000 wounded, and refused to assault again. It is said when an assault was afterwards ordered at Petersburg that General Meade replied, "it is useless to order it, these men will not do it."

But I diverge from the story of my personal transfer of duty, and, I might add, my personal contact with General Lee—not introduction, as I did not have that honor until some time afterwards. As soon as the enemy brought up their siege guns, or heavy artillery, which was only a few days after taking their position, they opened on the city with shell without the slightest notice, or without giving opportunity for the removal of non-combatants, the sick, the wounded, or the women and children out of range of fire. The fire at first seemed chiefly directed toward the Old Market, presumably on account of the South Side Railroad depot, which was situated near there, and about which troops would naturally be collected. But they soon enlarged their operations, and swept Bollingbrook and Lombard Streets, Bank Street and lower High Street, and Sycamore Street as high as the corner of Washington. The steeples of Tabb Street Presbyterian, St. Paul's Episcopal, and Washington Street Methodist Churches offered targets for their fire, and the Post Office and Custom House also came in for their part of the compliment.

To persons unfamiliar with the infernal noise made by the screaming, the ricochetting, and the bursting of shells, it is impossible to describe the terror and the demoralization which was immediately created. The shelling on the first day continued only for a few hours in the morning, though subsequently we were treated usually with a morning and evening serenade. Many of the citizens left at once, not standing upon the order of their going, and fled to the country to the west of the city wherever they could find a house to harbor them. Others left more leisurely, taking a few necessary articles of furniture, and made themselves as comfortable as possible under the circumstances, whilst others, whose homes were least exposed to the fire, made bomb-proofs in their yards or gardens, into which they betook themselves as soon as the firing began, and from which they would emerge when it was over, and return to their usual business. It usually continued for only two or three hours.

These bomb-proofs were holes dug in the ground about five or six feet deep, of dimensions commensurate with the number of persons they were supposed to accommodate, and were covered with heavy timbers, and these with earth, the door or entrance facing to the west, the direction opposite the batteries from which the shells came. Some of these bomb-proofs were made quite comfortable, and ladies could take a book or their sewing into them. But though some parts of the city were more exposed and more unsafe than others, yet it was evident that no portion of it was secure from danger, and General Lee, calling attention to this fact, directed me on the 3rd or 4th day of his arrival to empty every hospital, and to remove the sick and wounded, with hospital stores, furniture, attaches, etc., and place them on the cars of the Southside R. R., their destination not committed to me.

There were then about three thousand on the morning roll from the hospitals. To remove this number with the limited means of transportation at hand was no small job. I commenced the work promptly, however, but on the second or third day some surgeon who thought his wounded were not being moved with sufficient alacrity, reported the fact, and I received a message from General Lee that he "hoped it would not be necessary to order me a second time to remove the wounded from under fire." I knew pretty well where the complaint came from, as it was reported that morning that a shell had fallen in one of the hospitals, and that a soldier had taken it up and thrown it out of a window before it exploded. This incident, of course, was demoralizing, but every effort was being made to remove the wounded as soon as possible, and I thought it ungenerous in one of my corps of assistants to make such a report. I replied to General Lee that every effort was being made to comply with his order, but with the limited means at hand three thousand sick and wounded men could not be removed very expeditiously and that many could not be moved without more danger to their lives than they risked from the shell. Then came a rejoinder from the General that after no battle which he had ever fought "were there three thousand men who could not be moved." To which I replied, calling his attention to the fact that men just wounded in battle and falling in full strength and health would easily bear transportation, but that the men whom I was called upon to move at this juncture were men who had lain in Hospital, many of them for months, debilitated from the heat and festering wounds, or from sickness, and that some of them would die upon the stretchers if taken out; that two had already died, and many had begged to be permitted to take their chances with the shells rather than to be taken away; and asking that he send inspectors from his staff to relieve me and to take charge of the work. He sent Majors Breckenridge and Winfield, who, after seeing the situation, not only declined to relieve me, but made their report and advised that the whole matter be left to my discretion.

I removed in a few days all that would bear transportation, and reserved the Confederate States Hospital, and the hospitals at West End Park, and the Central Pavilion, reporting that they were but little exposed to fire, and that I thought it judicious to keep these hospitals open for the desperately wounded that were now coming in daily from the lines. The General accepted the report, I presume, as I never heard anything more from it, and received no further order to remove the wounded or to close the hospitals. The hospital at Central Park I did not close until after the fight at the Crater on the 30th of July following. This hospital was reserved mostly for the wounded Federal prisoners, and with the Federal wounded brought in from the Crater it was crowded even beyond its capacity, and it was impossible to supply medical officers to take charge of those needing immediate attention.

There were five Federal surgeons, prisoners taken not at the Crater, but belonging I think to Wilson's Cavalry Raiders, which Fitz Lee had cornered and cut to pieces, or captured, near Reams Station a few days before. I approached these doctors and asked them if they would not like to take a hand in some surgery, offering them as inducement all the liberty and privileges compatible with the rules of war. They said they would be glad to do so, and I put them to work in the hospital under Dr. Robert Page, who was the Confederate surgeon, allowing them a detail of Federal unwounded prisoners to act as nurses and assistants, and directing Dr. Page to make requisition for all the chloroform, morphine, etc., which they might need. The wounded prisoners, mostly negroes, were being brought back and laid on the grass preparatory to examination, and such operations as seemed necessary.

I did not visit the hospital until the next day about noon, when I received a message from Mr. George W. Bolling, whose mansion was very near the hospital, telling me that he thought "I had better look after matters there." On reaching the place I was shocked beyond expression to find about an hundred and fifty wounded negroes, who had been brought in since I left, and were lying about on the grounds, most of them naked; and with every conceivable form of wounds and mutilation, were shrieking, praying, and cursing in their agony and delirium, their wounds undressed and festering under a summer sun. My first thought was, "is this Christian civilization."

The Federal surgeons whom I had engaged the day before were lounging in front of their quarters, doing nothing. Dr. Page, a sturdy and reliable officer, but not a mild-mannered man, was in altercation with them, using language more pertinent to the occasion than polite, and after suppressing him I took a turn myself, and pointing to the scene of horror, the result of their neglect, asked them what it meant, reminding them of their promise to take charge of their wounded and of the especial privileges accorded to them. Their spokesman replied that they "were sick, and tired, and disgusted, and that they were prisoners of war, and were not in duty bound to do any work." "Very well," I replied, "but you should have said this yesterday when I approached you. As prisoners of war I know very well what to do with you," and calling an orderly directed him to go to Major Bridgeforth, General Lee's provost marshal and ask him to send me a sergeant and a guard to take away five medical officers. One of them asked immediately, "Major, where are you going to send us?" "To the prison at Andersonville, Georgia, to-morrow morning," I replied. "Do not send me," he said, "give me another opportunity," a request which they all joined in, "give us another opportunity." I was but too ready to acquiesce, as I could not possibly, with the medical force under my orders, have given prompt attention to these poor creatures, and I gave them the opportunity. The next morning everything was in ship-shape order. Surgery had triumphed and all the survivors were comfortably bedded in the hospital. Among the requisitions necessary to render them presentable was one for one hundred and fifty suits of underclothes to replace those stolen from them during the first night of their captivity, and before they came under the hospital guard.

After a few days, and before I could remove the patients, my surgeon friends complained that they had nothing out of which to eat the poor fare furnished them except tin dishes and tin cups; moreover, that their quarters were not safe from shelling or even bullets; and finally, that white and colored soldiers were bunked together indiscriminately in adjoining beds.

I gravely asked them to submit their grievances in writing, and that I would forward the paper to headquarters, which I did without comment, knowing very well what the result would be. On receiving the paper, General Lee sent Major Breckenridge, of his staff, to investigate the matters of complaint. I never heard what report he made to the General, and presume, from the line of remark which was submitted to the complainants, that he exonerated me. He said to them in language as polite as the peculiar circumstances would permit, that it came with bad grace from men who had marauded the surrounding country with Wilson's Raiders, destroying the food of the innocent and unarmed people, pillaging where anything was left to pillage, stealing and carrying away spoons and table ware, and breaking such ware as they could not carry away, to complain that they had but little to eat, and no vessel out of which to eat it. Moreover, that in being assigned to hospital treatment, General Lee had ordered that no distinction be shown between white soldiers and colored soldiers, that if they could fight side by side, they could sleep side by side. To the last subject of complaint, that it was not a safe place, but exposed to occasional fire, I called them to note that the missiles endangering their lives endangered ours also, and that they were not fired by our men, but theirs, who knew as well as we where the yellow flag floated, or, if ignorant of our locality, I would but be too glad to send a flag of truce to signify our position. Soon after this date the hospital was closed, the sick and wounded transferred to other hospitals, and the prisoners who were well, including the surgeons, were turned over to the provost marshal. I never knew anything more of their fate.

Two other hospitals were kept open, however, and were constantly filled to their utmost capacity with the ill and badly wounded. Besides this, many private residences were opened to soldiers and officers who could not get hospital room, or who were fortunate enough to have friends in circumstances to receive and take care of them. Many soldiers owed their lives to the tender ministrations of women, who in their own homes nursed them and shared with them their little store of food. And if there be a God who looks down from heaven and registers such deeds of love in His Book, many an entrance has been already administered by the Master to them who gave the "cup of cold water in His name."

We have spoken of the failure of the Federal army to enter Petersburg on the night of the 15th of June and morning of the 16th,—it could hardly be said to take Petersburg, when so little resistance could be made,—a failure which their own historians denominated the "fiasco of the war." But there were two other occasions on which an entrance could have been effected even more easily. On one occasion, during the first week in May, 1864, about the 6th or 7th, I think, Butler, after landing at Bermuda Hundred, where he had been sent by General Grant to lead a column against Richmond on the south side of the James, where the Army of the Potomac had fought its way down from the Wilderness on the north side, dispatched a brigade of troops to threaten Petersburg from the Richmond Turnpike. This force reached Swift Creek, and halted on the hill, just north of the bridge on the turnpike which spans that stream. Had they pushed on immediately I do not know what force we could have mustered to oppose them, but fortunately troops from the south had been ordered to Beauregard, who was holding Butler in check in his "on to Richmond" from the south side of James River, and a regiment from South Carolina, the Twenty-second, I believe, Colonel Hey-

ward, arrived in Petersburg just at the right time and
was hurried through the city to the scene of action.
After a hurried march of three miles which brought
them to the bridge, they crossed and charged up the
hill to find they had encountered a whole brigade of
Yankees. There was a fierce fight, and the houses on
the pike, especially the old Arrow-field Church, showed
the marks of the contest for many years after the war.
The South Carolinians were terribly cut up, but they
held their own and drove the enemy, or at least the
enemy retired, as far as Walthall Station, or its vicinity,
on the Richmond and Petersburg Railroad.

The next day another regiment from South Carolina,
Colonel Graham, arrived, and Hankin's Battery of light
artillery from Sussex or Surry County, Virginia. I
showed these troops out of the city in the direction of
the enemy, and the following day battle was renewed
at Port Walthall, with the lines of the enemy on the
east and ours on the west of the railroad to the north of
the station. The battle must have been very hotly contested, and at very close quarters, judging from the
positions of the dead and the accounts of the wounded.
Night closed the affair and both parties fell back; our
troops for nearly two miles, the enemy not so far. The
next morning a countryman came into the city and said
that the wounded were still uncared for and were crying for help. Taking a surgeon, an ambulance, and
one or two hospital stewards, I started for the battlefield. Upon reaching our line, about two miles from
the scene of the fight of the day before, I was told that
the enemy was somewhere before me, but no one
seemed to know where. Taking, by permission, a
dozen of Dearing's Cavalry, which had been brought
up, I proceeded, showing them out to the right, where
I thought the enemy would be found, if in the vicinity.
I went nearly two miles, when I came to a large open

The War

field, where I could see the white flags (handkerchiefs on ramrods), and could hear the calls of the wounded. Dismissing my escort, believing that on my mission I would be safer without them, I followed the turnpike until I came to where the railroad crossed it, and found myself on the extreme right of their line, and left of ours, where the battle had evidently been the hottest. Here the dead and the wounded of both parties lay not an hundred yards apart. But the wounded were Federals exclusively, our wounded having been taken away I suppose by our surgeons. Moreover, I discovered that we were technically within the Federal line, as they, or their pickets, could be seen under cover of wood, not a mile distant. My first thought was to leave and get out of sight with my little party, but the wounded begged me not to leave them to die without an effort to save them. I referred them to their own surgeons, who had left them, but who were not far off, and would probably return for them. "No," they said, "they left us last night, and they are afraid of being killed or captured if they return." "Well," I answered, "who is to insure that we shall not be killed or captured? Your men are in sight." However, they begged so earnestly that we could not resist their importunities, so we got them together under the shade of a tree, and gave them water and brandy, preparatory to getting them away.

Though only the 7th or 8th of May, it was one of the hottest days I ever felt, and I was lying down in the shade, almost overcome with heat, after the work, when I heard a tipping in a dense little piece of wood near me, and the next minute a Confederate officer and a file of men stepped out of the bushes, and the latter brought their pieces up as if to fire on me. "Don't fire," I shouted. "Who are you?" asked the officer. "A Confederate surgeon," I replied, "trying to help these poor wounded men." "You look d—d little like it," he returned, and his doubts were reasonable. I wore only a linen short coat and a pair of blue trousers, with gold braid, and was amongst men in full Yankee uniform. I then gave him my name and rank, and told him his. (I knew him.) He was a Captain Woolrich, of that county, belonging to the Thirty-second Virginia, I think, and knowing the locality well was scouting for Beauregard trying to find the enemy. I said to him, "You have found the enemy now. They are in that body of pines in the distance, and I beg that you will take your men back under cover, or you may draw their fire on us. He had discovered all that he wished, and, saluting, left me. The men were all badly wounded, and one or two died before we could get them away. On the extreme right of the Federal line a gun had been disabled by our fire, but must have been gallantly defended before it was abandoned, as the dead lay, some piled on, others about it. On pulling off the bodies to see if any were still alive, some papers dropped from the pocket of a young lieutenant, amongst which was a letter addressed to a lady in Bremen, and written in the German language. On reading it, I found it was to his betrothed. In it he informed her that his term of service had expired, and that he should leave for New York City, giving her the street and the number where she should meet him on her arrival in this country. Poor fellow! This was his last fight, into which he went, no doubt, voluntarily, as he was about to leave the Army. I made an attempt to send this letter through the lines, but I do not know whether it reached its destination and carried the sad news which I indorsed on it, or whether she read the fate of her love amongst the cold items of the "dead" at the battle of Walthall's Station. One of the wounded that we picked up and brought off was a tall, red-headed captain from Connecticut, his arm shot off at the shoulder joint. Though desperately wounded, he had not lost his pluck, and the first question was, "What fool fought that artillery of yours yesterday?" On questioning him as to what he meant, he replied that "he knew no more about his business than a school boy. He fought his guns right up to our lines." "Well," I said, "he seemed to have done some execution." "Yes," he replied, "and we did some execution also." This was but too evident.

The yellow, butternut clothes and stitched-down shoes of Hankin's artillerists as their dead lay almost amongst their enemies, bore sad and striking contrast to the gaily-decked dead of the enemy. The Federal troops were of regiments which had been brought around from Florida, and their uniforms were bright and new. One man, especially, I noted amongst the dead in a position which I did not believe any dead man could maintain, and I thought he was alive until I went to him. He was sitting up, leaning his back against a tuffet of stiff bamboos, with his gun in his grasp as if about to discharge it. He had been shot through the breast, and his tin cup attached to his belt had caught his blood. His dress was not that of a private soldier, nor of an officer, but it was simply elegant, and his fine shirt was an article to be coveted by a poor Confederate. Some one had taken his shoes, which were the only articles about his person that had been disturbed.

Our Connecticut captain maintained his bravado to the last. When, on getting him to the city, some ladies offered him wine and such delicacies as they had, as they often did to the wounded when brought in, irrespective of the color of the jacket, he scornfully replied, "No, keep your good things for your Rebel brethren, they will need all they can get before they get through with this scrap." He died that night,

Maj. Hankins, a modest and gallant gentleman, who commanded the artillery that did such execution at close quarters, lived through the war to be killed soon after its close in a personal rencontre in Surry county.

I never knew who commanded the infantry in that fight. They were greatly outnumbered by Butler's forces, but they drove these back upon their base on James River, and joining Beauregard at Chester and Centralia, participated a short time afterwards in the heavy fighting near Drewry's Bluff, by which Beauregard "bottled up Butler" at Bermuda.

Another occasion on which the enemy in overwhelming force failed to get to Petersburg was on the 9th of June following the preceding attempt. This day has been one of sacred memory since, and annually, in commemoration thereof, the people of Petersburg lay aside their cares, their duties, and their pleasures, and assemble at the old Blandford Cemetery to deck with flowers the graves of their martyred dead, and to give thanks to God for the special deliverance vouchsafed unto the city at that time, and continued in so many miraculous ways during the interim of war which for eleven long months was waged to the very lintels of their doors. It is a day made historic by noble deeds, whose recital, handed down from father to son, stirs the blood to proud and patriotic resolve. And well may it be so; and long may it be so!

Butler, in further futile attempts to capture Petersburg, had sent a brigade under General Kautz, from City Point in a southeasterly direction, expecting them to reach the city from the Jerusalem Plank Road. News was brought that morning from our scouts that a column of Federal troops was in motion and was under orders to approach the city from the direction indicated. The Court-House bell was rung about nine o'clock in the morning, and couriers were dispatched to get together all the local militia, old men passed the age, and boys too young to be enlisted in the regular service, with any convalescents at the hospital well enough to bear arms, and any other men willing to volunteer, and to order them to repair at once to our works near the Rives House on the Jerusalem Plank Road, about a mile from the corporation line, and to report to Col. F. H. Archer, who was in command of a small force at that point. Hon. Anthony Keiley, now one of the judges of the International Court in Alexandria, Egypt, at that time a member of the General Assembly of Virginia, and exempt from military rule, happened to be in the city, and volunteered in the fight. He was captured, and whilst in prison he wrote a most graphic account of the affair, "In Vinculis," which was published after his release. I reproduce it in part, as follows:

I was sitting in my office, peacefully engaged, and endeavoring to extract from the Richmond papers, just received, something like an idea of the situation, when, as though our city were blest with a patent fire telegraph, all the available bell metal in the corporation broke into chorus with so vigorous a peal and clangor so resonant as to suggest to the uninitiated a general conflagration. * * * The general understanding, if not order, was that this signal, theretofore consecrated to the enunciation of fire, should thenceforth in Petersburg serve the purpose further of heralding the approach of another devouring element—the Yankees. Thus it came to pass that in most indecent haste I let fall my journals and went into the street, to learn from the first excited passer-by that the enemy's cavalry, to the number of twenty thousand, so ran the tale, were approaching the city and were already within two miles of where my informant stood. The usual discount of seventy-five per cent still left the tale uncomfortable to a degree. "What forces have we on the Jerusalem Plank Road [the road by which they were approaching], do you know?" I questioned. "Not a d—n man [we had not had, I remark parenthetically, a revival of religion in our town for some time, and Confederate whiskey would make a nun swear] except Archer's Battalion, and not a hundred and fifty of them," was the reply. [Archer's Battalion consisted of old men past sixty and boys under eighteen.]

I immediately turned my face in the direction of Archer's Battalion, but a mile southeast from the cemetery, and on reaching there found all in preparation. Reporting to the first captain I met he made the obvious suggestion that I should get a musket, and I hastened to the ordnance officer to supply myself. This gentleman courteously invited me to make an intelligent choice between three specimens of smoothbore military architecture known in the army as "altered percussions." One of these formidable arquebuses had a trigger with so weak a spring that the tenderest cap ever turned out of a laboratory would successfully resist its pressure; the second was so rusty that its ramrod shrank from sounding its oxidized depths; while the third proved on examination to be so bent and wrenched that you could not see daylight through it when the breech-pin was unscrewed! I now began to be overwhelmed with the apprehension that I was destined to act exclusively as a lay figure in the drama about to be put upon the boards, when a friend, commiserating my perplexity, handed me a gun left in his tent by a comrade that morning who had gone to town on leave. Armed and equipped as the law directs, I stepped forward to the breast-works.

We had not long to wait. A cloud of dust at our front told of the hurried advance of cavalry, and the next instant the glitter of spur and scabbard revealed to us a long line of horsemen rapidly deploying under cover of wood that ran parallel to our line about half a mile in front of us. Our venerable muskets were not worth a tinker's imprecation at a longer range than a hundred yards, and we were compelled per force to watch the preparations for our capture or slaughter. * * *

The enemy determined to feel us with a small portion of its command, and on came at a sweeping gallop a gallant company of troopers. * * * We possessed our souls in patience till we could see the chevrons on the arm of a non-commissioned officer who led them (a brave fellow), and then there broke forth from such amiable muskets as could be induced to go off a discharge that scattered the cavaliers like chaff, three riderless horses being all of the expedition that entered our lines. Meanwhile the long line of foemen were stretching around us, many fold more than we in numbers, and armed with special rifles repeating sixteen times. And there we fought them till we were so surrounded that the two men nearest to me were shot in the back while facing the line of original approach; till our camp in the rear of the works was full of the foe; till the noblest blood of our city stained the clay of the breast-works as they gave out their lives with gun in hand and face forward on the spot where their officers placed them. * * * Their faces rise before me now, all gallant gentlemen and true, one of whose lives was well worth a hecatomb of the bummers and bounty-jumpers before them. One by one my comrades fell around me, Dr. Bellingham the last; and as I turned at his request and stooped to change his position to one of greater comfort, the enemy trooped over the earthwork behind me, and the foremost one, presenting his loaded carbine, demanded my surrender with an unrepeatable violence of language that suggested bloodshed.

All avenue of escape being cut off, I yielded with what grace I could to my fate, captive to a hatchet-faced member of the First District Cavalry, greatly enamored of this opportunity of going to the rear.*

The old men and boys who made this defense, unparalleled in this or any other war, belonged to the best citizens whom the city of Petersburg and its vicinage could claim—men and boys who had behind them mothers, wives, sisters, sweethearts, whose fate in case of falling in the hands of the enemy was foreshadowed in the cruel orders of Dahlgren's Raiders.† They had the highest incitement to hold their positions, even unto death, and nobly they filled the fatal requirement of duty. They fought—one hundred and twenty-five, badly armed, and untrained, and behind their frail defense—one hundred and twenty-five against two thousand three hundred of the enemy, until, as Mr. Keiley says, "surrounded, men fighting the enemy before them were shot in the back by the enemy behind them." But with their blood they held the enemy at bay for nearly two hours, until the impetuous Graham, himself a Petersburg boy, who had been hurriedly sent for from the forces in Chesterfield, dashed through the streets of the city at full gallop, with his four guns that he had carried away three years before, at the very beginning of the war; and the gallant Dearing with his intrepid troopers following just after him. They

---

*As a peculiar incident belonging to this affair, I will note that Professor Staubly, one of the volunteer militia who fell in the fight, was a particular friend of Colonel Dahlgren, of the Federal army, who had lost his life a few days before in a raid which had for its object the capture of Richmond, and who had upon his person orders, in case he succeeded, to kill President Davis and the members of his Cabinet, and to give the city over to sack and pillage. Professor Staubly steadily refused to believe that his friend Dahlgren could be guilty of so atrocious a design, and at the time that he fell had an application filed with the Confederate authorities, asking permission to find and return Dahlgren's body to his friends.

† See Appendix.

formed on Cemetery Hill, and, later on at Water Works Hill, sent a few well-directed shells into the head of the Federal column, and drove them ignominiously back from the coveted prize of "beauty and booty" which they thought they held in their dastardly hands.

The names of the men and boys who made this memorable fight are written in imperishable record in the archives of the city, and, better, in the hearts of hundreds of the helpless ones who were rescued that day from a calamity worse than death. After thirty-eight years but few of that little band of men or officers are left to recall the tragic scenes of that summer's day; but one, the undaunted leader, even then gray-haired and a veteran of the Mexican War, still lives and moves amongst us, honored, as he deserves to be, an example of the Christian citizen without cant, and the Christian soldier without fear, Col. F. H. Archer.*

When General Lee reached Petersburg the day after General Smith, with his thirty thousand troops, had failed to enter the almost defenseless city, and confronted the Federal forces encircling it with their lines of ditch and fosse and dirt, it is said to have been a question mooted amongst those in authority whether the Confederate forces should not attack Grant's army with vigor at once and, forcing back his extreme right near Hare's farm, thrust themselves between the remainder of his army and their base at City Point, and thus compel them to surrender. It was said that Beauregard urged this course upon Lee, telling him that his army was flushed with continuous victory from the Wilderness down to their present position; that they had rendered hors de combat within six weeks more of the enemy in numbers than they counted in their

---

*Col. Archer has recently died and gone over to meet his comrades.

own ranks; that the enemy was discouraged by constant defeat, and demoralized by great losses in battle, and would prove ready victims to further disaster, and in the meantime that his own army, in event of a long siege, would be daily diminished by the casualties of constant combat, by division, by desertion, etc.; and that though the enemy, inactive in the trenches, would be subject under the circumstances to equal losses, yet that he had the world to draw from, could always put two men in the place of one lost, whilst our resources, virtually exhausted as far as reinforcements were concerned, would not permit us to keep our army even to the present standard.

Other reports were that General Lee advised the surrender of Richmond and Petersburg, and a continuance of the tactics begun at the Wilderness, viz: to move upon Grant's left, fighting him every day when opportunity favored, and thus subjecting him to daily loss greater than we incurred, and leading him constantly away from his base of supplies into an unknown, inhospitable, and hostile country. It was said that Mr. Davis opposed this plan on the ground of giving up the seat of Government, and the loss of Richmond and Petersburg, and the continued falling back of the Confederate forces would give encouragement to the enemy and be followed by discouragement and demoralization on the part of the Southern people. I do not know how far these reports, current at the time, were sustained by facts.

A few days after General Lee had reached Petersburg and established his lines and filled them with his veterans, and confident of present safety had set up a sense of such casual peace as often pervaded the air (there is no other description for it, when two great armies are facing one another and taking respite of mutual slaughter), I invited his medical staff and several other general officers to breakfast at my quarters. After waiting for an hour for my guests, General Lee's staff and some others not appearing, those present sat down to the table; but our party was soon disturbed, even to dissolution, by a terrific cannonading on the left of our lines, near the iron bridge on the City Point Road, and in the vicinity of the old race track, followed by musketry, continuous and heavy, indicating that a battle of no mean pretensions was on. We had assaulted the enemy's works "with vigor," had failed to carry them, and after some considerable loss our men were withdrawn. Whether this attack was made in accordance with the advice said to have been given by Beauregard, to "break the enemy's right and double him up," or whether it was merely a feint, I never had any definite means of determining by information gotten from those who alone knew. The attack was determined on the night previous, I am sure, as General Lee's medical officers, in apologizing for their failure to be present at my breakfast, stated they received orders the night before not to leave their quarters the following morning.

No other sortie was made by the besieged, and strangely enough, it would seem, no assault by the besiegers in their overwhelming numbers, until the 30th of July following, when they sprung a mine under our works at the Elliott Salient, now known as the Crater. With this exception the fighting was done behind their works, or in open field to their left,—always and persistently to their left,—and though always in number greatly superior to our own, and often repelled with fearful loss, they would reinforce and reappear with a pertinacity and courage worthy of a better cause, until our thin lines were finally enveloped in their anaconda folds, and the tragedy of Five Forks ended the scene of the immortal defense of the beleagured city of Petersburg. We have referred to the assault of the enemy on the 30th of July. It could hardly be called an assault on our lines, as they had been destroyed by the explosion of 8,000 pounds of powder introduced through a subterranean gallery of 520 feet, extending from the Federal works to our own, and placed under a salient occupied by Pegram's Battery, of this city, and a part of the Eighteenth and Twenty-second South Carolina Regiments. These troops were blown up, but few left alive, and in the place of the fort there was left a crater 200 feet long, 60 feet wide, and 30 feet deep. There were literally no works to assault for a space of 150 to 200 yards, and no men to repel an assault at this point, and the way was open to Cemetery Hill, a few hundred yards distant, and to the doomed city about the same distance from its crest. The explosion occurred about four o'clock in the morning, and this portion of the works was in possession of the enemy until about nine o'clock, when they were retaken by Mahone with three brigades—his own, and Wright's of Georgia, and Saunders' of Alabama. That is, for about four hours the Federals, with our works broken for some two or three hundred yards, failed to advance or take any advantage of their position. According to the report on the "Conduct of the War," General Ord estimates the troops that really got into the Confederate works at ten or twelve thousand, and of this number forty-three hundred were colored troops; behind these were massed, according to McCabe, 65,000, not in immediate vicinity, of course, but accessible if necessity should arise for re-inforcements.

It is not to be wondered at that a very sharp correspondence arose during that time between General Meade, whose quarters were at the house occupied now by Mrs. Brown, about one and a half miles from the Crater, and General Burnside, who had immediate charge of the attack, and that the failure to capture Petersburg on that occasion was called by their historian, Swinton, the "fiasco of the war."

Now let us estimate the number of Confederate troops to whom was assigned the duty of recapturing and reestablishing our lines. When the explosion occurred at four o'clock in the morning and the enemy rushed into our broken works, information was sent at once to General Lee, whose quarters were then at the Turnbull house, about a mile to the west of Petersburg, and near the present Insane Asylum. He directed Colonel Venable, of his staff (afterwards Professor of Mathematics at the University of Virginia) to ride rapidly to General Mahone's position, which was on our lines, near the Wilcox house, about a mile to the left of Elliott's Salient, and to order him to send two of his brigades, the Virginia, under Colonel Weisiger, and the Georgia Brigade, under General Wright, to report to General Bushrod Johnson, whose quarters were in the old Mingea house on the hill just to the northeast of the cemetery, and who had charge of our lines at the point where the explosion occurred and where they were in the possession of the enemy.

General Mahone, who always exercised the most jealous care of his brigade, said to Colonel Venable that he disliked to send his brigade, and with approval of General Lee he would lead it himself. He then ordered his men of the two brigades to fall back out of the works, one at a time, so as not to attract the attention of the enemy to the working of our lines at that point, and as soon as he had gotten them out of sight of the enemy, formed them into line, and sent them out along the continuous ravine leading to the east of the Cameron house, and on to near the present location of the water works, from which there was a covered way, partly natural and partly ditched, and with protecting traverses leading to our works a few hundred yards southeast of the cemetery, and used for the carrying of rations, ammunition, etc., to the troops in the works. He rode forward himself and reported to General Johnson, where it seems he found General Lee, who cordially approved of his leading his brigade, and asked to be shown the way to the captured salient. General Johnson sent a young lieutenant, Harris, with him, and when they reached the point where the covered way crossed the Jerusalem Plank Road, a few yards south of the termination of the present electric road, he found his brigade coming up. Leading them up to within some two hundred yards of the covered way and stepping out, he said, describing it afterwards: "I found myself in full view of the portion of the salient which had been blown up, and of that part of the works to the north of the salient, and saw that they were crammed with Federal soldiers and thickly studded with Federal flags. A moment's survey of the situation impressed me with the belief, so crowded were the enemy and his flags,—eleven flags in less than one hundred yards,—that he was greatly disordered, but in large force. I at once sent back for the Alabama brigade to be brought up by the way in which the two brigades had come." In the meantime it was evident that no time could be lost, and he directed Captain Girardey, of his staff, to form the brigade in line of battle in a gulch or depression of ground, parallel with our works or nearly so, about two hundred yards distant from the enemy—the Virginians on the left and the Georgians on the right. Hardly had they gotten into position when Girardley called to Mahone, "General, they are coming" (the enemy showing some intention of charging), and Mahone called back, "Tell Weisiger to forward!" And then, says Mahone, "with the steadiness and resolution of regulars on dress pa-

rade, they moved forward to meet the enemy." On
their arrival at the works there was a hand-to-hand
fight with bayonet and butt of musket, and with horrors that no one can readily appreciate who was not
engaged in the conflict, until the works to the north or
left of the traverse were taken, the enemy still holding
the pit, which proved to them a veritable trap of death,
and holding in addition some fifty feet to the right of
the pit. The Virginia brigade had done its work, the
Georgia had failed; nor did it take the enemy's lines
in its front until the coming of the Alabama brigade,
with Colonel Saunders. About one o'clock P. M.
our lines were re-established, the enemy still holding
the pit, from which he could not emerge without almost certain death. This pit was crowded with Federal troops who, failing to advance when our works
were broken, had cowered under the fire of shell and
shrapnel poured in from our batteries to the north and
to the south of the Crater, and sought safety behind
the boulders and walls of that immense opening in the
earth.

McCabe, adjutant of Pegram's Battalion of Artillery, an eye witness of and participant in this fight,
says (address before the Association of the Army of
Northern Virginia): "And now the scene within the
horrible pit was such as might be fitly portrayed by
the pencil of Dante after he had trod 'nine-circled
Hell.' From the great mortars to the right and left,
huge missiles, describing graceful curves, fell at regular intervals with dreadful accuracy and burst amongst
the helpless masses huddled together; and every explosion was followed by piteous cries, and oftentimes
the very air seemed darkened by flying human limbs.
Haskell, too, had moved up his eprouvette mortars
among the men of the Sixteenth Virginia, so close, indeed, that his powder charge was but an ounce and a

half, and without intermission the storm of fire beat upon the hapless men imprisoned within. Mahone's men watched with great interest this easy method of reaching troops behind cover, and then with imitative ingenuity of soldiers, gleefully gathered up the countless muskets, with bayonets fixed, which had been abandoned by the enemy, and propelled them with such nice skill that they came down upon Ledlie's men [in the pit] like the rain of the Norman arrows at Hastings. And this horrid butchery continued until our lines were retaken in their continuity about one o'clock P. M., when a white handkerchief was displayed from the end of a ramrod or bayonet, and the response being to 'come in,' a great number of prisoners came pouring over the crest, which, including a few that had been captured before, footed up 1,101." The Federal accounts of this affair of the charge upon their works, and of the slaughter which ensued, and of the horrors of the pit into which they were driven shows that McCabe did not exaggerate in his statements.

Capt. Freeman Bowley, of San Francisco, in an address before the California command of the Loyal Legion of the United States November 8th, 1889, said: "When driven back, with a dozen of my company, I went down the traverse to the Crater. We were the last to reach it, and the Johnnies were not twenty yards behind us. A full line around the crest of the Crater were loading and firing as fast as they could, and the men were dropping thick and fast, most of them shot through the head. Every man that was shot rolled down the steep sides to the bottom, and in places were piled up four or five deep. The cries of the wounded pressed down under the dead were piteous in the extreme. An enfilading fire was coming through the traverse down which we had retreated. General Bartlett (who had been disabled by the crushing of his wooden leg) ordered the colored troops to build breastworks across it. They commenced the work of throwing up lumps of clay, but it was slow work, and some one called out, 'put in the dead men,' and acting on this suggestion, a large number of dead—white and black, Union and Rebel—were piled into the trench. * * * The artillery on Cemetery Hill kept up a constant fire of grape, and kept the dust flying about us. A mortar battery also opened on us, and after a few shots they got our range and the shells fell directly among us. Many of them did not explode, but a few burst directly over us and cut the men down most cruelly. Many of our troops now attempted to leave, but nearly every man who attempted it fell back riddled with bullets. The white troops now were exhausted and discouraged. Leaving the line, they sat down, facing inwards, and neither threats nor entreaties could get them up again. * * * From this time the fire was kept up mainly by the negro troops, and officers handling muskets. A few Indians* of the First Michigan Sharpshooters did splendid work. Some of them were mortally wounded, and drawing their blouses over their faces chanted their death song, and died, four of them in a group. Of the men of my company who rallied with me, all but one, a sergeant, lay dead or dying. * * * The rebels planted their battle flags on the edge of the Crater-front, and on both sides, not six feet from our men, muskets, with bayonets, were pitched back and forth in harpoon style."

Any one wishing to read an enlarged and accurate account of this fearful hand-to-hand conflict will find it, under contribution from many soldiers and officers,

---

*Some of these poor fellows fell into my hands after the fight was over.—J. H. C.

Union and Confederate, in "War Talks," published by Geo. S. Bernard, Attorney, Petersburg, Virginia, himself one of the 800 of the Virginia brigade which charged and carried by the bayonet and butt of musket works manned by tenfold their number.

In stating that Wrights' Brigade of Georgia failed to carry the post of the enemy's lines in their front, it is but just to add that Colonel Hall, who commanded the brigade, in a letter to the *Petersburg Express* of August 1st, 1864, stated that only a regiment and a half of his brigade had emerged from the covered way when Mahone's men charged, and that by order of Capt. Girardey they charged on the right of Mahone's Brigade; and one of these regiments planted its colors on the edge of the Crater, and remained there until ordered away. This is confirmed by Lieut. Laighton, of Richmond, who commanded the sharpshooters from the Twelfth Virginia. He says that he distinctly remembers that "a small number of Wright's Brigade charged along with the Virginia brigade, immediately on the right of the battalion of sharpshooters." The casualties of two hundred and thirty-one reported in the Georgia brigade is sufficient evidence that they somewhere met a very murderous fire.

The regiments of Elliott's Brigade, on the north of the Crater, which had escaped the explosion—especially the Seventeenth South Carolina—made a gallant fight in restraining the advance of the enemy, after they had taken our works, and suffered severely. So did Ransom's and Clingman's North Carolinians make a brave stand, as the North Carolinians always did, and suffered severely, and with them several regiments of Wise's Brigade.

To Mahone's Brigade, however, was given the honor of the day, and he was rewarded by the thanks of General Lee, and received the stars of a major general.

Weisiger was made brigadier general, a tardy but well
deserved promotion, and Capt. Girardey jumped from
a captain to brigadier. He was a gallant officer, and
was given charge of a Georgia brigade, but was killed
soon after this in the first fight into which he led his
men. The Alabamians, who charged about 1 P. M.,
and recaptured the works in their front, came in for
high commendation, but bought their laurels dearly.
The remnant of this brigade, about an hundred men,
possibly less, I succeeded in getting off at Appomattox
Court House after they had been mustered and counted off to be sent to a Federal prison. Of this I shall
speak later.

There is no doubt but that the Confederate artillery,
—Wright's Battery, Haskell's, Coit's, Lambkin's, Davidson's, Otey's, Flanner's, and others which I cannot
recall,—by the promptness with which they opened
fire on the enemy as they appeared at the rupture of
our works made by the explosion of the mine, and by
the skill and undaunted courage with which they
handled their guns, and the execution done, as their
fearful missiles of shell, and grape, and canister fell
amongst the Federals crowded into the small space
through which they were compelled to advance, did a
great deal to delay the enemy until the arrival of Mahone's infantry.

Capt. Flanner, in the "Historical Papers," May 1878,
says: "I claim that the battery commanded by me, and
composed entirely of North Carolinians, is entitled to
the credit of preventing the Federal army from entering Petersburg on the morning of the springing of the
mine." This battery was located at what was known
then as the Gee house, which stood on the Jerusalem
Plank Road near the intersection of the Baxter Road.
The Captain says: "Immediately on the advance of the
army we opened on them with shell and canister, when

they soon sought shelter in their trenches. In a few minutes they again formed, and commenced advancing. We again opened on them with our six guns. They pressed steadily forward, when our guns were doubly charged with canister, and a deadly fire poured into their ranks. Their lines were then broken, and they fled to their works, and there remained until the arrival of Beauregard with the troops commanded by Mahone. The fire of the enemy from one hundred guns was concentrated upon my company for nearly two hours, but amid this terrible rain of deadly missiles the brave North Carolinians stood to their guns and repulsed any advance of the enemy."

Captain Flanner probably does not exaggerate the weight of the metal against him, as in Captain Kirtis's book, "Heavy Guns and Light," he says on authority of Col. Henry L. Abbotts, who commanded the siege artillery of the Army of the Potomac, that "eighty-one Federal guns fired in this action 3,833 rounds of shot and shell, missiles aggregating over 75 tons of metal." We would not rob the gallant Captain or his brave North Carolinians of one feather from their plume. Where there were North Carolinians, there were brave men always, and none who ever saw them in a fight, or noted the return of their casualties after a fight, will gainsay that; but there were other brave men, of the infantry and of the artillery,—men whom we have mentioned,—who rallied promptly after the demoralizing explosion of the mine, and who shared with our Captain and his game crew that generous rain of metal so abundantly poured out upon their devoted heads.

Major D. N. Walker,* of the Thirteenth Virginia Battalion of Artillery, and who commanded the Otey Battery from Richmond, whose guns were located to

---
*Letter to Geo. S. Bernard—"War Talks."

the right of the Crater, said that the battle was an "artillery fight," and that "the enemy were practically whipped before Mahone took part in the action." It would be difficult to prove this fact to the infantry of Elliott's Brigade, of Ransom's Brigade, and of Wise's Virginia Brigade, who to the north of the Crater repelled the advance of the Federal troops, and who suffered so severely. In the Fifty-ninth Virginia, of the ten officers commanding the ten companies, nine were killed on the field. These must have borne some humble part in the repulse of the enemy.

It would be more difficult to convince the men of Mahone's Brigade that the fight was practically ended, who in that charge with a dash and courage "never surpassed" and seldom equalled (according to Capt. Walker himself, who witnessed it from his battery), and who with bayonet and clubbed musket rushed upon ten times their numbers of the enemy, and drove them back upon their lines, and who suffered a loss which was unaccountable if the fight was over. The fight was not practically over until Mahone's second charge, under Colonel Saunders, of the Alabama brigade, recaptured our works in their entirety. This was about twelve or one o'clock P. M. The time of the first charge was about 8.30 A. M., but has been reported as being later. Colonel Venable, who took the orders from General Lee to Mahone, says that the "charge was made before nine o'clock A. M." This was corroborated by any number of the participants in the fight on both sides, but the Federal record, as found in the testimony of General Meade before the "Committee on the Conduct of the War," establishes the fact beyond question.

General Meade says: "At nine A. M., July 30, I received the following dispatch from General Burnside: 'General Meade—Many of the Ninth (9th) and Eighteenth (18th) Corps are retiring before the enemy. I think now is the time to put in the Fifth Corps promptly.' At 9.30 A. M. the following dispatch was sent to Gen. Burnside: 'Headquarters Army of the Potomac, July 30th, 1864, 9.30 A. M. To Major General Burnside, commanding Ninth Corps: The Major General commanding has heard that the result of your attack has been a repulse, and directs that if, in your judgment, nothing further can be effected, that you withdraw to your own line, taking precaution to get the men safely back.' At 9.45 A. M. General Burnside received a peremptory order to withdraw his troops."

The troops were not withdrawn, however, before 1 P. M. Then ensued a correspondence between Generals Meade and Burnside, by telegrams, of such spice and vigor as to be almost as interesting as other incidents of the fight. Indeed, it is not difficult to believe that such a correspondence between two major generals of the Confederate Army would have led to a transfer of the scene of action, so far as they were concerned. After the war, when the participants in the whole affair had given their versions, differing of course in many things, as if it were possible under such strain and excitement and peril for men in different portions of the line to see things alike, jealousies and bitterness arose, not to be wondered at, but regretted. As far as the Confederate soldiers and the Confederate leaders were concerned, there was surely glory enough to go around to all, and to satisfy the most exacting.

An absurd question arose as to who gave the command to charge as the Virginia brigade arose to their feet and rushed upon the enemy,—whether Weisiger, Mahone, or Girardey,—as if the order of one man could be heard along two hundred yards of line of battle, amid the bellowing of cannon and the pandemonium of shrieking shell, and whistling shrapnel and hissing minies. The men of that command were not only men of the highest intelligence, but trained soldiers, and tried in half an hundred battles, and were capable, nearly every man, of being a leader, and doubtless would have arisen without orders and charged, by soldierly instinct, at the most opportune time for victory. Some of the men testified that they heard no command to charge, but saw that the time had come.

A more absurd question arose as to whether Mahone was really in command on that occasion, or present at the charge. One would think that such a statement would not receive the credence of any man. Yet I heard a general officer—a lieutenant general—say ten years after the war that Gen. Mahone was not present at the affair of the Crater. This officer was not present and of course knew nothing about it. The men who were present speak with no uncertain voice. General Mahone was not there by *orders*. He was *directed* to *send* his brigade to Gen. Bushrod Johnson, who had immediate command on the part of the lines broken. He *volunteered* to *take* them in himself. But what say the men whose presence and whose gallantry none can ever question? Major Jones, now president of a college in Mississippi, and who led the Twelfth Virginia, says (letter under date of January, 1877, to General Mahone): "On getting my regiment in position, your courier delivered me a message to report to you at the right of the brigade. Walking in front of the brigade and reaching you, I found all the other regimental commandery before you when I arrived. * * * Turning to the officers, you delivered a stirring address to this effect: 'The enemy have our works. The line of men which we have here is the only barrier to the enemy's occupying Petersburg. There is nothing to resist his advance. Upon us devolves the duty of driving him from his strong position in our front, and reestablishing our lines. We must carry his position immediately by assaulting it. If we don't carry it by the first attack we will renew the assault as long as a man of us is left, or until the work is ours.' "

This statement of Major Jones has never been questioned, but in an editorial in the *Richmond Commonwealth*, in June, 1880, prompted by a bitter correspondence between General Mahone and General Weisiger, it was more than intimated that General Mahone was not entitled to the credit of the success at the Crater; but that he "was in the covered way at a time when he ought to have been somewhere else." Upon the appearance of this editorial, some old members of Mahone's Brigade, Capt. J. E. Tyler, of the Twelfth Virginia, Lieut. J. E. Phillips, of the Twelfth Virginia, Sergeant Leroy S. Edwards, of the Twelfth Virginia, and Private Jos. A. Gentry, of the Sixth Virginia, whose presence in the battle was never questioned, collected a number of statements from a number of officers and soldiers participants in the same affair, and published them in the *Richmond Whig*, in August, 1880. Amongst these statements, one from Capt. W. A. S. Taylor, Adjutant of the Sixty-first Virginia, says: "Whilst waiting for the command 'guides post' I saw Girardey wave his hand above his head and shout 'charge.' I presumed the command came from General Mahone, and with the command I started for the works [of the enemy]. * * * Arriving at the works, the command delivered its fire, and finished with the bayonet. In a few minutes thereafter General Mahone was at that portion of the works occupied by the Sixty-first Virginia, and I heard him say, 'The work is not over, we must retake the balance of the line.' "

Colonel Rogers, who commanded the Sixth Virginia Regiment, after describing the charge and the fearfull loss in his command, says, "Almost upon the instant of reaching the entrenchment, Gen. Weisiger called to me that he was wounded, he thought mortally, and, turning over the command to me, retired with assistance from the field. The brigade was in great confusion; our loss in the charge had been very heavy, the work of death was rife in the trenches, and our men were suffering from an enfilade fire. * * * Then I met General Mahone in the trenches, and received from him timely instructions, and orders to hold the position at any hazard, and under any loss, until he could bring another brigade to our relief."

Mr. Thos. H. Cross, of the Sixteenth Virginia Regiment, says: "I saw General Mahone just before we started on the charge, and saw him again in the breastworks."

Mr. W. W. Caldwell, of the battalion of sharpshooters of the Twelfth Virginia Regiment, says in a statement on the same day, June 30, 1880: "I had not lost sight of him (Mahone) five minutes, when the enemy commenced firing outside the captured portion of our front. * * * In the movement to the trenches which we captured I did not see Mahone, but in less than five minutes after we were in the works, he was in our midst, encouraging our men in the thickest of the fire."

I have selected these from a number of statements to the same effect from men who testified of their personal knowledge. I have personally a melancholy reminder of Mahone's presence in the trenches in a note which he sent to me in the rear, with the body of a nephew of mine, R. E. Butts, a young lawyer of the Petersburg bar, and a member of Co. E, Twelfth Virginia Regiment. He stated in words of sorrow that "my gallant nephew" had just been killed at his side. It was at the time probably referred to by Colonel Rogers of the Sixth Virginia, immediately after the capture of the works, when Mahone appeared amongst them, placing men in position, especially the sharpshooters, to pick off the Federals who were annoying our troops with a fatal fire.

Mahone replies to the incident in a report published in "War Talks of Confederate Veterans." He says: "The Virginia brigade having made its charge, I put the Georgia brigade in position to meet any possible reverse to which the Virginia brigade might be subjected, then hurried across the field to the works which the Virginia brigade then occupied, and after making a thorough examination of the situation, so disposed the same as to increase the ability of the brigade to hold the works retaken, at the same time causing the sharpshooters to be so posted as to make death the penalty of the enemy attempting to escape and get back to their lines. It was here that I remember young Butts [my nephew] being killed in my immediate presence. He had just cautioned me, whilst I was looking through an opening in the works, not to expose myself. I told him I would look after that, and almost immediately afterwards he received a bullet in his forehead which killed him instantly, and he fell on the floor of the trench at my feet." This incident was told me also by David Meade Bernard, also a lawyer, and after the war judge of the Hustings Court of Petersburg. He said that he and Butts were engaged at the request of General Mahone in picking off the men who were continually attempting to get back from the Crater into their own lines, and that Butts remarked just as he was shot, "I got that one," the man jumping up into the air and rolling down the hill as he was struck.

Mr. George S. Bernard (in his "War Talks"), a brave soldier of the Twelfth Virginia, a participant in the immortal charge of the Virginia brigade, an honest and potent collector of facts, and who noted in his diary some of the incidents of the fight, even before the fight was ended, says: "When the Virginia brigade made its charge, General Mahone of course remained in his position in the ravine along which the Georgia brigade was filing to take its position at the right of the Virginians. To have charged with the Virginia brigade, as was the duty of its commander, General, then Colonel Weisiger, would have been evident that he had lost his head, and with the Georgia brigade moving along under his eye and needing his presence to put it in position, would have been criminal indiscretion. The Virginia brigade having made its charge, and the Georgia brigade having filed into position from which it was intended that it should charge, General Mahone hurried across the slope over which the Virginia brigade had just charged to the breastworks, and was in the breastworks a few minutes after the Virginians had gotten into them, encouraging the men, posting sharpshooters, etc."

With facts like these, which cannot be disputed, supported as they are by so much evidence, the allegation that Mahone on this occasion failed to do all in the way of personal presence at the scene of conflict, and post of danger, that should or would have been done by the bravest of division commanders under like circumstances, is utterly untenable, and should be abandoned as false and untenable.

I have collected this testimony in reference to Mahone from sources so abundant that I scarcely knew how to select it, and from men, who, at his right hand and under his eye, for four years were witnesses of his courage and skill and devotion as a soldier, because even now, when the bitterness of partisanship is passing away, there are still some persons disposed to deny him his well-earned honors.

At the time this evidence was gathered together the unfortunate controversy which arose between Mahone and Weisiger after the war in reference to the affair at the Crater had been over for years, and was deeply regretted by the friends of both, and by none more than by the men who had followed them both in four years of unparalleled hardships and unprecedented peril, and who were witnesses of the undaunted courage with which they both met difficulties apparently insuperable, and overcame odds that threatened the extinction of their command. Neither of them were men of personal magnetism, and both were strict and uncompromising disciplinarians, and the hold they had upon their men was born of the consciousness that they would be handled with skill, that they would be cared for in disaster, and that they would be required to incur no dangers which their officers were not willing to meet.

After the affair at the Crater, at which the Federal loss, according to their own returns, was some five thousand killed, wounded, and missing, no further assaults were made immediately upon our works. The siege continued, with the daily cannonading of our lines and of the city, and the daily story of suffering and wounds and death, and the stretching out of the Federal lines to their right, fortifying them, not only in our front, but in their rear, lest Mahone, who had become their terror, should flank them, as he had done more than once to their great loss. The city was shelled generally at certain hours of the day or night, and those who remained in their homes, and some who had returned to their homes, driven back by the discomforts of refugeeing, would go into their bomb-proofs, and wait until the firing ceased before coming out again.

Though the city at some localities was almost knocked to pieces, yet there were few casualties amongst the citizens, or amongst the soldiers who were detained in the city on duty. The wisdom of keeping two hospitals open was soon demonstrated by the fact that they were kept filled by the badly wounded and the sick who could not be made comfortable in the field hospitals adjacent to the city, and by the additional fact that no casualties occurred in any of them. Two nurses were killed, but not whilst they were on duty at the hospitals, and no medical officer was hurt with the exception of myself, and I was not near a hospital at the time. My ambulance men used to say that the Yankees always knew where my quarters were. It is certain that they shelled me out of them more than once—once when I was located in the building now known as the High School, and which I had just vacated on orders from headquarters informing me that "the enemy had gotten my range." I did not vacate too soon, as the chair on which I was sitting was knocked to pieces by a shell which came through the Iron Front on Sycamore Street a very few minutes after I left. My quarters after that were in the small brick house on South Street, adjoining the South-side Box Factory, in the yard of Collier's mill. But I slept at night at the house on Farley and Hinton Street now owned and occupied by Mayor Pleasants, where I had some furniture stored, and which was often the comfortable resort of officers coming in from the lines. Hinton Street had not then been laid off, but there was a wide open valley extending from Friend Street west to South Street, and the shells intended for Tabb Street Church steeple and the Post Office ploughed that valley before becoming exhausted, and made the locality

The War

very unsafe. Of course they shrieked and pounded above and around the house in a most unpleasant way, and finally drove every one away from their firesides, as desirable as they were, except myself and my valet Romulus.

On the night of the 30th of August, after the affair of the Crater, and on the day on which General Hampton had gotten into Grant's rear and driven into our lines some 3,000 cattle, depriving the Federal army of their beef for some time, the officers, naturally very indignant, and unable in any other way to vent their spleen, opened on the city, apparently with every gun, and prolonged their cannonade far into the night. About ten o'clock I was lying down on a lounge and watching the shells as they flew past the windows, those at least which had fuses lit, and listening to the music of the others. The situation became more sublime, as far as the terrible is an element of the sublime, and I said to Romulus, my servant, who was lying on his blanket near me, "Boy, we will run Providence one more night, but to-morrow we will change our base again," when suddenly two planets of the first magnitude seemed to come together right in my face, and to break into a million stars of smaller magnitude. I felt myself whirling over in the midst of plaster, laths, glass, broken timber, and the dust of debris indescribable. Then followed Cimmerian darkness, and I became conscious of a stinging pain in my left shoulder and left foot, and of an ominous trickling down my back—on the whole a sense of being generally used up. My first sensible thought was, "I am not killed, it hurts too badly." As soon as I could get the dirt out of my mouth I called to Romulus to know if he was hurt. "Not touched, sir," he answered. "Well, I am," I replied, "come and get me down under the lee of the wall in the basement." "Better lay still, Marster," he

said; "shell never come in the same hole twice." That
seemed a reasonable calculation of chance, but I pre-
ferred not to take it, and directed him to drag me
down to the basement, out of the dirt. After getting
me into a safer place, and striking a light, he saw some
blood on my shirt, and became demoralized and wanted
to go for a surgeon at once. I told him no, that I was
but a little hurt, and that if he attempted to go for a
surgeon through that fire he would be killed himself, or
the surgeon would be killed before he could get to
me. He made me as comfortable as he could and I
soon fell asleep.

On awakening the next morning my faithful valet
was still watching over me. Finding my wounds very
slight, I simply reported unable for duty and asked for
an officer to be assigned to my place temporarily. However, it gave me a short furlough, and I was surprised
to receive a note from the War Department a few days
afterwards, thanking me for my services, and noting
me "for courage, steadiness under fire, and devotion
to duty." This was a salvo for the slap I got from General Lee for not removing the wounded from under fire
with more diligence when he first came to the city, but
it was a compliment I did not deserve. I never went
under fire when I could honorably avoid it, and I always retired " as soon as a patriotic sense of duty permitted." I never loved danger for danger's sake, and
never put myself in the way of it, either for amusement
or for curiosity. Some surgeons occasionally indulged
in such diversion in the early years of the war, but they
soon became wiser as their experience enlarged; and
though no men whom I met in the four bloody years
of our strife more faithfully and more courageously
stood to their places under the call of duty, yet they
learned not to court unnecessary exposure to danger.
Besides, though many a medical officer paid the penalty

of a limb or of his life for his constancy and courage, not often was one gazetted or promoted therefor. Without the animus of the fight, or the opportunity of retaliation which the armed soldier had, yet quietly, bravely, the doctor knelt in the field, by friend and foe alike, and sought to save, without thought of self, the mutilated and the stricken. It was not for him to cheer, with the shout of the victor—his office was only to hear and to help the fallen and the dying, enemy or comrade.

In the first fight before Richmond, General Lee, noting, I suppose, the disposition of some of the non-combatant staff, surgeons, quartermasters, etc., to go to the front at a fight, commented on the fact and reminded them in an order that their place was in the rear. It was a compliment as delicate as it was deserved. The veteran soldiers had a belief, almost amounting to a superstition, that no man could change place with another in the presence of the enemy without incurring especial danger. Mr. Geo. S. Bernard refers to this fact in his "War Talks," and says that in the line of battle, just before the charge at the Crater, young Butts, who was killed, occupied his (Bernard's) position, and that they exchanged places just before Butts was killed. At the bloody affair at Crampton's Gap, Harrison, of the Twelfth Virginia, whose position in the line of battle brought him behind a stone post, where he was comparatively safe, with an unselfish courage, rarely equalled, vacated it, and gave it to the next soldier in line, who, not a veteran yet, showed some evidence of wavering. Before the fight was over this poor fellow was killed behind the stone post, and Harrison escaped without a scratch.

During the siege of Petersburg I sent on one occasion for a detail of men to guard some hospital stores in transition to a safer place, and two soldiers of a

Georgia regiment were sent me. I directed them where to go. It was by chance a dangerous service, and to these poor fellows an unusual one, which in the soldier's vocabulary generally meant a dangerous service, so one of them hesitated a little and asked to be permitted to get some chewing tobacco from a commissary near at hand. I said to him, "Go on! In twenty minutes you will probably have no mouth to put your tobacco in." It was not spoken in unkindness, but it was an idle speech which cost me no little self-reproach when he was brought back in perhaps less than that time, mortally wounded—a good part of his face carried away by a shell, according to my unhappy prediction. But tragic incidents were so common, and so crowded themselves upon us during the siege, that they often ceased to impress us as they should.

During the winter of 1864-'65, amidst the sorrow and the suffering, which can hardly be exaggerated, gaiety amongst the young people was rife. There were parties, starvation parties, as they were called, on account of the absence of refreshments impossible to be obtained; ball followed ball, and the soldier met and danced with his lady love at night, and on the morrow danced the dance of death in the deadly trench out on the line, and the comrade who reported his fate took his place the following night in the festive hall, and often met the same fate the following day. The belles wept the fallen beaux, but comforted themselves with the recruits who hurried to "close up ranks," to the music of some regimental band, at the dance.

During the latter part of the siege a young friend of mine, a lieutenant-colonel of artillery, came by my quarters one Sunday morning and begged me to go out with him to his battery on the lines and see some fun; saying that the Yankees were going to have dress parade, as they usually did on Sunday, and that he was going to train one of his rifle pieces on them and "see them scatter." I reminded him that training rifle pieces was a game that both sides played at often, and that a rifle piece might possibly be trained on us. "Oh!" he said "no danger, not half as much as here where you are, and where you have to go. Besides, you have had several narrow escapes where you are, and been wounded once, and a man is rarely struck behind my works." I replied to him that if I were killed anywhere that my daily duties called me, it would be all right, that it would be the time and place for me to die; but that if I were killed out in the lines with him some one would say "he had no business there, it was just what might have been expected." In a few hours the body of my poor friend was brought back, a rifle shell having carried away a good part of his head. To complete my story, I must add that he was to have been married soon, and that his intended, a beautiful young belle of the city, wept him for a short time, and then consoled herself with a gallant colonel of infantry. He in turn was wounded, and in the head, but he survived his hurt, and came back from Appomattox, and claimed his bride. They both are living still, in a distant city, and when I saw them within a year past, time had dealt so lightly with them that he was still as handsome as when he wore the "buttons and the gray," and she had simply exchanged the beauty of the ball-room for the maturer charms of matron and mother.

To this day many stirring incidents of that memorable winter of 1864-'65 come trooping through my brain—some pathetic, and some of grimmest humor, as memory and the strange power of association calls up one and another.

"Awake but one, and lo! what myriads rise;
Each takes its image as the other flies."

And then as I sometimes sit in reverie, communing with the past, there comes before me, as if I saw it all only yesterday, an army of heroic figures.

Lee, the peerless, passing along Washington Street on "Traveler" toward some officer's quarters, near the lines in Blandford, riding alone, without courier or staff, as was his wont; of mien so dignified that no man could presume on familiarity, and yet so gracious that a child might approach him.

A. P. Hill, the preux chevalier, riding with easy grace, alert, as if looking for the enemy, and facing generally to the right, seeking probably to inspect his lines where the weak point lay, and where finally he met his end charging alone upon the Yankee pickets and demanding their surrender. A. P. Hill, the intrepid leader for four years of the Light Division of the Army of Northern Virginia, and the only man upon whom both Lee and Jackson called as they fought their battles over in their dying delirium, "Tell A. P. Hill to prepare for action."

And Jeb Stuart, the dauntless trooper,—of whom a Federal general said, "that he was the greatest cavalry officer ever foaled in America,"—dashing along with the careless abandon of a school boy, a smile on his face, but the light of battle in his eye, ready for frolic or fight, and shouting to the foot-sore infantry, "If you want to have a good time, join the cavalry."

And Beale,—sturdy, bronzed and grave, at the head of his steady Ninth Virginia troopers, passing my quarters,—ordered to-day to the extreme left, and to-morrow to the extreme right, as dangers seemed to threaten our flank, separated by twenty miles, and always exposed to especial danger.

And the Lees. Rooney—quiet, conservative, courageous, at the head of his trusty horsemen; whom I once heard say, when advised to make a certain movement, with the assurance that it would give him promotion, though he would gain nothing else and would probably lose heavily: "I would not have the little finger of one of my men unnecessarily hurt for all the glory that could come to me."

And the other Lee—Fitz Lee, the "nephew of his uncle," as his political enemies after the war dubbed him, but the dashing cavalier, the hero of a hundred fights, and the fortunate survivor of all; the man whom his State elevated to honor after the war, and whom his former enemies received with enthusiastic applause, and whom his reunited country rewarded with place and position in acknowledgment of his worth and talents—but the man whom a political ring of the New Virginia took down from his pedestal and placed one of their own number upon it.

And General Cook, of Georgia, coming out of the hot battle of Hare's Farm, Fort Stedman, and riding up Lombard Street, itself swept by the shell of the enemy, his bridle arm hanging by his side, and saluting the surgeon as he approached him, "I never dreamed of being struck, sir." Never dreamed of being struck! When our troops, after carrying the Yankee works over abatis and ditch that seemed impassable, were left without support by somebody's blunder, and were driven back with a loss that was akin to slaughter: when regiments were decimated, some, as Ransom's North Carolinians, almost destroyed—and the gallant Cook "never dreamed of being struck!"

And Gordon—his wife, who had never left him during all of his bloody campaigns, but had shared his hardships and his dangers, almost literally in bivouac and in battle, now sick at Mr. J. P. Williamson's, on Market

Street, whilst he, on the last bitter days of the siege, was fighting fiercely, leading a forlorn hope, and sending in a courier now and then to tell her of his safety; and finally, when all was lost and his stubborn veterans were falling back on their last march to Appomattox, coming himself, his face blackened with powder, and seamed with stains as if the tears had forced themselves through, coming to say "good-by" to the faithful, brave woman whom he was compelled to leave behind. I never realized before, as I did then, those inimitable lines of Bayard Taylor—

> "The bravest are the tenderest,
> The loving are the daring."

And Mahone as he appeared in those last days! I rarely saw him during the war except at his quarters. He seemed to leave them seldom, except for some fight which he was pushing out on the right. Quiet, uncommunicative, absorbed in his own thoughts, taking care of his men; such a dyspeptic that he could not eat of the ordinary fare of the soldier, but keeping his cow and his hens, for which provision was made that they should be moved when he moved—but not interfering, as nothing interfered with the persistence and pertinacity with which he pursued his ends, viz: to find the Yankees and to drive or capture them. Whilst obedient to the commands of his superiors, he exercised a most liberal right of private judgment when he was sure of his facts.

It is not inopportune, in evidence of this element of Mahone's character, to relate an incident which has never gone out of my mind. After our bloody repulse of the enemy at the second battle of Cold Harbor, in June, 1864, and when both armies were at bay, Grant, thwarted at every move to throw himself between Lee and Richmond, and Lee watching his right with ceaseless care, and ever present to intercept, as he had at the Wilderness, any move of the Federal army to turn it, General Anderson reported to General Lee that the enemy had disappeared from his front, and Mahone was ordered to pursue with his division and to attack. Mahone knew that Hancock with his corps was still in his front, and to throw his division upon them could only end in disaster as cruel as it was unnecessary. He informed General Lee of the fact, but Anderson, as corps commander, insisted on the accuracy of his information, and the order was reiterated to charge. Mahone then directed the adjutant of his old brigade, and the adjutant of Posey's Mississippi Brigade, to select fifty men from each brigade, one hundred in all, who would go wherever he ordered them. When they reported, he sent for Captain Chappel, of the Forty-first Virginia, a Marylander, who had proven his courage on many a field of carnage, and said to him, "Captain, take these men and charge the enemy in your front." "General Mahone," said Chappel, "do you order that we should charge Hancock's Corps? That is in our front." "Yes," replied Mahone, "and it it due you, Captain, that I should give you an explanation. I know that Hancock's Corps is in your front, but Dick Anderson [General Anderson] has told General Lee that they have retired, and he has ordered Mahone's Division to pursue. To obey that order means the annihilation of my division. I cannot afford to do that. It is much better to sacrifice one hundred of you than the whole. I have sent for you because I know that you will lead these men into the face of the enemy, and because I know that they will follow you. You have my orders, Captain. Good-by." The charge was made, and in perhaps less than half an hour Chappel returned to Mahone's tent with eleven only of the hundred left, and, touching his cap, said, "General, your order has been obeyed." "Thank you, Captain; take the men to their quarters." The others had all been killed or captured. I know of two men still living who will bear me out in this remarkable statement. One, Col. Hugh Smith, an honored citizen, and Commissioner of the Revenue of this town; the other, a prosperous and active business man, Mr. Patrick Raftery.

But incidents of that fearful winter crowd so fast upon the memory that one wearies of a retrospection that he would fain put aside. Privation, hunger, cold, sickness, wounds, death—the daily menu in a daily entertainment—the recollection of which, like Banquo's ghost, will not down at one's bidding. Dr. H. A. White, in his "Life of Lee," says of that winter: "Winter poured down its snows and its sleets upon Lee's shelterless men in the trenches. Some of them burrowed in the earth. Most of them shivered over feeble fires kept burning along the lines. Scanty and thin were the garments of these heroes, most of them being clad in mere rags. Gaunt famine oppressed them every hour. One quarter of a pound of rancid bacon and a little meal was the daily ration assigned to each man by the rules of the War Department. But even this allowance failed when the railroads broke down and left the meal and bacon piled up along the tracks in Georgia and the Carolinas." [This was not so much the result of the railroads breaking down, as the fault of negligent and incompetent agents and officers. The iron hand which had made itself felt in impressing corn and meat from the citizens, relaxed its grasp when the material was gathered at the depots.] "One-sixth of this daily ration was the allotment for a considerable time, and often this supply failed entirely. But with dauntless hearts these gaunt-faced men endured the almost ceaseless fire of Grant's mortar batteries, and the frozen fingers of Lee's army of sharpshooters clutched the musket barrel with an aim so steady that Grant's men scarcely ever lifted their heads from their bomb-proofs."

But these "dauntless, gaunt-faced veterans" held their post until Lee—Lee whom they worshipped—gave the order to leave the trenches, when they stepped out with martial tread, and entered on their last march to Appomattox with cheerful, hopeful spirit, with jest and cheer and song, as if assured victory were awaiting them somewhere, anywhere that Lee called a halt and formed his line of battle. Lee, sturdy of heart, but not buoyed with hope,—for he knew what was before him,—led them on with the same matchless skill and the same unflinching courage which he had shown from the Wilderness to Petersburg, and no man could look in his face and read of the irreparable disaster which he knew but too well awaited him. And when the enemy had turned his right by their final desperate effort at Five Forks, and broken his lines in front of his quarters at the Turnbull house, and nothing was left him but to retire, riding back toward Petersburg he said to one of his aides, "Colonel, this is a sad business, but it is just as I told them at Richmond. The line has been stretched until it has broken."*

"And as he continued slowly riding to the rear, the shells from the enemy's advancing batteries bursting about him," quoting from White's "Life of Lee" again,—"he turned his head over his right shoulder, his cheeks became flushed, and a sudden flash of his eye showed with what reluctance he retired before the fire directed upon him; and he continued riding slowly toward his inner line, a low earthwork in the western suburbs of the city, where a small force was drawn up, still ardent,

---

* See Appendix. "Last Fight at Five Forks."

hopeful, defiant, and saluting the shells now bursting above them, with cheers and laughter. It was plain that the fighting spirit of his ragged troops remained unbroken; and the welcome with which they received him indicated their unwavering confidence in him, despite the untoward condition of affairs."

What manner of man was he? What manner of men were they? Words cannot paint the courage and constancy of the leader, nor the confidence and devotion akin to worship with which he inspired his followers. At the beginning of the year 1865 Lee had barely 40,000 men in the trenches extending forty miles from the Chickahominy to Hatcher's Run. Grant had 110,000, and from these he could draw at any time enough force to continue his hammering upon our right, which he knew must eventually beat down any resistance that our decimated ranks could offer. On the 5th of February he sent a larger force to capture or turn Lee's defenses at Hatcher's Run, but this was met by the Confederates, who, though outnumbered ten to one, fought with their old-time vigor and fire, and the enemy was driven back upon their lines. After this fight, lasting two days and nights of the severest weather, General Lee wrote of his men: "Under these circumstances, heightened by assaults, and fire of the enemy, some of the men had been without meat for three days, and all were suffering from reduced rations and scanty clothing; exposed to battle, cold, hail, and sleet. The physical strength of the men must fail, if their courage survives."

It was about this time, just after this fight, that Mr. Davis made General Lee Commander-in-Chief of all of the Confederate armies. Too late. President Davis was ex-officio Commander-in-Chief of the armies of the Confederate States, an office whose functions he had filled, as far as possible, to the letter, since his removal to Richmond; and when he laid down his baton the armies of the Confederate States were but a small command; and besides this, General Lee was a strict constructionist of the law which required of a subordinate officer unquestioned obedience to his superior. Had he been Commander-in-Chief, few believe that he would have sat down in front of Petersburg, suffering a siege in which he had everything to lose and nothing to gain. He knew but too well that his resources were well nigh exhausted when he reached Petersburg; that the brilliant battles he had fought on his way were but victories of Pyrrhus; and that whilst he had inflicted upon Grant losses quadruple to his own, yet the Federal commander could replace every soldier lost with four in his place, whilst the ranks in his own brave battalions, thinned by continuous fighting, could never be refilled. It was doubtless with the design of retiring from his trenches that he made the last sortie on the 25th of March, when Gordon, at the head of the Second Corps, made that brilliant charge on the enemy's works at Fort Stedman, his soldiers tearing away the abatis as they advanced, and carrying the enemy's works by the bayonet. Longstreet, again too slow with his supporting attachment, as he was too slow at Gettysburg, failed to give Gordon his help, and our victory was as ashes on the lips. Gordon was compelled to retire with a loss of 3,000 true and tried men, worth more than twice the 2,000 which he had killed or captured from Grant. Lee doubtless struck this blow, hoping to cripple Grant temporarily, so as to get an opportunity of taking his troops away safely and joining Johnson, then making his way northward. If it be a maxim of war to do always what you know that your enemy does not wish you to do, this is the correct conclusion which I have made.

Grant says, writing of this period of the war: "I had spent days of anxiety lest each morning should bring the report that the enemy had retreated the night before [from Petersburg]. I was finally convinced that Sherman's crossing the Roanoke would be a signal for Lee to leave. With Johnson and Lee combined, a long, tedious and expensive campaign, consuming most of the summer, might become necessary under these tactics."

Grant sent three divisions of the Twenty-fourth and Twenty-fifth Corps on the 27th of March to Hatcher's Run, and on the 29th the Fifth and Second Corps, and, on the same day, Sheridan to Dinwiddie Court House, with 13,000 picked and well mounted cavalry. To match this force Lee had transferred Pickett from his left to his right with 10,000 infantry, and Fitz Lee with 5,000 cavalry on their "skeleton horses," who confronted the enemy on the night of the 30th. The next morning, after such fighting as can only be imagined, Warren's Corps was forced back behind Gravelly Run, and Sheridan from near Five Forks back to Dinwiddie Court House. But to no avail. Both soon returned, and with their overwhelming numbers enveloped our thin gray lines and drove back all who were not killed or captured.

Pickett's Division, which under its gallant leader had been the pride of the army, and which was so nearly destroyed at Gettysburg in their fatal charge at Cemetery Hill, came out of this last fight with but few upon its rolls. Five days afterwards, on the retreat to Appomattox, I saw one who had been amongst its most gallant staff officers, dispirited and oppressed with its losses, throw himself on the ground and swear that he would never again draw his sword from its scabbard. Fitz Lee, with his horsemen, though losing heavily, came out better, and with the remnant of his un-

The War

daunted cavaliers hit the enemy many a hard lick during the seven days' retreat before the final surrender.

A staff officer in Fitz Lee's cavalry, a man who had seen all the fighting and been a participant in every battle in which Lee's Brigade of cavalry had ever been engaged, a man whose courage and dash was the admiration of the army, told me that he had never witnessed such desperate fighting as Lee's troops made on the last charge on that fatal 1st of April; and that nine colonels of cavalry went down in a space that he could compass with his eye. A lady upon whose plantation this last fight occurred told me that in her yard and lawn, covering not more than a dozen acres, the dead horses were so numerous that it required days to haul them away and bury them, and that the stench of the carcasses was intolerable. It would seem that Five Forks was really the Waterloo of the Confederacy in Virginia.

After the repulse of Fitz Lee and Pickett at Five Forks on the morning of the 1st of April, and the breaking of our lines near the Turnbull house on the morning of the 2d, it was evident, of course, that we would be compelled to evacuate both Richmond and Petersburg, and Lee sent a dispatch to Breckenridge, Secretary of War, at Richmond, which was delivered to Mr. Davis at St. Paul's Church about eleven o'clock. The purport of this dispatch was that there was no prospect of holding his position here longer than night, if as long as that; that he should withdraw to the north side of the Appomattox at night, and advised the withdrawal of all the troops from the James River at the same time, with the view of concentrating all of our forces near the Danville Railway at some point to be designated later. This point was designated later in the afternoon as Amelia Court House.

The troops were safely withdrawn from both Petersburg and Richmond, owing to the skill with which they were handled, or to the lack of promptness and energy of pursuit on the part of the enemy. On the 5th the most of them had reached Amelia Court House, where they were told that supplies awaited them, and that food would be supplied for the whole army. On reaching the Court House this was found to be a mistake. The supply train, either through bad management or treachery, a question never yet satisfactorily settled, had been sent on to Richmond, and the enemy got our rations. This was a fatal blunder. Lee was detained twenty-four hours, endeavoring to collect subsistence and horses, and in the meantime Grant had arrived with two corps, the Second and Sixth, and had reached Jetersville, on the Richmond and Danville R. R. above Amelia Court House, and thrown this superior force across Lee's track. Had Lee been able to provision his army at Amelia Court House he could no doubt have cut through Sheridan's cavalry, which was in his advance, and made his way to Danville, as he had intended to do when he retired from Petersburg and Richmond; and joining Johnston would have given the enemy a protracted and desperate struggle, perhaps have won a telling victory.

Grant had left his base of supplies also, and could not have followed far with his large army, dependent upon the country for subsistence which Lee drained as he marched before him. Indeed, I heard a general officer of the Confederate Army, who after the war became a member of Congress, say that it was currently believed in the Union Army that Meade did order the pursuit to be stayed at Amelia Court House, and that Sheridan sent a courier to find Grant wherever he could be found, and to beg him to set aside this order and to

The War

press the pursuit. Moreover, Grant now held the inside track en route to Danville, and could mass a heavy body of troops at any time in Lee's way if he persisted in his effort to push through to Danville. Nothing was left the latter then but to turn northward of west, and making the old stage road from Richmond to Lynchburg his way, strive to reach the latter city, where he could draw supplies and where he would meet with some reinforcements. Under these circumstances he left Amelia Court House on the night of the 5th, taking the route indicated. The next day, the 6th, Sheridan, ever active, indefatigable, and audacious, interjected a body of his troops between Lee's column, and then with the Second Corps, or Sixth, or perhaps a part of both, fell upon the rear of the Confederate Second Corps under Gordon, and captured 8,000 of our men, including six of our generals—Custis Lee amongst them. This was at Sailor's Creek, and the troops were those who had been withdrawn from Richmond and its defenses at the same time that Lee had withdrawn his forces from Petersburg. Amongst them was the Naval Brigade, or Reserves, under Admiral Tucker, of the Confederate Navy. It is said that this old hero of the quarter-deck did not relish the idea of "giving up the ship" and of being included in the surrender of the forces with which he had kept company for four days, and drawing his men up, prepared to give the enemy the marline-spike and cutlass, and to force his way through to Lee. I was told that it required not only the authority of the senior officer commanding the Confederate troops now lost to the army and laying down their arms, but the earnest protest of some Union general, who had gotten amongst them, to convince him that he was surrounded, and that to attempt to cut through would end in wholesale slaughter.

In the confusion following this catastrophe, the blocking of the roads with wagons and artillery, and the rushing of stragglers, or of some who had fortunately and honorably gotten out of the difficulty, I met General Lee, without especial escort, as I had so often seen him, riding apparently back toward the rear, as if seeking by his presence to stay the rout and bring some sort of order out of the hopeless chaos. Thas was the last time that I ever saw General Lee during the war, and his face was as placid and his manner as perfect as if on dress parade he was reviewing his victorious platoons. The next and last time I ever saw him was in Petersburg, whither he had come to witness the marriage of his son, Gen. W. H. F. Lee, to Miss Tabb Bolling. I dined with him at General Mahone's, who then occupied the house on the corner of Sycamore and Marshall Streets, now occupied by Mr. R. B. Davis. Dignified, but grave, he was accessible to all, yet left upon all the same impress of his own superiority.

CHAPTER V

THE SURRENDER AND EVENTS FOLLOWING.

The 2nd of April, 1865—I Prepare to Evacuate—A Pathetic Scene—I Note the Absence of My Dog Jack—A "Borrowed" Horse—On to Amelia Court House—An Invitation from Mahone—Romulus Given His "Free Papers"—A Brave Quartermaster—I Lose All My Possessions Through a Yankee Cavalry Raid—The Asset of a Broken Concern—"A Swig From the Same Canteen"—The Best Forager I Ever Saw—Signs of Demoralization—Fall Into the Hands of the Enemy—I give Away a Pair of Spurs—Interview With General Devlin—An Invitation to a Much-Needed Breakfast—I Show the "Sign of Distress"—Ordered to be Paroled—A Night Adventure—Mahone Again and a Parole Blank—An Inhospitable Reception and the Very Opposite—A Question of Boots—With My Wife and Children Once More—A disagreeable Incident—The Finale of the Old Regime.

But to return to Petersburg and follow the fortunes which befell me on that direful day of the 2d of April, 1865, and the seven consecutive days of the retreat to Appomattox Court House. My quarters were then on West Washington Street, on the south side, and about half way between South and Dunlop Streets. About eleven o'clock A. M. on that day, Col. Peyton, of General Lee's staff, riding rapidly in from the direction of the Turnbull house, General Lee's headquarters, drew up his horse at my door and informed me that Gen. A. P. Hill had been killed, our lines broken, and that Petersburg would be evacuated that evening. He had no orders for me, but said that mine would come later. They came pretty soon afterwards, and were to the effect that, taking all the surgeons and all the hospital attaches that could be spared, with any wounded officers that wished to go, and were able to travel, I should leave as early as possible, and go to

Amelia Court House, where we would find further orders, and where transportation would be furnished to Danville, Virginia.

After looking into matters, I saw that but few surgeons or hospital attaches could be spared from the post, and I ordered to be ready for marching, four surgeons, as many hospital attaches (nurses), two ambulances, one chaplain, and several young colored men who had been serving in various capacities about the hospitals. One of these was my valet Romulus, whom his mother brought to me just before I left, with the injunction to "follow marster to the end of the earth; and if he don't come back, don't you come back either." Early in the afternoon I started my little cortege over the river at Campbell's Bridge, and directed them to take the road to Chesterfield Court House, and to pursue that until I overtook them. In the meantime I waited at the door of the Confederate Hospital, located in a large tobacco factory at the corner of Jones and Washington Streets, as if stayed by the horrible fascination of the sights and sounds of that terrible Sabbath afternoon. The city was environed on the east, the south, and the west, and the fighting was as fierce as if men could not be satiated with blood.

As I stood at the hospital door, loath to leave my home and city,—for I felt that I should never see either again as I saw them then, if I ever saw them at all, the wounded were being hurried in from ambulances and upon stretchers, their moans mingling with the cries of women, the shrieking and bursting of shell, and the hoarse orders of men in authority,—two scenes caught my eye, as indelibly fixed there now as on that Holy Sabbath eve which the great God had seemingly given up to the devils in pandemonium. A stretcher was borne in the gateway by four soldiers, just from the near front, one of them crying, "My poor Captain, my poor Captain; the best man that ever lived." A large, finely-made man he was, his right arm shot away at the shoulder joint, and the quivering, bleeding flesh soiled with dust and stained with powder, and filled with the shreds of the gray sleeve that had been hurriedly cut off. Something moved me, as the bearers halted, to uncover the face over which some rude but kindly hand had thrown a piece of dirty blanket. Great God! There lay before me a friend of my earliest boyhood. Years had passed since we parted. I had known him as the gentlest, most lovable of men, living in a quiet, country home amidst a simple-hearted, peace-loving people, an Arcadia in which war was not even a dream. But he did not know me. His honest, brave life was fast ebbing away, and the mist was gathering over his eyes which could only be swept off in the sunlight of that country where the nations shall learn war no more.

I turned away from the scene heart-sick, when a poor woman caught me by the hand, crying, "Doctor, will you not get some one to help me carry my poor husband home? I can take care of him and nurse him better than any one here—there he is." And there, lying only a few feet away in the hospital yard, where with others he had been hurriedly brought in and put down anywhere that space could be found, was a private, an humble citizen, not subject to regular service, but belonging to the second-class militia, who had been summoned to the defense of the city when our lines grew so thin. He had fallen in battle at a spot near where, in peace, he had lived with his wife and little ones, and now he lay, a fourth part of his skull carried away with a fragment of a shell, exposing his brain, leaving him with some little automatic life, but of course not conscious, whilst his poor wife was striving to get from him some sign of recognition, and begging that he might be carried home. I could only stop to tell her that my right to order was at an end; but if a thousand men were at my beck none could help her now. I could see no more, but mounting my horse and riding slowly along, I crossed the river at Campbell's Bridge, and on the heights at Ettricks took one last look at Petersburg as it was—Petersburg, the city for a hundred years of happy homes, of brave men, and of fair women. When I returned two months afterwards, the collar was upon the neck of the freemen and the serf held the chain.

Following the road toward Chesterfield Court House, I soon overtook my little cortege, and found all present save one. This was a bob-tailed, bob-eared, rough-haired Scotch terrier, about twelve years of age. He had seen no little service, and he showed it. When it suited his views to answer at all, he would answer to the name of Jack. He was irritable, self-asserting, frail as to virtue,—his name disagreeably associated with any number of scandals,—but full of faith in his master, and irrevocably attached to his master's fortunes or misfortunes. I had given my chief of ambulance orders, before leaving Petersburg, that whoever might be left behind, Jack should go; and that proper transportation should be furnished him. He had always had too high an appreciation of himself to walk, and had ridden more thousands of miles, had fallen out of more vehicles, and been run over oftener than any other dog in the world. I assert this without fear of contradiction. He had but few friends, and but little capacity to make them, and some difference of opinion on the subject of riding had occurred between him and the chief of ambulance before the start from Petersburg, and hence Jack had been left behind. I said to the chief, "Return to the city at once, and bring me my dog, or fall into the hands of the enemy yourself." The man looked at me for a minute as if he would question such an order; but four years of discipline and obedience had not lost its force on the first night of the retreat, so he turned off and retraced his steps to Petersburg. I never expected to see him again; but late at night, after we had gone into camp about five miles from the city, he returned on horseback, and leading Jack by a chain of white handkerchiefs. He said that he had *borrowed the horse*. Soldiers generally had but little difficulty in *borrowing* a horse, provided they could find one without a rider in hailing distance, so that I did not inquire where he had borrowed it. I did have some curiosity to know where he got the handkerchiefs though, and ventured to ask him. "Well, sir," he said, "they are breaking up everything in town, and looting the stores, and I found these handkerchiefs at the head of Old Street."

We were all very tired after the stirring events of the day, and were soon sound asleep. We were awakened, however, in some two or three hours by firing a few miles to our rear, and finally a heavy explosion in the same direction. We rose to our feet, and thinking there was danger of pursuit, determined to move on. Jack, however, who had been sharing my blanket, became demoralized, and sought individual safety in individual flight. I never saw him again until my return to Petersburg some two months subsequent to this date, when he was one of the first to meet and greet me, and his expressions of joy were very effusive. Some one had evidently taken good care of him, and I heard from some of the hospital people whom I had left behind me that he had gone over to the enemy, as did some other dogs of whom we had a right to expect better things. However, the prodigal returned to stay, and when I left Petersburg a few days afterwards in an ambulance, seeking my family in central North Carolina, he was ready to secure his place in the vehicle. When I reached my wife and children he went to them as faithfully as if he had never turned his back on a friend; but for the balance of his life he would never follow me again. I suspect he had the memory of many hot places into which I had led him. His subsequent history is not without interest, but its details would lead me farther from my subject than its importance would justify. I will only add that he was ever a poor soldier, and always left when the firing began,—not always without company,—impelled by thirst or some other consideration of a personal character. But his service in civil life in a long career entitled him, in my opinion, to civil sepulture, and his grave may be found in the section marked "Claiborne" in the Old Blandford Cemetery, and his epitaph in the third chapter of Ecclesiastes, 20th and 21st verses.

But to return to our story. With the exception of Jack, therefore, our party moved, and after a tedious night's march over execrable roads (the country roads were no better ante-bellum than now), we reached Chesterfield Court House about nine or ten o'clock next morning, and found Mahone's Division drawn up at right angles across the road. They received us with cheers, and opened ranks for us to pass through. With these bronzed veterans, the heroes of an hundred fights behind us, we dismissed all fear of pursuit, and passing along a few hundred yards, laid down to rest and await further orders. After some hours they came. "Take the right-hand road to Goode's Bridge; rendezvous at Amelia Court House, there rations and transportation by rail to Danville will be furnished you."

We re-commenced our march, but did not reach Goode's Bridge that night, bivouacking somewhere near, just on the side of the road. We had not yet struck the stream of the retreating army, with its impedimenta of baggage wagons, ambulances, ammunition trains, etc., but late in the afternoon we passed a typical old Virginia mansion near the road, and on the well-kept lawn, under patriarchal oaks, General Mahone was seated, with his staff, evidently awaiting something. He recognized me—indeed, I had been one of his early friends—and called to me to dismount, tie my horse, and "come and get something to eat." My habits of obedience were too well established, after four years of service, to permit me to refuse, so I joined the party, telling my people to go on, but to await me before going into camp. Butter-milk, fried chicken, and ash cake were soon brought out under the shade of the trees, and we enjoyed the hospitable repast as only soldiers could do "who had nowhere to sleep and nothing to eat for days." As soon as we had finished our repast the General said, "It is time we were off."

I rode along with him leisurely for an hour or so before we came up with our men, talking more of the past—in which we had many things of interest in common—than of the future, upon which neither of us looked as of much promise. After a little time he reined up his horse, and looking at me gravely said, "Doctor, what are you going to do now?" I told him of my plans, or rather of my orders. He replied, "Take my advice, send your detachment along with one of your surgeons, and stay with me. If any troops get out of this trouble, Mahone's Division will get through." I had great confidence in Mahone, and in his resources and his men, scarred and bronzed in campaign and battle for four long years; I believed in him and I believed in them; but my little company had gone on under my orders and I felt that I had better follow them, and so I said, "General, you have a very good surgeon on your staff." "Yes," he said, "there is Wood." "Well then, as you have no need of my service, I will go on, though I thank you for the compliment you pay me, and appreciate your kindness." "Go on then," he replied; "but you will be sorry that you did not remain with Mahone's Division." We shall see in the denouement how far the wisdom of my course was justified.

We went into camp that night near Amelia Court House, and next morning I arose early, and mounting my horse rode to that place for the purpose of getting further orders and the transportation which had been promised me. Just before reaching there I came upon a bivouac of officers—two generals and several other officers of high command. I recognized Maj. Thos. Branch amongst them, who introduced me, and as they were just going to breakfast, invited me to join them. I declined this civility, but asked where I could see or communicate with General Lee, or one of his staff, making known the object of my wishes. They could give me no information except that the rations which we expected to get there had gone on to Richmond, and that as to transportation by rail, that the Danville Railroad was in the hands of the enemy. More than this, that if the army continued to follow the road—the country road—to the left and parallel to the one which we followed yesterday, a fight would be in order very soon. Indeed, a desultory firing was heard just then, and the officers mounting their horses moved off to the front, Major Branch and I retiring.

On getting back to the road which we had been following the day before, we found that the whole army train had been ordered to follow the same road, as promising more safety, or less probability of being interrupted by the enemy. I got my cortege into line —wagon, ambulance, buggy, etc.—after some scurrying and swearing (the latter done only by the inferior officers), and took up the line of march, we did not know whither. Only one who has followed a large army can know how slowly, and with how many halts, a wagon train can move. A broken axle or a balky horse can detain the whole line for hours. One wagon can hardly find opportunity to pass another, and when such a thing is attempted, it is met with a storm of obloquy and opprobrious language that even a quartermaster's nerves become shaken. Being well mounted on a fine black mare which I had gotten from an impressing officer the day before, and which was too high strung for artillery, I rode along the line to and fro for some hours, exchanging views with an occasional comrade with whom I would meet.

I soon became convinced that unless our enemy were of the most listless and unenterprising character, that the wagon train would soon come to grief, and my little party with it. I called to Romulus—the colored boy, who had been a favorite servant at home, and the one whom his mother had brought to me upon leaving Petersburg and bidden him to "follow marster to the end of the earth"—and said to him: "Boy, no Yankee shall ever claim that he gave you your freedom. I will free you right here." Getting down from my horse, I wrote for him what was known at the South before the war as his "free papers," and giving him a knife as a memento of his master,—if he never saw him again,—and as much money as I could spare, I told him to follow me as long as it was safe for him, but when things became too hot to skedaddle in any direction which seemed to be the safest. He pocketed my bequests and went along with the cortege, but evidently the whole affair seemed to him a good joke.

I remained talking to some friends, knowing that I could overtake the party in five minutes at any time, and had ridden forward not more than a mile when I came to an open space on the side of the road, just at the beginning of which some one had evidently been camping, and left a good deal of forage on the ground when leaving. I got off my mare and took the bit out of her mouth, determined to give her a good square meal. She had just begun to eat when some one cried "Yankees!" I looked across the field, and a few hundred yards away, coming from a road that ran at right angles to ours, there was a company of Yankee cavalry, and there was a general rush of teamsters and stragglers back to the rear. I remembered that the sergeant from whom I got my mare the day before had told me that she was "hard to bit," and I thought that if she should be a fool now, we both would have a short shrift. She behaved very well, however, and I soon bitted her and was on her back, but in mounting I dropped one of my gauntlets, a scarce article at that time, and one which I could illy afford to lose, and started to dismount and recover it; but never did cavalry arrive so rapidly and in such numbers! I had just time to dash out into the woods on the opposite side of the road, and make my retreat as fast as the impediments of riding through the woods would permit, which was not very fast, but which gave me an opportunity to see that the enemy were comparatively few in number, and lining along the road were shooting the mules and horses, with no other idea than obstructing the road and disabling us by destroying the teams.

There were a number of our men rushing back through the woods, many of them armed, and I begged them to halt and save the train; calling their attention to the small number of the enemy, and to the fact that they were not shooting at the men but at the horses and mules. One old soldier whom I tried to stop looked at me in a dazed kind of a way, and said, "If you are fool enough to believe that, you can stop, I am going on." I looked at the stars upon my collar, and thought

The Surrender and Events Following 269

of endeavoring to enforce my authority, when a stream of stragglers rushed by, increasing in number, and making a panic that was irresistible. In a few minutes a goodly number of us came out together in the road, a little out of range of the fire. Here I noticed a colonel of our cavalry, afoot and trying to stay the rout; but they paid no more attention to him than to me. Just then my attention was directed to a quartermaster who had gotten his wagon as a sort of a breastwork in a very narrow part of the road, on either side of which was a growth utterly impenetrable to cavalry, and seeing the advantages of his position, was begging the men to "stand and shoot." One man said he had no gun. "Plenty of guns and ammunition in my wagon," said our doughty quartermaster, and seeing me at the same time, he jumped upon the pole of his wagon, or something near it, and shouted, "Major, you have been to the front, speak to the men and tell them how few of the enemy there are who are attacking us." Continuing his harangue (his words are as fresh in my memory as if yesterday were that eventful day), he cried: "Stand, men! Stand, men! Right here! Five determined men can stop this whole rout! Stop; for your country's sake, stop! For General Lee's sake, stop! For God's sake, stop! For my sake, stop!"

In the meantime I was so attracted by his earnestness, if not moved by his eloquence, that I did not note the situation as accurately as I should otherwise have done, and I was rather startled into consciousness of the real condition of things by two or three of the enemy riding up in most disagreeable proximity, and pop, pop, pop (not at the horses this time) from their carbines, which purported to shoot sixteen times without reloading, but which seemed to me to shoot more nearly sixteen hundred times. My quartermaster made fight, I think—at least somebody fired a gun; then the quartermaster went down with a broken arm, I heard afterwards, though I never saw him again. My mare not relishing the situation and being under fire for the first time, whirled around with me, and I discovered that I held the field alone; she discovered the same thing, and several other things it seemed, which lent wings to her feet, and without at all consulting my wishes, but in full accord with my desires, she left incontinently, I lying upon her neck and not knowing what minute I should receive an inglorious wound in the most exposed portion of my person.

The fugitives must have made very good time, as it was nearly a quarter of an hour before I overtook any of them, and then I ran into an officer, whom I recognized by the richness of his expletives as a North Carolina quartermaster and an old friend. Then there were several other officers, one with three stars upon his collar, before whom I had appeared in a court martial a few months before. Some one of the stragglers called out, "fall in, Company Q," but it was noted as a piece of pleasantry not at all appropriate to the occasion, and as a liberty for which any private should be condemned. My quartermaster friend and I left the road and went across the field in the direction of a parallel road, where we thought we might be able to place ourselves under the aegis of some of Lee's fighting men. We had gone but a few hundred yards when a regiment of infantry came at a double-quick right toward us from a valley to our left, and in some peculiar light reflected upon them seemed dressed in blue, so we prepared to surrender to the Yankees. It turned out, however, to be the Twelfth North Carolina, sent to rescue the wagon train; and they were followed by a regiment of cavalry, sent to interrupt Sheridan's ubiquitous troops. We followed them back to the location where we had left our eloquent quartermaster

The Surrender and Events Following 271

on the pole of his wagon; but the enemy had gone, and so had the quartermaster. We heard afterwards that he had escaped, though with a broken arm. Passing farther on we found that they had shot a number of horses and mules, though somebody had evidently stood their ground,—some wagoner I suppose,—for several dead troopers with their grayish yellow-trimmed uniform lay on the ground. One who had fallen off his horse was so drunk that we could not conscientiously kill him, or conveniently take him prisoner, and we left him lying near the road. My little cortege was struck just about this place.

Romulus had been taken prisoner, with several others, but the surgeons had escaped into the woods, and came up as we arrived. One of our party, a handsome young lady of Suffolk, Virginia, Miss R., who was taking care of her brother, Capt. R., a cavalry officer with a broken arm, and who was seated by him in my commissary wagon, refused to leave the wagon when they ordered her, and defied them to burn it, and so saved a few of our pitiful stores. She also gave evidence that somebody had done some shooting, as she showed several bullet holes in her dress. They took her brother away from her, however, and made him a prisoner. I regretted that she had not had her place in my quartermaster's wagon, as stored in my baggage was a military cloak of great value, too fine for any officer under the grade of lieutenant general, which I had never worn, and which I had hoped to save for my three little girls, who had been refugeeing during the war in Louisburg, North Carolina. This cloak had been sent me as a present. It came from abroad, I presume, through the blockade, and its price in Confederate money was estimated at fifteen hundred dollars. Besides this, I lost every article of clothing I had in the world except that which I had on my person. My greatest loss was a diary, kept from the days of the Charleston Convention, 1861, which inaugurated the war of secession. This was bound in vellum and bristled with facts that none could gainsay. I have felt its loss particularly in evolving these reminiscences.

We got our young lady friend aboard the wagon of a quartermaster of the North Carolina regiment, where she found agreeable companionship in a Miss D., of New Orleans, and a Mrs. S., of Raleigh, North Carolina, who with some other ladies were trying to get out, or keep out, of the enemy's lines. I saw this wagon party the next day, and judging from the music and laughter which issued from under its cover, their misfortunes had not seriously affected their spirits. The day after we met these ladies again under different circumstances. With the surgeons of my little party, four of us, I had gone forward to the front, and after a short time came upon General Longstreet and several of his staff, apparently lounging at rest. Still going on and suspecting nothing, we suddenly came upon a line of battle, the men strung out diagonally across the road at an eminence. Infantry; no artillery to attract attention, but some little stir going on in the front. Just then an ambulance was hurriedly driven up, and a lady in it cried, "Don't take me right into the battle! Don't take me right into the battle!" I rode up to see what service I could render, when a young infantry officer took hold of the mules and rapidly drove them down under the shelter of the hill. We followed and found other surgeons there rigging an extemporaneous table, and evidently preparing for sanguinary work. Strangely enough there had gotten together our lady friends of the day before at the same place—Miss D. and Miss R., and the lady in the ambulance was Mrs. S. Feeling secure from the firing, which began in earnest, we made our arrangements to stop and give what assistance we could as surgeons. Indeed, one poor fellow had just been brought in, shot through the knee, and we were contemplating amputation, when a courier rode up hastily from General Longstreet, or General Lee, with orders for the surgeons to leave at once and to leave the ladies and the ambulance and the wagon and everything, showing us a path through the woods by which we could make our way out safely. We left at once, of course, after a hurried adieu to our friends, who soon fell into the hands of the Yankees. We subsequently heard that they were treated with great courtesy, and were sent back to Petersburg.

But we must go back to the scene of our personal disaster. Of my cortege, besides the surgeons who escaped into the woods and returned as the fighting troops came up, there were two colored hospital attaches who came also, preferring, as they said, to take their chances in Dixie rather than go North; and my orderly, a Moravian from Salem-Winston, who would not fight on account of religious scruples, but who as a forager and factotum was invaluable. Indeed, the reason why he was not captured was that he was off on a foraging expedition when the train was attacked. He returned on a very fine young horse, which I suspect the enemy had taken and found unmanageable and released. Buchhart—that was my man's name—rode him during the balance of the route to Appomattox, though I saw him get some hard falls. However, one animal was left—a mule belonging to the Confederate Government, but which I had hitched to a buggy belonging to myself, and used as a supplement to my means of transportation. He had escaped the bullets of the enemy, and was standing just out of the road, in the midst of the general destruction, with appearance so forlorn and lugubrious that it was impossible not to smile. There was also near him a sad and seedy-looking darky. I called the man to me, and hastily writing, on the pommel of my saddle, a note in doggerel, directed him to take the mule and buggy to a handsome residence a few hundred yards away, and deliver both to the gentleman who lived there. I had no idea who this gentleman was, nor did I dream of ever hearing from mule or man again. But I did. The gentleman was an honored member of my profession, who must have thought such a note very absurd and very unfitting an occasion of so much disaster. But in the June following I received a letter, sent somehow by the doctor,—mails were not reestablished then,—saying that he had a mule and buggy in good condition belonging to me, and that if I would send for them he would take pleasure in returning the same. I persuaded an impecunious Confederate comrade, who had just been released from Point Lookout, to go for them, sending my most grateful acknowledgments, and an humble apology for the levity of the ill-timed doggerel with which I had committed them to his charge. It is perhaps now difficult to understand how one could retain such lightness under circumstances so depressing, but soldiers—poor fellows—often lightened their misery by merriment. Many a joke was made amidst the fiercest fighting, and many a brilliant sally was spoken by lips sealed the next moment in death. My comrade came safely back in a few days, escaping on the road the dangers of Yankees, and stragglers from both flags, who had the most peculiar and free notion of the sanctity of private property, especially if such property were represented by horse or mule flesh. For some time after that date horse stealing was not rated as grand larceny. Comrade S. drove up to my quarters, and alighting from the buggy announced laconically, "Here's your mule," and disappeared. I think he had possibly been weighing in his thoughts some of the difficulties which perplexed mine, and as he had no interest in settling them, withdrew from the scene.

The question was, to whom did the mule belong? He was the asset (no pun) of a broken concern—the Confederate Government,—which had gone into the hands of a receiver; and many a representative of that receiver appeared on our streets in the person of a Yankee quartermaster. I really felt some conscientious scruple myself; besides, my old comrades, who had gotten hold of the story, jeered me, and so I concluded that I would seek counsel of "my friends the enemy," stating a supposed case. I did so, and approached an officer, whom I did not know, but who seemed a good fellow, and asked him his views. He took hold of the question promptly and practically, made it appear at once that he understood the situation, and paid me the compliment to say, "If you have a mule of that sort and don't sell him at once and put the money at once in your pocket, you are a bigger fool than I take you to be." I acted upon this suggestion without delay, sold my mule for seventy-five dollars, and my buggy for seventy-five (in greenbacks), and with this capital stock commenced life anew.

But again I anticipate my story. Let me go back to the scene of the wreckage of the train of which I have spoken. It had been struck by one of the marauding bands of Sheridan's picked cavalry which hung on the flanks of our army night and day, and which under guides knew the country well—the cross-roads by which they could fall on one side or other of our wagon trains, capture, burn, disable and destroy, and safely retire on the appearance of fighting men. The especial prize which attracted them on this occasion was a battery of six new Brook guns which had been brought out from Richmond at the evacuation of that city, and which were drawn by very fine horses, impressed for that purpose, belonging to parties in Richmond. It is unnecessary to say that the guns and horses were carried off by the enemy. Besides, more than one hundred wagons and ambulances were burned and a number of mules and horses shot, so that it was some hours before the march could be resumed. As but few of our party were left, and we had nothing on wheels to encumber us, we did not wait for the general move, but resumed our way, light of baggage.

But few incidents worthy of record occurred under my personal observation during the next day. One, I remember, impressed me so strongly that it never has been erased from my mind. During Thursday night,—sometime during the small hours,—at a creek, or double creek they called it, a panic occurred; and with wagons such as were left, stragglers, retainers, and not a few soldiers, there was a blockade of the way, and confusion worse confounded. It took us a little time to get out of it; but, unincumbered, we found ourselves more fortunate than many others, and were just coming out when I met General Lee riding slowly toward the rear, possibly, I thought, with a purpose of trying to straighten out the inextricable tangle into which matters had gotten. I passed him near enough to look into his face. He rode erect, as if incapable of fatigue, and with the same dignity of carriage that I had so often noted on the streets of Petersburg. From his manner no man could have discerned that which he knew so well, viz: that his army was fast melting away, that his resources were exhausted, and that in a very few days he would be compelled to deliver up to the enemy, which he had defeated so often, the remnants of those ragged jackets who had followed him for four long years, and who had never failed except "in their own annihilation."

Another incident entirely personal I record. During the night, which was quite cold, one of my surgeons chanced to meet a quartermaster friend who had some whiskey. He brought up this gentleman, and under stress of our misfortunes we found excuse for indulging in a drink all around, "a swig from the same canteen." It was the first drink that I had taken in many months, and though I suppose the whiskey was as good as any, it had the most peculiar and unhappy effect upon me. I had congratulated myself up to that night that I was immune to hunger, to fatigue, to scare and to sleep; but after that drink I was so hungry, so tired, and so scared that I was ashamed of myself, and withal so sleepy that I had to get off of my horse and walk for some distance to keep myself awake.

We reached Farmville early the next morning, and here my untiring and irrepressible orderly, Buchhart, discovered that Major Fred Scott, one of the assistant commissary generals, was issuing rations. How he discovered it I never knew; but the Major was handing out to such soldiers as passed him pieces of bacon, and such portions of flour or meal as they could find means to carry along with them. Buchhart got hold of a middling of Virginia meat and some quarts of flour, but where he found the bag into which he received the flour has never been accounted for to this day. I have stated already that he was the best forager I ever saw, but I am inclined to think that he never signed a requisition for the supplies which he was fortunate enough to get. He insisted after getting these rations that we should halt, and that he would go into somebody's kitchen and cook perhaps a three days' supply. We consented, and I turned aside into a narrow street, and lying down tied my horse's reins around my body and was soon asleep. I used this precaution because a brother officer had lost his horse

two nights before, stolen from his side whilst asleep.
When my faithful orderly awakened me and we had
gotten our little party together again, nearly the whole
of Lee's army—the infantry and artillery, I am sure—
had passed through the streets of Farmville and crossed the bridge over the Appomattox River, placing
themselves again on the north side of that stream.
Some of the cavalry was left and was having a lively
time holding the Yankee advance in check that was
coming inconveniently near the little town.

We had no time to eat then, of course, but hurried
down to the bridge, but with our rations cooked, and
went over the river with the rear guard. This was
nothing like as numerous as were the Yankee prisoners of whom they had charge, and who crossed over at
the same time. There seemed to be several thousand
of them. I noticed that many of them carried joints
or middlings of bacon, such as I saw issued to our soldiers, and I have no doubt that Major Scott very generously divided his last commissary stores with them.
A soldier could no more bear to see a fellow-soldier
hungry, whether friend or foe, than to be hungry himself. And did not our enemies, after we had surrendered at Appomattox Court House, divide their rations
with us? These amenities soften the bitter passions
engendered by the cruelties of war, and prove after all
that human hearts are ever akin when trouble and sorrow come. After the rear guard, with the prisoners,
had passed over the bridge, orders were given to burn
it, which was done at once by a member of General
Lee's staff, Major Cook, who was sent back for the
purpose. The cavalry was left to take care of itself,
which it did by crossing the river at a ford a short way
above Farmville.

When we reached the hills above Farmville, on the
opposite side of the river, we found a great many guns,

The Surrender and Events Following 279

not drawn up in a position for firing, but more like going into park. This we did not understand at the time, but which we remembered when we learned that General Lee had sent a note to General Grant that morning asking upon what terms he would accept the surrender of the Army of Northern Virginia. Nothing came of the note, which was probably intended as a ruse by General Lee, in order to gain a little time and to get his forces together, for a few hours afterwards he sent another note to Grant saying that the time had not arrived, in his opinion, when it was necessary or proper to surrender his army. In the meantime the army had been hurried up on the roads on the north side of the river, leading westward, and we followed. In a few hours we came upon General Lee's headquarters, wagon and ambulance, and his carriage. This was the first time I ever saw his carriage, or ever knew that he had one. He must have resorted to it very rarely, though one of the headquarters men told me that he had used it once or twice during the retreat.

They were tearing up and throwing out from his wagon and box numbers of papers and letters, etc., evidently a clearing up of the ship for action, and preparing for the worst. Dr. Guild, General Lee's medical director, was also present, with his wife, in another ambulance; and knowing me very well, invited me to remain with them to the last, which could not be far off. I thanked him, and intended doing so, but there was a hurried "forward," a daily and nightly reiteration, and in the move we lost sight of him and his ambulance and never saw him again.

In the meantime, being unincumbered with baggage, and independent of orders, we moved forward, keeping with the advance of the army, and determined to get away and go to join General Johnson in North Carolina, if possible.

We moved on, without especial incident to us, until Saturday afternoon preceding the surrender. There were signs of demoralization and disintegration of our forces on every hand. Soldiers who had been men and who had faced death in every form, upon a hundred fields, without flinching or dismay; officers, even of high grade, without command, and assuming no authority; muskets thrown aside along the highway, or sticking in the ground by the bayonet, evidenced this fact. Not that there were no fighting men left. The old veterans, like the old guard at Waterloo, knew how to stand and how to die. When called to halt and keep back "those people," as General Lee ever spoke of the Federals, they rallied with the old joyful light of battle in their faces, *gaudamen certaminis*, delivered their withering fire, and sullenly moved on again; but though always inflicting fearful loss, yet always leaving some faithful comrade of their own "dead on the field of honor," until their numbers grew so thin that the end or annihilation was evident to all.

Up to that time the surrender of the Army of Northern Virginia had not entered into my conception. To me, as to every Southerner,—as to every man, woman and child in the Confederacy,—it had been the embodiment of courage, and fortitude, and heroism. The cause for which it had fought for long years was the cause of liberty, and truth, and right. God could never let those brave battalions go down before might, whose standards had been held up for so many years by the hands of our heroes; those battle flags could never trail in the dust, which, kissed and consecrated by Southern women, had been baptized by the blood of the truest and best of earth. Surely the prayers of a million of Christian men and women, proving their faith by their works of self-abnegation and self-surrender, could not fail to have a hearing above, where the destiny of nations was determined and ordained! Ah, many a heavy-hearted old soldier, trudging his way home after the surrender at Appomattox Court House, believed, with Bonaparte, that Providence was always on the side of the heaviest ordnance!

On the afternoon of the 8th, the day preceding the surrender, our little party, keeping to the front with some sections of artillery, which, mostly out of ammunition, had been ordered to push ahead on the Lynchburg road, came upon Colonel Peyton, one of General Lee's inspector-generals, putting in position a small body of infantry upon a knoll commanding a considerable view of the surrounding country. There did not seem to be more than two hundred in all. As he was an especial friend, I rode up to him and asked him what command it was. He replied slowly and sadly, "That is what is left of the First Virginia Regiment, and it is the sole guard of the left flank of the Army of Northern Virginia." At a long distance beyond range there could be seen a body of Federal horse, hovering around as birds of prey, and awaiting opportunity. Within range of my eye there were many muskets stuck up in the ground by the bayonet, whose owners, heart-sick and faint from hunger and fatigue, had thrown them away and gone—none knew whither. God help the poor fellows and forgive them! Four years of peril and fatigue and fighting had proved their metal, but gaunt hunger had at last overcome them—overcome their manhood—and they had scattered through the country anywhere out of range of the enemy, to any house or hut that promised a piece of bread. I saw men whose rations for days had been corn stolen from the horses' feed, and parched, and munched as they marched and fought.

I said to Colonel Peyton, "Does General Lee know how few of his soldiers are left, or to what extremities they are reduced?" He replied, "I do not think that he does." "Then, whose business is it to tell him, if not his first inspectors." "I cannot tell him," he replied, "I cannot." For the first time my fortitude failed me, and choking with tears I said to my little party, "Let us push on, we can be of no further use here. Maybe we can get to Johnston's army in North Carolina, or maybe some leader beyond the Mississippi will raise the stars and bars, and liberty find there a rallying point and refuge." To that time my faith in the final success of the Confederate cause was strong; but when the sun went down behind the hills of the Appomattox I looked upon life as a bauble, and the only blessed ones those brave men who were sleeping in soldier's graves without knowledge of defeat, without the taste of the ignominy of walking under the victor's yoke.

As I rode along, some of the classic readings of a happy past haunted my memory, and I thought of Ulysses, after the siege of Troy, wandering the world a wretched waif, and of Homer's lines:

> "Happy, thrice happy, who in battle slain
> Pressed in Atrides' cause the Trojan plain.
> Oh! had I died before that well fought wall,
> Had some distinguished day renowned my fall;
> Such as was that when showers of javelin sped
> From conquering Troy around Achilles' head."
>
> Odyssey, Lib. 5, verse 306.

And I thought of the grand Latin epic, and of the laments of the unhappy Æneas, and his song—

> "Oh! terque, quaterque beati,
> Quis ante ora patrum Trogae
> Sub moenibus altis
> Contegit oppertere."

The Surrender and Events Following

> " 'Thrice happy those whose fate it was to fall!'
> Exclaims the chief before the Trojan wall;
> Oh! 'twas a glorious fate to die in fight,
> To die so bravely in their parents' sight.
> Oh! had I then beneath Tydides hand,
> The bravest hero of the Grecian band,
> Poured out the soul with martial glory fired,
> And in the plain triumphantly expired,
> When Hector fell by great Achilles' hand."
>
> Virgil, Æneid, Book 1, ver. 91.

But there was no time for sentiment. We hurried on, and reached Appomattox Court House just before sunset—passing the little village and going into camp a mile, perhaps, beyond it, near some guns of the artillery, broken sections of which had been ordered on to Lynchburg. I had taken the bridle off of my mare that she might enjoy a little forage, and was lying down with my head on my saddle, asleep, supposing that we had gotten beyond the Yankee column, which we knew was pursuing and plundering on a parallel road. I had hardly gotten to sleep when my faithful Buchhart awakened me, crying, "The Yankees be upon thee, Doctor." I had just time to escape, with two of my comrades, Doctors Smith and Field, into a thicket of dwarfed oaks,—"black jack," as it is called in that section, and which is impenetrable by cavalry,—when the enemy came down, whooping and yelling, with clanking of sabres, and made for the artillery, which was a few hundred yards to our rear. Immediately there was a sharp firing of carbines and of artillery, a rebel yell, and a hurried retreat of the troopers; then another charge, and an irregular discharge of field pieces, and a general scattering as far as we could see. We put ourselves at once farther from the field of action, by retreating through the woods, and coming to a high fence climbed over that, placing it as well as the "black jack" between us and the enemy's horse.

Darkness coming on, and ignorant as we were of the topography of the country and the relative position of the opposing forces, we thought it best to remain quietly and to lie down until daylight.

The next day, after we had fallen into the hands of the enemy, we got a good account from some of our fellow-prisoners of the affair of the night before. It seems that the Yankee cavalry, grown careless by constant and unresisted raids upon our stragglers and trains, had charged down the road where they passed us,—charged in column,—and that some of our artillerists, getting wind of what was coming, shotted their guns to the muzzle with what relics of ammunition, grape, and canister they had, had opened on the column at short range.

Sergeant Dibrell, of the Richmond Howitzers, who served one of the guns, told me that the havoc was dreadful. The Yankees were repelled, but seeing the insignificance of the force arrayed against them, they came back as assiduously as before, led by a bronzed old major on a gray horse, who with many others met his death with a reckless courage worthy of a better cause. The second charge was successful; the cavalry running down the gunners, capturing some, whilst others dodged into the woods, following the tactics of the three surgeons. The casualties of our side were few. Dr. Nash, however, of Norfolk, the surgeon of one of the companies, got a pistol bullet in his face.

But returning to the fortunes of the three surgeons. Awakening by daylight in the morning, we started through a field adjoining our resting place, and took the direction in which we supposed we could find our people. With no compass but our wits, which were not at all sharpened by the night's experience, we took the wrong course, and in a few minutes walked upon a vidette sitting quietly upon his horse, and apparently looking for news. Thinking that he was one of our men, we approached him in a very friendly manner, naively mentioned the fact that we were three lost Confederate surgeons, and asked to be shown where we would probably find Lee's lines. We started in the direction indicated, when he snapped out a sudden "halt," and something equally persuasive—an ugly-looking Colt's revolver of the regulation size,—and ordered us to come forward. We did so, and showing his uniform under his cavalry overcoat, we perceived that we were taken in. He gave at once a curt order, "Right about, face; march quick!" We obeyed unhesitatingly, and strode forward in the opposite direction to "Lee's lines," our escort advising us to that effect, and closely accompanying us, selecting me as "next man" and keeping his pistol very unpleasantly near my head. I ventured to remark that we were unarmed, and that I doubted if it were necessary to keep us so closely covered by his weapon, but he made no reply.

We went hurriedly on over the rough ground, his pistol bobbing up and down near the right side of my head, and I really apprehended some danger of an accident, and said, "Sergeant, you will shoot me presently," to which he cheerfully replied, by way of allaying my fears, "I don't care a d——n if I do!" I said, "But, Sergeant, I do care very particularly; it would be a very unpleasant death to be shot here this cold morning, with so few witnesses of my fortitude." But he did not change his conduct, and I saw that any little irregularity of the ground causing his horse to stumble might send a bullet crashing through my brain, and so I changed my tactics. I reopened the conversation on a different scale, and said, "Sergeant, those are poor spurs which you wear, for so fine a trooper. I have in my overcoat pocket a beautiful pair, made out of copper taken from the old *Merrimac*, which your people burned at the evacuation of the navy yard at Norfolk. If you will permit me to stop and get them out of my overcoat pocket, I would like to make you a present of them." He smiled, and said "All right." I took the spurs out of my pocket, and handed them to him, and greatly to my relief he put his pistol back in the holster. I valued those spurs very highly, and if by chance my captor be still alive and these few lines should fall under his eye, I would take it as an especial favor if he would return them to me; and I will forgive him for the scare which he gave me that morning at Appomattox.

Well, our captor carried us to the picket lines, and turned us over to General Devlin, who was afterwards Attorney-General under Grant. He received us very courteously, and on finding out who we were introduced us to his surgeon, who was also very courteous; and knowing that we had not breakfasted, had coffee served us, and regretted having "nothing more substantial to offer." Indeed, the whole staff was so kind that we might have thought ourselves in no hostile camp, but amongst friends, except for one little circumstance—one contretemps, which they no doubt regretted as much as I did.

General Devlin was questioning me, asking, amongst other things, "Why does not General Lee surrender? How long is he going to keep up this foolishness? If he falls back to Lynchburg, does he not know that he cannot escape?" I replied to all of these by telling him that I was not in General Lee's confidence; that I had not attended his council of war; and that I was really unprepared to say what were his intentions. He then asked me how many men, of all arms, General Lee had left? How many prisoners he had with him? What his position was, and what roads bore upon it? and other questions of a similar character, which I could not answer, and which I would not have answered if I could. I did say, however, for mischief, that when I left the main body of the army there were more prisoners than we had troops. This was not really much of an exaggeration, and was received in good humor, except by a dapper little officer who stepped up and said, "General Devlin, that fellow is lying to you; he does not want to tell you." Such language was not tolerated in the class to which I belonged at that day, and to be called a "fellow," and to be told that I was "lying!" I felt myself burning down into my boots, and in resenting the insult probably very soon should have made a fool of myself, had not the General and several of his staff turned upon him with such a look as to cause him to shrink back from decent company. Very soon after, the General called up an orderly and directed him to take us to the rear. In a few minutes we reached the advanced lines of the enemy. There we met General Sheridan, splendidly mounted, and a number of officers with him,—his staff, I supposed,—all well dressed and with caparisoned steeds, presenting a very different appearance from our poor broken-down cavalry.

There was a large body of horse in an adjoining piece of wood, and as Sheridan rode up they were advanced in line. Some one said, "Now, boys, you are going to see something grand." A man near me said it was General Sheridan who spoke. The infantry, of which there seemed any number near by, and who, coming up, jeered the troopers, as our men used to jeer them sometimes, and said, "Oh, you will be back on us pretty soon." And "pretty soon" they were back, many of them, and we were hurried to the rear with the fugitives, to prevent, as I was told afterwards, recapture by Fitz Lee.

I was also told that Sheridan was not only repelled, but lost two of his guns in less than five minutes. There is abundant and authoritative evidence for this statement, but Sheridan does not mention it in his "Last affair at Appomattox," nor does he speak of having met me! Before we had gone back more than a mile we met a corps of infantry advancing, and then seemingly another, the soldiers appearing to come out of the ground, such were their numbers; and I can well believe that which history records—there were 75,000 of them! We were soon in the rear, as indicated by the number of prisoners under guard; by the hospital arrangements, and by a curious-looking cooking affair on wheels, which we were told belonged to the Christian Commission. This is all of the Christian Commission we ever saw. No doubt it had its presence and its functions, but they were never developed under our observation.

We were marched up, and merged into the body of prisoners, perhaps a thousand of them, and soon recognized several of our friends, whose misfortunes had antedated our own. Amongst them were Captain Lassiter, of the Norfolk and Western Road, who had been taken from his train, and Mr. S. L. Simpson, to whom we soon became indebted for courtesies. During the afternoon the "Rebel" prisoners were marched in a body, which had grown in size during the day, to a piece of woods a few hundred yards distant. The limits of the prisoner's camp were designated, the dead lines drawn, and details of prisoners ordered to bring in fence rails for fires, or temporary shelter; and with the instincts and ingenuity of old soldiers, many had soon fixed themselves in tolerably comfortable quarters. There was also a barn of splendid tobacco near by, of which we were invited—by our enemies—to help ourselves.

The day passed (Sunday) and no rations of any sort were served to the prisoners. My party, now reduced, had dwindled down to three—Doctors Scott, Field, and Claiborne. As we had had a cup of coffee at sunrise, we were better off than most of the prisoners.

Monday forenoon; no rations were issued. Friend Simpson, however, whose place in camp was very near our own, came to us and divided with us some compressed vegetable cake, and showed us how to make a sort of a soup, and gave us a piece of cornbread, for which we gave him grateful thanks, the only return in our power. Late in the afternoon a beef, perhaps more than one, was driven up and shot on the outskirts of the camp, and skinned and flayed on the ground. Just so much of the hot and quivering flesh was dispensed to each mess of the prisoners as our captors could spare, and found convenient, and one member of each mess was sent under guard to get it. We received ours with gladness, broiled a portion of it on sticks before the fire, and having no closets or commissary chests into which to stow the balance, divided it amongst ourselves, and each man placed his part within his cap and slept with it. This was the only safe place we had, and was not surely safe, at that, as Capt. G., of Richmond, who bunked on the ground near us, had both hat and rations stolen by some enterprising and hungry Rebel that night.

The next morning a Yankee soldier, who had been in and out of our camp all day the day before, asking a thousand questions, and making himself a nuisance generally, came to my mess, and singling me out, brought me an invitation from a Dr. Richardson, of New York, to breakfast with him, handing me at the same time a permit to pass the lines and return on my honor. How my Yankee friend discovered whom I was, or to what I was indebted for this mark of distinction, I could never find out. I found Dr. Richardson with some half dozen other officers,—surgeons, quartermasters, etc.,—all about to sit down to a substantial breakfast of broiled pig, bread, and coffee, at an extemporized table under the trees. They all received me courteously, though there was no introduction, and as we sat down the Doctor remarked, "Help yourself, Doctor; your people furnished the menu. We have no rations; your Fitz Lee burned our wagon trains on Sunday, and I don't know when you will get any more." It is unnecessary to add that I made a square meal, and having talked very pleasantly for a few minutes, both sides avoiding subjects which might lead to discussion, I thanked my stranger friend and returned to camp.

This was my last invitation. A portion of beef, just killed, was issued to us every day, without bread. Until Wednesday we did not know that General Lee had surrendered, and then we could learn nothing of the terms. The guards with whom we could speak either knew nothing or did not care to tell. Indeed they were a listless, careless set, who seemed to be attending to their business in a mechanical, perfunctory way, without any especial interest in affairs generally. The prisoners continually jeered and guyed them, and broke the dead line recklessly, without challenge or rebuke, and I think that almost any Confederate could have walked away who wished. Possibly some did. But without money, without friends, and without rations, and knowing nothing of the country or the condition of affairs, it was safer, the most of us supposed, "to bear the ills we had than to fly to others we knew not of."

But on Thursday afternoon a change came. An officer appeared in the camp, and ordered the officers to be enrolled and mustered ready to march. I noticed that the adjutant of the guard, who was making preparation to get us off, wore on the lapel of his coat a Masonic emblem, so as soon as I could get an opportunity I gave him the "sign of distress." He came to me and asked "what he could do for me." I replied by asking "what he was going to do for us." He said that the "officers would be sent to Fort Lafayette." Then I said, "I do not wish to go. I have a family refugeeing somewhere in North Carolina,—a wife and four children,—and I would greatly prefer to go to them." He seemed to think it not unreasonable, and said that "he would do anything for me not inconsistent with his honor as a soldier," and asked upon what plea I could hope to be released. I said that I was a non-combatant, as well as my two friends who stood in line next to me. "Were you the surgeons who were captured with some artillery on last Saturday evening when your men played such havoc with our cavalry?" I told him that we were, but that we had not pulled a lanyard or fired a gun. "Well, he replied, "you were taken with fighting men. You were in bad company and will have to take your chances with them." He came to me again, however, after a little while and told me that all of the men and officers who were captured within so many miles of Appomattox Court House, and within so many hours of the surrender, were entitled to their parole. "If that be so," I said, "then not only are we three surgeons, but there are here more than eighty men of Gracie's Alabama Brigade, with their colonel, who are entitled to it." (These men, I think, had kept up their fire some little time after the surrender, ignorant, of course, of such; but I saw no necessity to add this information.) Calling up the Colonel, a gentleman by the name of Saunders, I think, I put him in communication with the officer of the guard. My adjutant friend then produced pen, ink, and paper, and directed me to make a statement of the case, which he

forwarded immediately to General Meade. In an hour
or two an order came that eighty-four of us, including
Gracie's Brigade, should be sent back to Appomattox
Court House and report to General Bartlett, to be
paroled.

Accordingly we were marched back to Appomattox
Court House, under guard, in the rain and in the dark,
and halted in front of the headquarters of General Bartlett. The General sent for Colonel Saunders and myself, and received us very kindly. After talking with
us a few minutes, he called an orderly, and directed him
to pass us through the pickets, and to direct us where
we would find General Field to receive our paroles.
The orderly did so, and after passing us through the
picket lines, told us to pursue the road before us until
we came to Confederate camps. As far as the "road
before us" was concerned, it had as well been the "road
behind us," for the darkness was Cimmerian, but we
trudged along, sometimes in the road and sometimes
out of it, as far as we could judge. We soon became
separated from our friends of the Alabama brigade, and
I never saw thèm again. I dare say that they spent the
night safely somewhere, and got back home safely some
time.

Dr. Field, and Smith, and I somehow drifted out of
the road, and seeing a light a short way off, went for it,
and found that it shone from the window of quite a
respectable-looking house. We advanced, and knock-
ing at the door, which was opened for a few inches
only, announced our rank, and asked permission to
enter and spend the night. A very curt reply informed
us that the house was already full of soldiers, wounded
and otherwise, and informed us, as one who spake with
authority, that we had better move on. We never
knew whether our ungracious speaker was friend or
foe; but a man who at that time spoke with the tone

which he assumed had doubtless some means of enforcing his orders, and we left without discussing the subject.

A few minutes after leaving the house, and getting well out into the darkness, we lay down to rest; but such a baptism, by pouring, as the clouds gave us, was not made the more saving by taking it on the ground, and we arose and moved on again for several hundred yards, in what direction we knew not, for we had lost our bearings. We discovered also that we had lost our third man, Dr. Smith; but it was useless to attempt to look for him then. Besides, wherever he was, he was in no worse plight than we were, so Dr. Field and I moved on again. We soon fell over one or two mounds of fresh earth, which we instinctively felt to be graves, and nearly stumbled upon the porch of a small house, the door of which we took to be open, for the reason that the darkness was darker in that direction than in any other. I said to Dr. Field, "Let us go in; here at least we can find shelter." It was a weird-looking place, I confess, but I repeated, "Let us go in." My comrade drew back, saying, "That is a dangerous looking place," to which I replied, "That from *you* beats all. The gamest boy and man [I had been his schoolmate and seen him tried] I ever saw, and now for you to talk about being afraid, borders on the ludicrous; besides, what have you got to lose except your life, and what is that worth? Come on." As we entered the door there came to my nostrils that ineffable smell of gore which no man can fail to recognize who has passed through the experiences of four years of a bloody war. Striking a match from a box which I carried in my pocket, sure enough we found ourselves in a field hospital, which had been utilized doubtless only a few days before during the last fight at Appomattox. There were the bloody clothes which had been cut off from the poor wounded fellows, the straw upon which they lay, a table, and even an open Anatomy, from which some surgeon had evidently been refreshing himself during the work of mutilation.

Well, we were at home, and there was no one to dispute our right. We utilized the straw and a broken chair to kindle a fire in the large open fireplace, and lay down to warm and to sleep, but were soon awakened by a large wasp's nest falling upon us. The house, I suppose, had not been inhabited for some time, and the wasps had taken possession and built their nest in the chimney. We were not long in getting up and getting rid of our new enemies, fortunately without a sting, and soon lay down again and slept until morning. We made a breakfast, as soon as we were awakened by the daylight, from some hard tack which Dr. Field had bought from one of our guards the night before, in exchange for a ring. It had been softened somewhat by the night's rain, and though wrapped in an old handkerchief of the Doctor's which had been innocent of the laundry for some days, was enjoyed with a zest real on that occasion, but difficult to understand at this lapse of time.

On coming out from our quarters we found Dr. Smith not far off, who said he had passed the night sitting up under a tree—not for the first time either, as he was an old campaigner. He had discovered the route to our destination. Taking up the trail then, we resumed our tramp. We soon found out that we would have to cross the Appomattox River to reach the camp of General Field, to whom we were ordered to report for the purpose of being paroled. By the terms of the "surrender" the Confederate generals were required to parole the men under their respective commands on paroles which were printed by the Federal authorities on an extemporized press at Appomattox. We were ordered to report to General Field, not that we belonged to his command, but because he was the only officer left of that rank who had not been able to get the printed parole up to that time, on account of some accident to the press.

On reaching the Appomattox River, which was but an insignificant creek when we crossed it the Saturday before, we found it swollen by continuous rains into quite a respectable stream. As there was neither bridge nor ferry, however, we waded in without the formality of undressing. The water did not reach much above the knees, and we felt no inconvenience from our morning bath. On following our route some half mile from the river, we came upon a group of Confederates breaking camp and about to take up the march homeward. Strangely enough, I knew every one of them, and in company with all save one I had commenced my military career four years before, lacking four days. The group consisted of General Mahone and staff, Major J. A. Johnston, Major O. H. P. Corprew, Capt. Samuel Stevens, Capt. Hamilton J. Stone, Capt. John R. Patterson, Quartermaster-Sergeant W. Edward Spotswood, and two orderlies. I only knew one of the latter, a young Kentuckian, by the name of Blakeman, who had gotten himself the soubriquet of "The Bravest of the Brave." As we reached the group, all of whom were well mounted and ready to move off, General Mahone accosted me, "Well, where in h— have you been?" "A cooler place than that," I said; "I am just out of a mud hole." "You look like it," he replied, and I expect that I did. If any old soldier should read these lines who was detained at Appomattox several days after the surrender, long enough to encounter the rain that wept over our defeat, he will bear testimony to the mud, and to the slipperiness of the roads.

During the night before, under the forced march to freedom our Yankee escort had taken mischievous pleasure in hurrying the prisoners, and how often I had fallen, and how often I was ordered "to get up, Johnnie," with a bayonet unpleasantly near my person, I cannot recount. But there was no time to discuss the present circumstances, and I said, "Boys, you are not going to leave me?" Mahone then said, "Did I not tell you not to leave Mahone's Division? Now you see what has come of it." "Yes; but, General, what became of your surgeon, Wood?" "Oh, that fellow got shot." I knew that myself, because I had seen him grievously wounded; and he had asked me to take care of his watch and instruments. But the enemy had been very good to him, had given him his ambulance, or an ambulance and mules, and I told him that he was safer, and would get out of trouble more surely than I, which was true. I heard that he made his way to Fincastle, Virginia, where he lived for many years afterwards.

Mahone then asked me if I was paroled, and that if I were, said he would take me home with him. I told him that I was not, but that with my two friends, and some sixty or eighty of his old Alabama brigade, I had been released, after we had been mustered for Fort Lafayette, and ordered to report to General Field to be paroled. He told me that I would find General Field about a mile down the road, but that I would have to show a blank parole. Captain Patterson produced one from somewhere, and the General, dismounting, bade me take his horse and ride down to General Field's camp, and get him to sign it, promising by the time that I returned he would have some means ready to take me home with him. We tried to find two other blanks for Dr. Field and Dr. Smith, but could not find another.

I lost no time in getting to General Field's headquarters, and as his was the only tent I saw, I had no difficulty in finding him. At the door of the tent was Captain P., of Richmond, an ordnance officer in his command, whom I knew very well, having been a fellow-student of his at the University of Virginia. He bade me get down, and giving my bridle to a soldier, took me into the tent and introduced me to General Field. My reception was anything else than cordial, but I was not prepared for what followed. I told him in as few words as possible that, with two other surgeons, and some sixty or eighty men of an Alabama brigade, I had been released from a prisoner's camp the night before and ordered to report to him to be paroled; that I had been fortunate enough to meet my friend General Mahone, who, giving me a blank parole, and loaning me his horse, had requested me to get his signature to it, as he wished to take me home with him. He heard me through, and then getting up (he was lying down), he went to the door of the tent, and putting aside a blanket that hung over the entrance to it, he said, "Do you see those poor men shivering in the rain, and scattered about in bivouac under those bushes? That is the remains of Field's Division. The Yankee press at the Court House is broken down, and I cannot tell when I can get any paroles, but until those poor men are paroled and sent away, you will remain here." "That is hard upon me, General," I said. "I am sorry for those poor men, but we have all suffered enough to give us some fellow-feeling for each other, and should be glad to have an opportunity of getting any one soldier out of trouble. I have this parole, and only await your signature to get me off, and to enable me to go home." "I shall not do it," he said. "As you please, General," I replied, and touching my cap, bowed myself out, determined to go with Mahone any way, even had I to sign the parole myself. He called me back from the door and said, "Let me see that parole." He took it from my hand, and after reading it, picked up a pen from his table and wrote "C. F., Major-General." That was enough Without awaiting further negotiations, or giving him an opportunity of changing his mind, I was off. But just as I mounted Mahone's horse to return, Capt. P. said to me, "Claiborne, can you get me one of those blank paroles?" I replied, "Captain, there was not one that we could find at Mahone's camp when I left; but if there were any I left two comrades there who would have first choice of them." "That is the way of the world," he said; "you are out of trouble now and are willing to leave an old comrade and collegemate, perishing of hunger and cold, the streams rising behind us, and no means of relief." This was spoken with tears in his voice and with a sadness that I have never been able to dismiss from my memory. Until I looked down from my saddle into the face of that brave man, I never realized what cold and hunger and hopelessness could bring one to. I said, "Do not talk so, P. Get on your horse, and go with me to Mahone, and if one parole can be produced for love or money, you shall have it." He did so, and we rode rapidly back to Mahone's camp; but after searching, no parole could be found, and my friend turned off and rode slowly back into what seemed literally the night of despair.

Drs. Field and Smith, after hearing of my interview with General Field, declined to report to him, and went back to the Court House, getting permission from General Bartlett to go back to Petersburg; riding on the railroad when the trains were running, and walking when the road was obstructed or torn up. I cannot think that the paroles amounted to anything.

General Mahone and his cavalcade, including myself, immediately left, and though we passed many Federals

The Surrender and Events Following 299

before we got well under way to Charlotte Court House, our destined stopping place for that night, no one ever asked to see a parole. Riding all day, just before sunset—cold, hungry, and tired—we came when within a few miles of Charlotte Court House upon a fine old country mansion in a grove of oaks, surrounded by every evidence of luxury and wealth. Turkeys, chickens, and other fowls; sheep, lambs, pigs, etc., roamed about the large lots, making a soldier's mouth water, and a corn crib, almost bursting out with the rich grain, stood in our way as we neared the mansion, evincing the fact that ruthless war had not visited that vicinity at least, and we thought, "What a haven for a tired and hungry Confederate soldier. No doubt but what we shall find comfort and welcome here." General Mahone directed his quartermaster, Major Johnston, to ride forward and ask the owner to allow us to remain all night, and say that we would need two rooms, with fire, supper for our party of seven, with corn and forage for our horses, and pay in gold (I suppose Mahone had some); and besides that our presence might insure safety and protection against stragglers. The Major rode forward, but soon returned, meeting us with evident disappointment, and reported, "General, Mrs. E. owns and lives at this place, and says that we can not stop here; that she does not want any soldiers about her, and that we must move on." The General replied in laconic style and with some impatience, "The Devil! Johnston, I have no doubt that you have made a mess of it. Dr. Claiborne, will you go to Mrs. E. and tell her who we are, and engage for us what we wish." "All right, sir," I said, and started on my mission, fully confident of a graceful and cordial reception.

I rode up, dismounted at the yard gate, tied my horse to the rack (which was at that time a feature of the landscape never omitted from the picture of a planter's home), went into the yard, and was met by a dignified and most respectable negro man, past middle age, and whom I recognized at once as the dining-room servant, gardener, butler, and factotum generally, that illustrated and adorned in those days every old Virginia mansion, and who invariably met the visitor and showed him to the house. This colored gentleman, with the grace and dignity of manner which such servants of a gentleman's house in old Virginia caught from constant contact and association with gentlemen, a character which is now almost extinct and which never can be reproduced, met me and said, "My mistress, Mrs. E., is a widow, sah; receives no company, and asks that you will excuse her." I should have retired at those words, but I had some pride in filling my mission, and I told him that my business was urgent; that times were troublous, and that it would probably be better for his mistress to see me. With an apology for not taking me to the front door, he carried me around to the rear of the house, and just as I was about to go up the steps of a long portico leading into the house, Mrs. E. appeared at the top of the steps, with an acrid voice, indicative of an acerbity of manner which her appearance did not belie, and said, "Do not come up those steps, we want no soldiers here." I apologized in a most polite phrase for my intrusion; said that I had no idea of entering her house without permission, but that General Mahone, with his staff, on his way home from the surrender of Lee's army, tired and cold, was approaching her premises, and begged gracious permission to remain all night; that he would like to have supper for the party, and forage for the horses, and that he would pay cheerfully in gold for everything he had, besides protecting her premises, which were exposed to the depredations of stragglers. "No, no," she said, "you cannot stop here."

The Surrender and Events Following 301

I was as tired as a man could well be, and I did not feel like going any farther, and thought I would try the patriotic and sentimental, so I said, "Madam, do you seriously propose to deny the rights of hospitality in an old Virginia home to one of the most famous generals and his staff; men who for four long years have fought your battles, and placed themselves as a living wall between yourself and the Northern vandals who have come down to seize your property and slay your people?" "I do," was her brief and unmistakable reply; "I don't know you, or General Mahone, nor ever heard of either of you before, and I want you to leave." "Never heard of either of us before!" What is fame? I returned to the General somewhat crestfallen, I confess, but Johnston was the only man who enjoyed my discomfiture.*

General Mahone remarked that it would be serving her right to encamp on her lawn, take what we wanted, and pay for nothing; but that it would be a bad example for us to set, especially in such lawless times, and that we must go on to Charlotte Court House, four miles. It was the longest four miles that ever I rode, and we were all pretty well fagged-out by the time we reached there. We were too many in our party to foist ourselves upon one house, and so we separated into two sections. General Mahone, Major Johnston, Capt. Patterson, and myself going to Mr. Selden's, formerly of Westover, on the James River, but who had taken his family to Charlotte Court House soon after the war commenced, as it was not believed that the Yankees would find that delectable village. The faith of the public was proven wise. For the same reason General Mahone had sent his family to refugee in

---

*I must do Virginia, and this Virginia woman, the justice to say that I heard afterwards that she was eccentric, almost to the degree of irresponsibility.

Clarksville, Virginia. It was not believed that any
Yankee would reach that riparian city, and one never
did, during the war. On going to Mr. Selden's we
found him not at home, but Mrs. Selden was, and received us as only a patriotic Virginia woman could receive a soldier; gave us a supper of hot rolls, broiled
chicken, and coffee—and such rolls, such chicken, and
such coffee! The savor of that supper has never died
away from my senses. After supper Mrs. Selden's
daughters, and one or two other young ladies, received
us in the parlor; and Captain Patterson introduced me
as Dr. Claiborne, of Petersburg, "the glass of fashion
and the mould of form." As I had not washed my face
and hands, or combed my head, or made my toilet for
ten days, and was muddy to my blinkers, I felt that I
was being trifled with, but I made my best obeisance,
took a proffered chair and distinguished myself by immediately going to sleep in their presence. They were
considerate enough to ask us to our rooms at an early
hour.

And now a very serious question arose which I feared
might cause some unpleasantness. There were two
beds in the room for us four. Mahone and I were
bunked together. I had not had the opportunity of
taking off my long cavalry boots for thirteen days, and
during that time they had been so often wet and dried
that they were literally moulded to my feet, and it
seemed almost impossible to remove them without cutting them off. And to have sacrificed a pair of boots
at that time without any earthly prospects of getting
another pair, was just a little less of folly than the sacrifice of the feet themselves. General Mahone, and then
my other comrades, refused to sleep with me with my
boots on, to say nothing of the scandalous impropriety
of occupying one of Mrs. Selden's beds in such foot
gear. A negro servant was summoned and the situa-

tion explained to him, and he guaranteed relief. After dragging me over the room several times, encouraged by the cheers of my companions, who saw more fun in the operation than I did, he finally succeeded in getting them off, and I slept with Mahone, for the first time and the last time in my life. The next morning Mrs. Selden sent us in a box of paper collars, the first I had ever seen; and with our faces washed, hair combed, clothes brushed, and collars on, we made quite a decent appearance. After breakfast, taking leave of our kind hostess, and gathering our little party together, we made a start on another day's journey.

Mahone, Corprew, Blakeman and I directed our course to Clarksville, Virginia, whilst others of the party turned their steps toward Petersburg. We reached Clarksville about dark, had a warm reception from Mrs. Mahone, as may well be imagined, and after a nice hot supper, went to bed—I, for one, more dead than alive. I had not only endured all the fatigue, exposure, and peril of the retreat, but my Rosinante, which I had ridden rapidly for two long days, was the roughest-riding animals which I had ever backed. It was equal to riding on a wooden horse. This was Saturday night, following the surrender, and it seemed to me that the events of a life time had been crowded into that short week. It was almost impossible to realize the changes that I had witnessed in that time; and the greatest marvel was seeing General Mahone sitting down in peace, playing with his children—the soldier whom one week before I had left at the head of his ragged veterans in fierce and hopeless fight. Sunday morning I was too sick to get up, but with the kindly ministrations of Mrs. Mahone, I was on my feet Monday morning, and Blakeman and I, the last paladins of our little group that left Appomattox together, about midday parted, he taking to the left to seek the home of an aunt in Mecklenburg County, Virginia, and I the road to the right leading in the direction of Louisburg, North Carolina, where my wife and children had been refugeeing during the most of the war. About night I reached Ridgeway, North Carolina, and found hospitable accommodations at the home of Dr. J., an old friend and college-mate.

The next morning I took the road to Louisburg, North Carolina, about twenty-five miles distant. During the day I met many of Lee's old soldiers, trudging their weary way homewards to different portions of the State—also several very fine teams belonging to the quartermaster's department, which had been out for weeks foraging, but whose drivers seemed to be at sea as to what they should do or where they should go. One man, a quartermaster's sergeant, had a splendid team of four mules, and said he had been for two weeks foraging and was just ready to go back to the army when the news of Lee's surrender came to him. He begged me to take the wagon and team and give him a receipt, and said he was going to leave them that day or the next with anybody who would take them, and make his way home afoot the best that he could. He lived in one of the far Southern States. Of course I had no more right to the team than he, and no more use for it, and I declined. About midday I came to a camp which had undoubtedly been left only a few hours, maybe the night before, and amongst the odds and ends which had been abandoned was a bolt of fine imported jeans. This was left by accident, I presume, but I picked it up and tied it behind my saddle. From this was fabricated the only underclothing that I had for weeks, all of my clothes having been burned or lost during the retreat to Appomattox. About six o'clock in the afternoon I reached Louisburg, and rode up to the house where I had sent my wife and children two years before, and soon had my loved ones in my arms. Four years before, almost to a day, I had taken them in my arms at Petersburg, my home, and giving them a last kiss and "God bless you," had gone out with my comrades and compatriots to the war, with brilliant uniforms and flying banners; with heart full of hope, if full of sorrow; with no fear of defeat, and no reckoning but that we should save to them, if not to ourselves, our fair Southern land—a heritage the best that Heaven ever gave. And now alone, ragged, unaccompanied by one single comrade; unheralded, without country, without home, without bread, without faith, I was before them, even a stranger to my little children! I leave the picture. Let some other finish it. The war was over—the war with men; but not over with that skulking crew of cowards and carpet-baggers which followed in its wake, nor with that foul flock of harpies who, hovering over the little left for starving women and children, polluted it with their noisome stench.

The hardships and exposure of the two weeks past and the hopelessness of the future brought on an attack of sickness, and I was detained for nearly a month at the home of the gentleman with whom I had boarded my family for two years. I had fortunately paid their board in kind, as it was termed then—that is, in bacon and flour—to about the middle of June; but as soon as I was able I went to Raleigh, seeking some opportunity of getting back to Petersburg and of further providing for my family. On reaching Raleigh I found an old friend and fellow-townsman, Mr. Thomas Branch, who had been refugeeing with his family in that city for a year or more. He took me to his hospitable house, where with him and his estimable wife I found good cheer. His house was filled with strangers, representatives of both armies—but there was no ripple of trouble between us. One of my room-mates was the Federal General Ames, of Massachusetts, who had distinguished himself at the taking of the forts below Wilmington. Like another Massachusetts General, Bartlett, he was especially kind and generous. A large body of Federal troops were quartered in Raleigh at the same time, but they, too, seemed especially quiet, and considerate of the feelings of the citizens. Having no other clothes, I was compelled to wear my uniform, and I never passed a Federal sentinel that he did not face about and present arms—a considerate attention which I entirely appreciated.

I told Mr. Branch that I was seeking some means of getting home to Petersburg, and taking my family there. He handed fifty dollars in gold to one of his younger sons, and bade him go to some place in the city and exchange it for greenbacks. He turned the proceeds over to me, which was the first dollar of Federal currency I ever had. Before I could get away from Louisburg, the place where my family had been refugeeing, a corps of the Federal Army passed through the town en route to Washington, to which place the whole army had been ordered to rendezvous for a grand review before they were disbanded or mustered out. They made a halt, or a part of them, several days in Louisburg, and a General Heth and his staff encamped in the yard of the gentleman's house at which we were staying. They held themselves apart from the inmates of the house, and placed a safeguard in charge of it. He was a poor miserable young boy, in feeble health, who, if he was armed, did not know where his gun was for half the time, and took great pleasure in playing with my children, insisting on dividing with them whatever he could get of anything good which would tempt them, and they were not very fastidious. I do not think that they had seen a particle of confectionery for more than two years. The children of any house were fortunate at that day to get enough of the plainest food.

A disagreeable incident occurred, however, before the Federal troops moved on; and one which threatened to get us into trouble. There were several ladies staying in the house, and as was usual these took no pains to appear before the soldiers or officers, or to conciliate them when compelled to be in their presence. On the contrary, they did not hesitate to show by word and manner more than a *mild* dislike. At the same time there was staying in the house a clergyman, a man of distinction in his calling, who had been quite noted, before the enemy came, for blatant abuse of the "Yankee," even in a manner not becoming a preacher of peace and righteousness. But when brought face to face with the verities of the present situation his views most suddenly and radically changed. One morning after breakfast, in the parlor with several ladies, he made himself very offensive to them, telling them that by such fools as they the whole trouble had been brought on; and that they would deserve no better than any indignity which the soldiers chose to inflict upon them. I happened to enter the room just as he was delivering himself of his pastoral talk, and seeing my wife amongst the ladies, requested her to withdraw, which she did, followed by the rest of them. I then closed the door and opened upon my clerical companion in language, I fear, even less chaste, and more decidedly expressive, than his reverence had indulged in; ending with a threat that if he opened his lips I would smash him and pitch him out of the window down upon his Yankee friends, who were just under it. Seeing that he was a brawny Irishman of nearly twice my weight, this was merely a *brutum fulmen*, and it was well for me perhaps that he did not give me an occasion to attempt to put my threat in execution. The proprietor of the house coming in at the time, I apologized for "making a fuss in his parlor"; but I had only time to speak a few words when General Heth, to whom his reverence had immediately reported me, sent an orderly to invite me to call at his tent. As it was my first invitation to headquarters, and partook, moreover, somewhat of the character of an order, I obeyed promptly. The General inquired what the trouble was about, and I gave him, candidly, the whole story. He only replied that he had no doubt but that my provocation was great, but suggested not very mildly himself, "that I have no further difficulty." The troops and my clerical friend both left the next day, and "there was no further difficulty."

In a few days I received a message from Mr. Branch to join him at Franklinton, the station for Louisburg at that time, and that we could get as far as Ridgeway on the Raleigh and Gaston road, and then he would have a carriage which would take us across the country to Petersburg, or rather to Blacks and Whites, now Blackstone, on the Norfolk and Western road, from which point the road was open to Petersburg. On getting to Ridgeway we found the carriage to be a wagon and two horses, and a riding-horse awaiting us. With Mr. Branch was one of his younger sons, I have forgotten which one; Mr. David Lyon, of this city, and the colored driver. In this company I began my pilgrimage home, or to the place which I called home some four years before, well knowing that there was no home left me; but with a brave heart to build me another one there or somewhere, and to gather again under one roof my loved ones driven away by the cruel fortunes of war.

On the second night of our transit across the country we reached a Mr. Haskins's, in Lunenburg County, and received a generous welcome. As this was only

The Surrender and Events Following 309

some twelve or fifteen miles distant from my father's, in the County of Brunswick, Mr. Branch kindly loaned me his riding-horse the following day, and I left my fellow voyagers, they going on to Blackstone and I to Roslin, the residence of my father. As my father had not seen me in many months, and as he had not heard from me since the close of the war and knew nothing of my fate, the joyous surprise with which he received me may be imagined, perhaps, but not described. Of his other son, who was an assistant surgeon in the navy, he had heard nothing, and knew nothing until he turned up as suddenly and unexpectedly in the month of July following. Only a few mails had been reestablished, and communication between points out of the regular routes was slow and uncertain.

After spending a few days with my father, and witnessing the finale of the old regime, when he called his slaves together and announced to them that they were free—free to remain with him as hired servants or to seek their fortunes elsewhere, I mounted Mr. Branch's horse, and riding over to Blackstone left him with Mr. Richard Irby, and took the first train for Petersburg. On the train, which was many hours late,—a tardiness, I may mention, which seems to have characterized the train from the west on the N. & W. road even to this day,—I found several hundred Yankee soldiers making their way North. The coaches and open cars were crowded, and many of the soldiers were noisy, and offensive in manner to the few Confederates who happened to be passengers. Mr. Williams T. Davis, of this city, and Major Boggs, of the Confederate artillery, were amongst the Confederates near me. One little Yankee lieutenant made himself conspicuously offensive, especially to Major Boggs. The Major had been a Methodist circuit rider before the war in the Virginia Conference, and though not a Southern man had

doffed the black for the garb of gray, and as a major of
artillery had given four years of hard fighting for the
cause of the Confederacy. As he had not yet had opportunity of putting off the gray, he still retained the
spirit militant, and arose to administer to the youth a
punishment not prescribed by army regulations. But
several of us interfered, and with the help of some Federal officers of high rank, declared peace. We were in
too decided a minority for any other mode of settlement.

CHAPTER VI

EVENTS FOLLOWING THE WAR.

My Dog Again—I Am Warned to Leave Petersburg—Make a Purchase and Start for Louisburg, N. C.—Back Again and to Work—The Condition of the South Before the War An Anomaly of Content and Happiness—The Military Government—The Carpet-Bag Government and Its Curse—Opinions of Some Eminent Northerners on the Reconstruction Period—Will History Reproduce Itself in the Philippines—The Evidence of Robbery.

On reaching Petersburg the first *person* that met me was Jack, my Scotch terrier, who had deserted during the retreat from Petersburg, and whom I had given up for lost. His expressions of joy in his mute language were pitifully effusive, and for the few days during which I remained in the city he could not be induced to leave me for a minute. Whether repentance for forsaking me, or fear of falling into other and less gracious company again, actuated him, I cannot tell; but he always had a wonderful amount of human nature mingled with his canine character. I went to the home of my brother-in-law, Colonel A. C. Butts, who was living on Lawrence Street at that time in the house now occupied by Mr. Alexander Wilson, and asked for quarters, which were cheerfully granted me. I had only been there a short time when I was waited on by one of my old servants, the mother of Romulus, who was captured during the retreat. She begged me to leave the city at once, saying that several Federal soldiers had been to her house repeatedly, and to the houses of other of my servants, looking for me, and that they would murder me if they could find me. I paid but little attention to what she said, thinking that the Yankees were only playing on her fears. But the next day a lady sent for me who had been thrown in company with the Federal troops a good deal, having had friends amongst them, and she begged me to leave as soon as possible; and not only that, but begged me to go to General Cadmus Wilcox, who she said was staying at Mrs. Robert Dunlop's, on Franklin Street, and to get him away. She vouchsafed the information, moreover, that we had been selected by the soldiers of a certain Northern regiment to be shot in revenge for the death of their colonel, whom they avowed had been bushwhacked and killed somewhere near Richmond since the surrender of Lee. She stated this with a minuteness of detail and with an array of evidence which led me to believe that there was some truth in it. I went to Mrs. Dunlop's, but General Wilcox had left the city; whether on account of anything he had heard of this matter, I know not. I told my lady friend that I would be glad to go if it were at all practicable, but that I had nowhere to go and no money to go with. It was my intention to go to North Carolina and take my family to my father's in Brunswick County, Virginia, until I could get to work again at my profession.

Going out the next morning, I met on the street a friend who had just bought a pair of horses and an ambulance, all in good condition, from a Federal sutler; and, telling him my story, asked him to let me have them. I told him very candidly that I had no money, but that I should have some as soon as I could get to work, and he generously turned the team over to me, and took my note for the amount of the purchase. As it was impossible for me to get out of the city that day, I went to the Federal Provost Marshal, whose office was at the Petersburg Railroad depot, and Colonel Potts, the ticket agent, who it seems had made a friend of him, introduced me and vouchsafed for my

Events Following the War   313

character I recounted the peculiar circumstances of my case, and told the Provost Marshal that I was getting ready to leave the city and go in search of my family in North Carolina, ,and that in view of the general condition of affairs I thought that I might be allowed to arm myself. He readily consented, and gave me written authority to procure arms and to use them in defense of myself if necessary. I have that paper now —the most remarkable paper, I imagine, ever given by a provost marshal to a paroled prisoner signed "———, Lieut. Colonel, ——— Artillery." Of course, had I been attacked it would have proven of but little avail, except to enable me to sell my life dearly, and to carry an enemy or two with me on my last campaign.

During the day I found one of my old servants, George Washington, and with him as driver, and Jack as passenger, we made an early start the next morning for Louisburg, North Carolina, where I had left my family. On the evening of the first day of our travel we reached my father's, who insisted on adding to my retinue his carriage and driver, and my bringing my family to his house and leaving them there until I could get a foothold again in Petersburg. This generous offer was gratefully accepted. As he had never been plundered, or his house visited, except twice by Federal raiders, who were hurriedly driven off by pursuit of our cavalry, he had suffered but little, and not a slave had left him. He had no money, as no one in the country had any; but food for man and beast was abundant, and the crops were luxuriant, as if sent by Providence to supply our wants in such times of need. We made the trip to Louisburg and back without incident, in less than a week, bringing my wife and four children—the oldest only nine years old. The children enjoyed the travel through the country greatly, and I think were disappointed when they reached their grandfather's and found that their wanderings were over. I left them with their grandfather and his wife, my step-mother, an excellent woman, who made for them a happy home until I had accumulated enough to send for them to come to me.

On reaching Petersburg my lady friend informed me that the regiment to which the soldiers belonged who had threatened my life, had left for the North and that the coast was clear. I proceeded to resume "work at the old stand," though not at the old house—that had gone into other hands; and opened an office in conjunction with Dr. J. J. Thweatt, and old friend and kinsman. Declining the many invitations to share the scant rations of my friends, I rented a room near our office for one dollar a week, paid a young lady in the house a dollar a week to take care of it, and bought me some tea, and crackers, and cheese. The same lady who took care of my room, made my tea, and for two weeks set out my humble menu. At the end of that time, gradually getting a little money from my practice, I took the liberty of indulging myself in a little dinner at some one of the many cheap restaurants with which the city was crowded, to catch the hundreds of soldiers and stragglers and sight-seers that abounded on the streets. But my breakfast and supper were of the same frugal provision. At the end of a month Dr. Thweatt and I thought we would combine, and constituting the office servant as cook, indulge ourselves in a more generous fare. In less than a month, however, we found that our joint finances would not justify two liberal meals a day, so we returned to our economies.

In the meantime, Mr. James B. Jones, of Chesterfield, an old friend of mine, and one of God's noblemen, seeing me practising medicine on foot, sent me his riding-horse and forage enough with him to keep him a month. With better opportunities of getting about, and with the return of the refugees who had been scattered through the country, and the free circulation of greenbacks by strangers, at the end of the month I bought me a horse for seventy-five dollars and returned my friend's. It was as late as October before I collected greenbacks enough to justify my bringing my family home. Then I rented two rooms for fifty dollars apiece from Mrs. Freeman, who owned and occupied the house now owned and occupied by Mr. Henry Roper, and which before its mutilation by some modern reformer was a beautiful and comfortable mansion. With Mrs. Freeman and her daughter, now Mrs. Benjamin Nash, of Richmond, we spent a happy winter, and formed ties of friendship which have only loosened as death has set his seal upon one or another of that little group. Indeed, there were many, many happy families that winter—the winter of 1865-'66. It is true that the most of us were poor, but who cared for the pinch of poverty when loving ones, regathered to homes from which they had been so long and so rudely driven, met heart to heart, and recounted the perils and privations which, now that they were over, had but drawn them closer in love's embrace. And though the city was filled with Federal soldiers, they were soldiers whom we had met in battle; men whom we had fought in war, and with whom we made up in peace; men whose respect we commanded, and who commanded our respect.

The bummers and bounty jumpers, the politicians and their measly crew of satellites, the little satraps from the kitchens and chambers of Washington had not been brought out and loosed upon us. And when the last body of Federal troops was ordered away, a regiment of regulars under a Colonel Randolph, who had been garrisoned at the Fair Grounds, now West End Park, I saw them go with unfeigned regret, and surprised some of my friends by saying to them that military rule was infinitely better for us than the hybrid combination of parasite and puppy which would surely follow. In a very short time they had gathered human testimony sufficient to convince them of this.

The real condition of the country which the Confederate soldier left when he left his home for the war was an anomaly of content and happiness, both for the individual and the masses. There were marked distinctions in society founded upon the patriachal regime, the result of slavery, where estates in land and negroes were handed down from father to son, and the families maintained for generations culture and command, which the peculiar institution had not only engendered, but made practicable and persistent. The gentlemen of the higher classes with gracious dignity maintained the noblesse oblige, and his humble neighbor accorded him the respect and reverence that such generous consideration awakened. The rich and the poor met together at the churches, on the Court-House green, at the political speaking, at the general musters—citizens all of one proud country, without arrogance on the one part or envy on the other. The slave only was the serf and the inferior, and he was proud of the shackles which his rich master had fastened upon him. And when the trumpet sounded the alarm of war all classes, every citizen, put down his calling, his trade, his profession without regard to rank, acknowledging a brotherhood that was only known in our Southern land, and rushed to the front, each as ready to give his life, as well for the rich man's mansion as for the poor man's hut. And even the poor slave begged to follow his master, and did follow him, administering, without pay, to his comfort on the weary march or in the chilly bivouac, caring for him when cut down in the blaze of battle; or left at home guarding the mistress and children with sleepless

Events Following the War 317

watch, and providing by daily labor for their daily sustenance.

Can any other country or nation show such an Arcadian life amongst its people? We of the South knew none of the fanatical teachings of our bigoted brethren of the North. Capital did not seek to throttle labor, labor did not strike for protection. There was no socialist stirring up strife with his vain and morbid dissenters; the anarchist did not stand with pistol and stiletto to stab any representative of honest government in his way. We did not have a church or a schoolhouse on every hill, but when we planted a church it did not preach heresy; when we built a school-house it did not teach a law higher than the "Constitution." Of a population of five million of whites, six hundred and twenty-five thousand had entered the Confederate Army, and these were the flower of Southern manhood; and of these, two hundred thousand had lost their lives, leaving in many instances helpless and dependent families. Many thousands had been maimed and were incapable of labor. Desolation was left in the wake of the Federal Army. One general, Sherman, had boasted that he left a swath miles wide in the course of his army, where nothing was left but the chimneys of the homes he had burned; and another general, Sheridan, declared that a crow flying over the Valley of Virginia would have to carry his rations with him. Everywhere in the South that a Federal soldier had put his foot,—and few places were so sacred or so distant from the highway that they were not polluted with his presence,—everywhere agricultural implements were broken up, mills burned, stock killed or driven off, fences and provisions destroyed. Indeed, nothing was left but the land, debts, and taxes, and not a dollar of currency to pay debts or taxes. Banks, banking institutions, notes, bonds had all been based upon the credit of the Confederacy—

and were all utterly worthless and insolvent. Worse than all that, the people of the late Confederacy were required to assume their full share of the debt of three billion of dollars expended in their subjugation, and to pay proportionately their portion of the millions of dollars of pensions to the soldiers who had plundered them for years. No conditions amongst civilized nations so pitiable and so damnable had ever arisen—not even in Prussia, at the end of her seven years' war, nor France at the end of any of her revolutions; only Poland, perhaps, when her nationality was absorbed by her cormorant tyrants, and when it was written, "Peace reigns in Warsaw." Peace also reigned in the Southern Confederacy, but it was a peace which will forever pass all understanding except by those who participated in its immediate blessings. When the remnants of the scattered and defeated army, disbanded and paroled, reached their respective homes,—those who were fortunate enough to find their homes left to them,—there was great joy, of course, and there was also merrymaking, and even marrying and giving in marriage, under circumstances seemingly very inauspicious to parties assuming such responsibilities. But privations and hardships of four long years of war had taught the sturdy survivors lessons of courage, and patience, and self-denial; and men who had faced so many dangers in the field, and women who had encountered so much trouble at home, did not stop to count the cost of the minor evils which a coming family might entail. Indeed, it has been said that "Cupid always follows in the receding steps of Mars."

As for the military government which was set up immediately after the war in the subdued States, it gave us peace and protection, as far as we had anything to protect; and as a rule dispensed equal justice to all.* It was infinitely preferable to the civic-military despotism created by congressional action according to the recommendation of the infamous "Committee of Fifteen" appointed with the specific and dastardly object of further humiliation of the Southern people, of disfranchising the white man, and of elevating the late slave over the head of his master. This committee of twelve Republicans and three Democrats Mr. Blair said "would have in its keeping in an especial degree the fortunes of the Republican Party." The northern Democrats, and some conservative Republicans, as Mr. Raymond, of New York, and even Mr. Seward, who said that "It is a plan not for reconstruction but for indefinite delay," opposed the report of this committee. But the majority of the Republican Party in Congress, ever bitter, relentless, and filled with malice toward an enemy which they had not met personally, and whose prowess had only fired their resentment instead of evoking their admiration, adopted its plans, and the reign of terror, the reign of the carpet-bagger, the scalawag, and the negro—the latter the best of the three—was inaugurated.

The military government which in this city had preceded the installation of the carpet bag and scalawag—civic-military, that is, civil by pretense, with the military behind it—was especially clean and just. The regiment, which remained for about two years, was encamped at the Fair Grounds, now West End Park, and was commanded by a Colonel Randolph, before spoken of, a gentleman and a soldier, who maintained order and dispensed justice "without fear, favor, or affection." The Federal troops, the returned soldiers of the Union,

---

*See an article by Hon. Hillary Herbert in *Atlanta Monthly*, February, 1867.

and the returned soldiers of the Confederacy met and hobnobbed in the most fraternal way, as men who had tried each other's steel. Indeed, some of our young men, returned soldiers, without means, without work, and without education, which the exigencies of war had prevented them from acquiring, having spent their young manhood in the field, joined the ranks of the Federal army when it left, and recommenced life as professional soldiers, drawing their sword only for pay and for hope of promotion.

I saw the last file of these Federal troops leave the city with regret, and when I expressed my regret to a friend, he seemed surprised, and said that he could not understand my position. I asked him to await events and watch the way from Washington. In a few days a new king carpet-bagger, to represent the civil law, and Adjutant Buttons, to represent the military, appeared. He lived to see and feel this change of dynasty, and there came down not one king, but a king for nearly every county and city of the commonwealth—and with every king an adjutant. The former, light of baggage, had one carpet bag, hence his name; but that was filled with provisos, and writs, and orders. Lieutenant Buttons was his executive officer; and a scalawag, a low fellow to the manor born, and bought with promise of spoil, was his suborned witness. These men were called sometimes and in some places "The Bureau," sometimes the "Freedman's Bureau." Even amongst these the military did occasionally contain a gentleman who, in the fear of God and without the fear of men, did defend the right and establish justice; but he was few, and not being appointed for the purpose aforesaid, was usually recalled at an early day. But no such saving example of truth, of honor, or of manhood ever appeared to my knowledge to break the monotony of the villainy which characterized carpet-baggers. The military appointee was generally a little lieutenant satrap, with shoulder straps, whose fine clothes proclaimed him innocent of the smoke of battle, and who, "dressed in a little brief authority, showed such fantastic tricks before high heaven as made the angels weep." These unfledged younglings, worthy of the cesspools from which they were taken, were usually the sons of sires holding high places in political office, and were sent down to set aside our honorable courts, to supplant the able and peerless judiciary which had construed our laws, and constituted themselves as judges, counsel, and jury to administer so-called justice in the land. As might have been expected, as was expected, and as was intended, trouble soon arose of a gravity commensurate with such untoward and intolerable conditions.

The first blow fell upon labor. The ex-slave early commenced to recover from the daze of freedom suddenly thrust upon him, and knowing and trusting the old master, had accepted service under him for stipulated wages and was helping to turn over the soil for the needed crops and to renovate the estates, broken and wasted by four years of war. He was at once informed that the "Nunion Burer" was sent for his protection, admonition, and instruction, and to that he should report for orders. He promptly and piously reported. There he was informed that it was not compatible with the character of a freeman to work for another man, especially if that other man was a white man. He was also told that the lands of his former master would soon be taken by the "Nunion" men and divided amongst his slaves, and that each negro would receive a mule and forty acres of land, and that he would have opportunity of working for himself alone. He believed and accepted this statement and promise in all of its fulness. And thus, not only was the ex-master stripped of his needed help in the time of his greatest necessity, but the old trusting and kindly relations between the races were broken and the way opened for future trouble and disturbance. No program for the production of trouble could have been better adapted to that purpose. The negro understood that he was the "Ward of the Nation"—the "Boss of the Burer" had told him so. As ward he had to be taken care of until he could come to his estate of forty acres of land and a mule. In the meantime, nothing was left to do in the daytime but to loaf, especially if the headquarters of the "Burer" happened to be at some little village or courthouse. And nothing could have so well suited him except the nightly office left him—to roam. This covered all the ground of his capabilities and desires; and in roaming of course he frequently over-reached upon his neighbor's property and invaded his neighbor's preserves, his pig-pen, his corn-house, or his chicken-house, and his neighbor would catch him in flagrant detection and would inflict upon him punishment both just and appropriate. And it was always a white neighbor, and for this his white neighbor was always reported at headquarters—headquarters being, in scalawag and carpet-bag lingo, the place where the "Nunion Bosses" held court. And then followed a travesty of justice which no pen or pencil could describe or portray.

Mr. Thomas Nelson Page has published a book called "Red Rock," purporting to be a novel, but an overtrue story, in which he has essayed to give some account of the assizes in one of these civic-military districts. He has failed to exaggerate, if it were his purpose to do so, the pollution, the corruption, the crime, the darkness of the deviltry which characterized the proceedings of these judicial sessions. At the mouths of their witnesses, suborned or otherwise, strife and contention were continuously stirred and promoted. And the more quiet, conservative, and respectable the citizen, the more it was their pleasure to persecute and humble him; and if he had any means, to pluck him, and to prosecute and fine and imprison him, under false charges of this pestiferous crew of cormorants, until many a man sorrowed that he had not laid down his life, instead of his musket, at Appomattox.

These were the days of Reconstruction, so called, in comparison with which the bloody days of battle were as pastime; and I know of no man now, whatever his party affiliation, who does not look back upon them with combined horror and indignation. And I hold now that the greatest achievement of the Southern soldier was not that, for four years, he faced death at such odds in an hundred fights, and ever held his own with foemen worthy of his steel, but that as a citizen, and unarmed, he had the fortitude to endure and to live down the humiliation of those bitter days, and that now he only holds them in his memory as a horrid hell-dream of the unreal.

The Hon. S. S. Cox, of New York, says "that no people ever suffered such humiliation and degradation as was suffered by the South from the rule of the carpetbagger. * * * The thesaurus of our English tongue may do justice to the plagues of Egypt, but here were plagues tenfold more numerous and worse." His language is vigorous and opulent, especially in invectives, but he confesses his utter inability to do justice to the subject, and he calls upon the Hon. Judge Jeremiah Black, one of the most eminent jurists of this country, "to eke out or wreak out his own *feebleness* of expression in describing the horde that flew down upon the South at the close of the war." Judge Black says:

These were called carpet-baggers, not because the word was descriptive or euphonious, but because they have no other name by which they are known amongst the children of men. They were unprincipled adventurers who sought their fortunes in the South by plundering the disarmed and defenseless people; some of them were the dregs of the Federal army, the meanest of the camp followers; many were fugitives from northern justice; the best of them were men who went down after peace, ready for any deed of shame that was safe or profitable. These, combining with a few treacherous scalawags and some leading negroes to serve as decoys for the rest, and backed by the power of the Federal Government, became the strongest body of thieves that ever pillaged a people. They swarmed all over the Southern States, from the Potomac to the Gulf, and settled in hordes, not with any intent to remain there, but merely to feed on the substance of a prostrate and defenceless people. They took whatever came within their reach. * * *

By force or fraud they controlled or prevented elections. They returned sixty of themselves to our Congress, and ten or twelve of the most ignorant and venal amongst them were at the same time thrust into the Senate. The pretended representative was always to vote for any measure that would oppress or enslave his so-called constituents; his hostility was unconcealed and he lost no opportunity to do them injury.

And quoting from Judge Black again in his essay on the Electoral Commission, the "Great Fraud of 1876," he said:

The greediest Roman Proconsuls left something to the Provinces which they had wasted, the Norman did not strip the Saxon quite to the skin, the Puritans under Cromwell did not utterly desolate Ireland; their rapacity was confined to visible things which they could handle and use; they could not take what did not exist. But the carpet-bagger had an invention unknown to these old-fashioned robbers, which increased his stealing power as much as the steam engine adds to the mechanical force of mere natural muscles. He made negotiable bonds of the State, signed and sealed them according to forms of law, sold them and converted the proceeds to his own use, and then "defied justice to go beyond the returns." By this device his felonious fingers were made long enough to reach the products of posterity. He laid his lien on property not yet created; he anticipated the labor of coming ages, and appropriated the fruits of it in advance; he coined the industry of future generations into cash, and snatched the inheritance from children whose fathers were unborn. Projecting his cheat forward by this contrivance, and operating laterally at the same time, he gathered an amount of plunder which no country in the world would have yielded to Goth or vandal.

This arraignment of the representatives of the Federal Government sent down upon the South after the close of the war, and the disarming of the gallant men whose heroism for four long years had commanded the wonder of the world, was not written by one of them nor prompted by partisan feeling, begot of the bitterness of oppression which they had been robbed of the power to resist; but it was the outpouring of a patriotic spirit in some noblemen of the North who dared to speak, and who defied the despots that, under the guise of the "powers that be ordained of God," hid the cloven foot of another party, and administered, in advance, the laws of another "kingdom, not of this world," but "where Satan sat enthroned."

But it may be asked, Why reproduce these bitter records? Why dig up from the dirt and expose to the light of day deeds of deviltry which the sun blushed to witness when they were born, and which Time, all-healing Time, with mantle of charity seeks to cover over with hopeful promise of a halcyon day when "might shall no more make right?" Ah! why write history at all? Is there nothing in the lives of the vicious and corrupt which the children of the generations following should be taught to shun? Is there nothing in the career and conduct of the brave and the virtuous which posterity should be taught to honor and emulate? Shall Nero and Caligula, shall Cato and Aristides, live alike in history, models for the young to imitate, examples for the young to follow? Does history never reproduce itself? Does the light which illumines the wake of the past project no shadows that teach the lesson of a sleepless lookout? Some wise men, even of to-day, think they see signals of danger in the political sky, warning of breakers ahead. From our new possessions of a people bought against their will and governed without reference to their wishes, and without regard to the teachings of the founders of this Republic that the genius of the Constitution demanded and guaranteed the consent of the governed, a wail of oppression and of cruelties has reached us even over seven thousand miles of sea, drowning the lesson of human liberty which for more than a century we have taught to every man who sought the aegis of our flag!

Let us refer to the Congressional Record. In the Senate of the United States, April 26, 1902, Mr. Carmack, resuming his speeech on the "Philippine Government Bill," said:

> By the terms of the pending bill, the islands were for the Filipinos as the pasture is for the sheep—they live and browse there in order to raise wool for others to wear, and mutton for others to eat.
>
> If the carpet-bag government you propose to establish in the Philippines is not a thousand times better than that which you established in your own country after the Civil War, the Lord God have mercy upon the people of those islands."

He then referred to the cabled reports from Manila that General Smith had acknowledged that he had given orders to make Samar a howling wilderness, and to kill all over ten years of age, as horrible beyond description. The program was to practise unheard of barbarities in the slaughter of the inhabitants, and to have the torch complete the work of slaughter. When the land is without a home and the country without a people, then the word pacified will be written upon the tombstone of the province of Samar.

It is now known that one hundred thousand people have perished in a single province in which there were only three hundred thousand, and yet the people of the United States knew nothing of this until recently. And what was that for? That a few rapscallions and carpet-baggers might have unlimited license to thieve and plunder! No wonder that the people are crying for their old masters from Spain! Senator Hoar, of Massachusetts, and General Miles, the ex-Commander-in-Chief of the Armies of the United States, neither one of whom can be accused of the love of the South or of the taint of the "sleeping treason of the Southron," have spoken in plainer words, if words can be made plainer, of the cruelties and barbarities perpetrated upon that simple and comparatively defenseless people whom the Government went seven thousand miles out of its way to persecute, and toward whom it violated every written and unwritten law under pretense of carrying to them the light of the Gospel and the blessing of citizens' freedom.

Is not history reproducing itself, and is it treason, is it a breaking of faith with the parole pledges of the past, for an ex-Confederate to note and to give warning of a danger which, under a mailed hand seven thousand miles away, has before this time been felt at home, and which is not restrained by principle nor palsied by age?

In going so far, I have gone beyond the intent of these Reminiscences when I commenced to record them. It is difficult for one who has witnessed the desolation of a country, his own by right of heritage from his fathers, whose blood had bought it, whose valor had defended it, and whose wisdom had crowned it with the best government which the world ever saw; who has seen the highest order of civilization, the structure of the bravest men and of the fairest women of all time, go down in a darkness upon which day can never again break; who has felt the steel in his own body and the iron in his own soul, to submit with meekness to it all, and to suffer in silence.

Mr. John Marshall, the author of the book referred to before, quoted from Giusti, "writes bitter things because his soul is bitter, for thy sake, O Freedom" ("The American Bastile"), and his motto is Γενεσθὀ Φῶς "Let there be light"; yes, light upon the past, light to illumine with the brightness of heaven characters whom envy and malice had sought to smirch or stain; light to illustrate, for the encouragement of the future, examples of truth, and virtue, and fortitude, and courage unsurpassed in history, in song, or in story.

The actors in the tragic drama of the Civil War,—and heroes there were, both Greek and Trojan,—are fast passing off the stage. There is no Homer to perpetuate in song the prowess of the mad courage of Hector or Achilles, but monuments are being erected of stone and of brass, North and South, to commemorate the valor and patriotism of the men who gave their lives in the battle for the right as they saw the right. For these men and for their memories we have nothing but praise and honor, but for the dastardly players in the miserable travesty of reconstruction which followed the war, the sooner their names and memories perish, the better for the world which their presence befouled for so many unhappy years!

The speech of Hon. Daniel W. Voorhees, in the House of Representatives, March 23, 1872—six years after the ostensible close of the war—depicts in terms of denunciation as severe as words can convey, but that words utterly fail to convey, the story of wrong, of contempt, and of oppression fastened upon the eleven States lately in rebellion against the Federal Government by the harpies sent down to fatten upon their vitals.

In evidence of the robberies perpetrated upon the impoverished citizens of these States by the carpet-bag and scalawag rulers placed over them, he tabulated the following figures and defies their contradiction:

States.	Debts and Liabilities.	
	At close of War.	January, 1872.
Alabama,	$5,939,684 87	$38,381,967 37
Arkansas,	4,036,952 87	19,761,265 62
Florida,	221,000 00	15,763,447 54
Georgia,	debts normal.	50,137,500 00

Louisiana,	10,099,074 00	50,540,206 91
North Carolina,	9,699,500 00	34,887,467 85
South Carolina,	5,000,000 00	39,158,914 47
Mississippi,	debts normal.	2,000,000 00
Tennessee,	20,105,606 66	45,688,263 46
Texas,	debts normal.	20,361,000 00
Virginia,	31,938,144 59	45,480,542 21
Grand total,	$87,039,962.99	$362,160,575.43

And to what purpose was this immense outlay ravished from a people broken by war; homes desolated; mills destroyed; farming utensils burned; old men and young men slain in battle, or helpless from wounds; labor taken from them, and currency worthless?

Mr. Voorhees says:

There was no monument erected to the public good; no colleges, no schools, no seminaries built with the stolen treasures; no lofty edifices or durable roads constructed; no massive bridges built; no rice swamp ditched; no harbors improved; no works of utility or patriotism erected. One monotonous desolation, which unholy avarice and unconstrained oppression had stamped upon the people; nothing to mitigate their degradation; stripped and robbed and left by the wayside.

The frogs, the darkness, the lice, and locusts left more blessings behind them in Egypt than these States received from their imported rulers, carpet-baggers, and detestable and more venal scalawags of home birth.

APPENDIX.

The Last Fight at Five Forks—Mr. Granier—What Manner of Man Was He—In the Interest of Justice to Mahone—Old Blandford Church—Personal Ancestry—American Bastiles—Dahlgren's Raid—"Who Fired the First Gun?"

THE LAST FIGHT AT FIVE FORKS

The following note, taken from "Reminiscences of Crenshaw's Battery," by Private J. C. Goolsby, of Richmond, who entered the Confederate service at 14 years of age and served until the last day at Appomattox Court House, giving an account of the last fight at Five Forks, will confirm the story of the tragic loss of life there, both of soldiers and animals. He says:

The battery took a position behind a fence, or rather we pulled the fence down, the grounds being separated by a space of about one hundred yards or more. In our front was an open field. * * * Standing in line the eye was first attracted by a neat frame house, situated in the right corner of the field, whose inmates were seen hastily leaving, making for the woods on the right; the field itself covering an area of some 500 feet or more in length by about the same in breadth, skirted on either side by a dense growth of trees. In our front for 500 yards the surface was even, after which it partook of a slight inclination, until it receded in a valley below, the ground upon which the enemy were massing for the desperate work of the evening. * * * We heard the sound of a bugle and presently our skirmishers were seen coming into our lines, followed by a charging column of Federal horsemen. What a sight! On they came, firing, shouting, the earth almost trembling with the heavy weight, the field being filled, as they aproached our lines, with the dead and wounded, the horses running in all directions, some with riders and some without. Our men could be restrained no longer, and the word "Fire" ran along our lines. Almost instantly the infantry poured in upon the horsemen a terrible volley; the guns of the artillery, double shotted, firing at the same time. But on they came, such was the power behind them; not being able to turn around, and running through the guns, only to be made prisoners. The destruction of life here was great, long lines being opened in

Appendix

their ranks as they attempted to break through. I had witnessed a good many exciting scenes in the army, but this surpassed them all. I really thought that we should never stop them. But whilst this assault was made in our front, Sheridan massed his infantry in three or four lines on our left, and swept up the works, capturing our left guns, stationed just at the spot from which this battle takes its name; but not without desperate resistance on the part of the cannonaders, one of whom knocked down a Federal soldier with the sponge staff. It was at this gun that Col. Willie Pegram was killed, the Christian warrior, the modest young soldier who had lived long enough to win the plaudits of the whole army.

The men behind these guns belonged to Pegram's Battalion, and their support was Corse's Veteran Brigade. It is unnecessary to add that the battle which they fought was hot and heavy.

MR. GRANIER

Mr. Granier (I cannot recall his initials) was a French nobleman who, with hundreds of others, escapes the massacre of the whites at the negro insurrection of San Domingo some fifty years before and sought refuge in this country. He had a beautiful daughter, a brunette, a little above the usual stature, of perfect figure, and with all the grace and vivacity of her race. She was of course greatly admired and sought after. She gave her heart and hand to Mr. James L. Dowell, a practical electrician and superintendent of the telegraph system in Virginia, and perhaps as far South as New Orleans. They lived in Petersburg, happily, until the breaking out of the Civil War, when Dowell's business calling him to Richmond, they removed to that city. Mrs. Dowell was a nervous, highly-strung woman, neurotic, subject to attacks of hysteria of an exaggerated degree, and withal very eccentric. I was not fully aware of her eccentricity, although I was her physician, until on one Sunday, sitting by her in church, I saw the butt of a revolver

showing itself outside of her pocket. I remonstrated
with her for going armed, but she laughed and said that
her husband was away from home so much that she carried a pistol to protect herself. After removal to Richmond she was divorced from her husband and married
Mr. E. A. Pollard, a giften but erratic man, and as eccentric as herself. He was at one time editor of the
Richmond *Examiner*, and co-editor with his brother,
Mr. Rives Pollard, of the "Southern Opinion," and author of the "Southern History of the War," "The Lost
Cause," "Lee and His Lieutenants," "Life of Jefferson
Davis," and several other books. Mr. Rives Pollard,
whose pen was as caustic as that of his brother, was
killed from ambush on account of some severe stric-
tures published in his paper in reference to a noted
young lady of Richmond. He was shot from a window
as he passed along the street. The young lady's
brother was arrested and tried for murder, but was
acquitted. Mr. Pollard's relations with his wife seemed
strained, and could not have been very cordial, as a few
years afterwards, in an apothecary store in Baltimore,
she shot him, wounding him slightly. After the death
of her second husband, Mrs. Pollard, whose eccentricities seemed to have increased rather than otherwise,
went to New York to live, but returned to Petersburg
on two occasions—once as an elocutionist, and once as
a temperance lecturer. On one Sunday afternoon, in
the course of a lecture at the Academy of Music in this
city, she invited any one in the audience who had
spoken at any time disparagingly of her to come upon
the platform and that she would treat him to a cowhid-
ing. It is needless to add that no one accepted the
invitation. That she meant what she said was possibly
in the memory of some persons, who knew that she
had on one occasion assaulted Senator Vest with a cow-
hide in the Capitol of the Confederacy in Richmond.

Appendix 333

These reminiscences are recalled by the publication of a telegram by the Associated Press in the *Index-Appeal* of last December: "Paris, Dec. 5.—The United States Consulate here is seeking the two sons of an American woman, Mrs. Marie Antoinette Nathalie, who was run over by a carriage November 30 and later died in the Beaujoir Hospital. It is said that she lived at one time in Richmond, Virginia, and in New York." She had disappeared from this country for many years, and seems to have dropped the name of Dowell and Pollard and Granier (her maiden name) and retained only the name of her girlhood, by which she was known to her friends in this city, Marie Antoinette Nathalie. Peace to her ashes! I knew her as a girl, piquant and pretty; as a bride, beautiful and happy; as a young mother, loving and devoted. What nervous strain broke the figment of her faith in truth and constancy of man, and turned her young life to that law of the neurotics bordering upon the irresponsible, God only knows, no other. Let that one who is without sin cast the first stone upon her grave. Her children died before her, and at her death she could probably have said with Loza, the Indian chief, in the bitterness of her soul, "Not one drop of my blood flows in human veins."

WHAT MANNER OF MAN WAS HE?

In reference to Lee and his men I have been asked, "What manner of man was he?—what manner of men were they? Let a Northern soldier answer. Brigadier-General Chas. A. Whittier, of the United States Volunteers, in a paper read before the Military Historical Society of Massachusetts, says:

The army of Northern Virginia will deservedly rank as the best army which has existed on this continent; suffering privations unknown to its opponents, it fought well from the early Peninsular days to the surrender of that small remnant at Appomattox. It was

always ready, active, mobile; without doubt it was composed of
the best men of the South, rushing to what they considered the defense of their country against a bitter invader; and they took the
places assigned to them, officer or private, and fought until beaten
by superiority of numbers. The North sent no such army to the
field, and its patriotism was of an easier kind. There was no rallying cry which drove all the best, the rich, and the educated to join
the fighting armies. We had Loyal Leagues and Christian commissions, and great war Governors (Andrew Curtin, and Morton),
organizers of victory; a people full of loyalty and of hatred for the
neighbors who differed from them as to the way in which the war
should be conducted, never realizing the fact that the best way was
by going or sending their brightest and best. As a matter of comparison we have lately read that from William and Mary College,
Virginia, thirty-two out of thirty-five professors and instructors
abandoned college work and joined the army in the field; Harvard
College, with its large corps of professors and instructors, *sent one
professor.* We thought our own Massachusetts a pattern of loyalty
and patriotism during the war. Read the record of Massachusetts
Volunteers as published by the State. The bounty paid (thirteen
million of dollars by the State and more millions by the cities and
towns, was a worthless expenditure to give Massachusetts a nominal credit; was paid to the deserters; to the host of men who never
joined their regiments; to the enlisting officers who put out on
their posters at one time something like this: "Enlist in heavy artillery regiments; no marching; no fighting; comfortable quarters,"
etc., etc.

General Whittier then furnishes a list of Massachusetts artillery and infantry, counting 20,959 men, *"of
which only 95 were killed in battle. This does not indicate a brilliant or a useful service."* Had General Whittier chosen to compare Harvard with the University of
Virginia, he might have noted that whilst the number of
students at Harvard was 833, against 630 at the University of Virginia, there are only 138 names graven on the
roll of honor of those men of Harvard alumni who gave
their lives for the Union; whilst the roll of the University men, when it shall be graven in brass, will furnish a
list twice as long as that of the New England University. Three out of every four of the alumni of the University of Virginia sprang to arms at the call of Virginia
in 1861, and of the fifteen hundred who served under
the banner of the Southern corps, three hundred and

fifty died for the Lost Cause; and to show of what fighting material these were, out of the fifteen hundred, thirteen hundred bore commission from the Secretary of War, from generals to second lieutenants, and these commissions were won by deeds of valor in the field. And a similar record may be written of every college and university in the South.

IN THE INTEREST OF JUSTICE TO MAHONE.

I have stated that after the bloody repulse of the Federal Army on the 18th of June, 1864, no other assault of any importance upon our lines was made during the Siege of Petersburg except on the 30th of July at the Crater.

Mahone's part in that affair has already been recorded. Subsequently, from the 18th of June, the fighting near Petersburg was always to the left of the enemy in the persistent attempt of Grant to turn our right and to envelope our forces in his anaconda fold. We met him always outside of our works, and in the fierce fighting which followed, Mahone was conspicuous above any other leader. We say that in no spirit of disparagement and with no intent to do injustice to any of the gallant men who so well played their part in the heroic but hopeless struggle in the last scenes of that memorable drama.

But to do justice to an officer who ever had tardy justice done him, to establish the truth of my statement, I have had recourse to the official records of the Union and Confederate armies.

June 22, 1864, General Lee to the Secretary of War (Serial 80, page 750):

The enemy's infantry was attacked this P. M. on the west side of the Jerusalem Plank Road and driven from his first line of works to his second, on that road, by General Mahone, with a portion of his division. About 1,600 prisoners, 4 pieces of artillery, 8 stands of colors, and a large number of small arms were captured.

Of this brilliant action General Grant says (page 14, same volume):

> The affair of the 22nd was much worse than I had heretofore learned. Our loss was nearly 2,000 men and four pieces of artillery.

The next engagement was on June 23. Of this General Lee says (page 750, same volume):

> Yesterday the enemy made a demonstration with infantry upon the Weldon Railroad, but before he had done much damage was driven back by General Mahone with a portion of his command. About 600 prisoners—28 commissioned officers—were taken.

Again, June 29, General Lee says (page 752, same volume):

> General Hampton reports that he attacked the enemy's cavalry this side of Sapony Church, and drove them beyond that point. The fight continued all night, and at daylight he routed them. When they reached Reams Station they were confronted by a portion of Mahone's division, who attacked them in the front, whilst their left flank was turned by General Fitz Lee's cavalry. The enemy was completely routed and several pieces of artillery and a number of prisoners were captured.

No further affair of importance occurred until July 30,—Battle of the Crater,—in which the part taken by Mahone has already been referred to.

The next engagement which we note from the same record was August 19 (page 851, et seq., Serial 872):

> Gen. A. P. Hill attacked the enemy at the Davis House on the Weldon Road. Heth's division in front, Mahone on the rear and flank, capturing 2,700 prisoners, flags, arms, etc.

And then on August 28th:

> Hagood's Brigade drove the enemy into their intrenchments, taking prisoners—Mahone not participating.

Appendix 337

And then, August 26, we note "the Battle of Reams Station" was fought. Troops engaged: Heth's and Wilcox's Division, aided by Hampton's splendid cavalry. Hancock's Corps was badly defeated—seven flags, 2,000 prisoners, nine pieces of artillery captured. Mahone not engaged.

Next, September 16, "Hampton's famous cattle raid" in the rear of the enemy; no infantry participating.

On October 1 Generals Heth and Hampton drove the enemy on the Squirrel Level Road, capturing 1,000 prisoners.

Then, October 28 (page 853, Serial 87), General Lee telegraphs of the battle of Burgess Mill, fought the day before:

> General Hill reports that the attack of General Heth made on the enemy the evening before, on the Boydton Plank Road, mentioned in my dispatch, was made by three brigades under General Mahone in front and General Hampton in the rear. Mahone captured 400 prisoners, three stands of colors and six pieces of artillery. The latter could not be brought off, as the enemy held the bridge. In the attack subsequently made by the enemy, Mahone broke three lines of battle, and during the night the enemy retired, leaving his wounded and more than 250 dead upon the field.

Again, October 31st, General Lee says (page 854, same volume):

> General Mahone penetrated the enemy's picket line last night, near Petersburg, and swept it for half a mile, capturing 230 men and officers, without losing a man.

Subsequent to this there was no collision of any importance with the enemy until February 6, 1865, when the battle of Hatcher's Run was fought. Of this General Lee reports to the Secretary of War (page 381, Serial 95):

> This morning Pegram's Division marched down the right bank of the creek to reconnoiter, when it was attacked vigorously. The battle was obstinately contested for some hours, but General Pegram being killed, confusion occurred and the division was driven back.

22

Evans's Division, ordered by General Gordon to support Pegram, charged the enemy, pressed him back, but was in its turn compelled to retire. Mahone's Division arriving, the enemy was rapidly driven back to his defenses on Hatcher's Run.

Soon after this Mahone was withdrawn from the flanking position on the Petersburg line that he had held so long, and was sent to the trenches on Bermuda front, relieving Pickett, who took his place on the right.

Thereafter: Gordon's splendid attack on Hare's Hill, February 26, which he carried, but could not hold for lack of supports, and the disastrous defeat of Anderson and Pickett a few days later at Five Forks completed the fighting around Petersburg.

This is not intended to ignore the attack made by the corps of Smith, Hancock, and Burnside on the 16th of June, before General Lee had established his permanent position at Petersburg, and before he had brought more than half of his army from Richmond. In this engagement the enemy lost 10,288 men, but the envelopment of the city followed. The regular siege of the city may be said to have begun on the 19th of June. On the 21st, Generals Wright and Birney inaugurated the famous left movement, losing three thousand men and being compelled to retire.

THE TRUTH ABOUT THE CAVALIER

Mr. W. H. Whitmore, in the "Cavalier Dismounted," says that the "people of the South were descended in great measure (through Virginia, of course) from indentured white servants sent from the jails and slums of England." And even Mr. Hugh Blair Grigsby, the "Bluelight Chronicler of Virginia History," says that the "cavalier was essentially a slave to the King and a slave to the church"; that he (Grigsby) "looked with contempt upon the miserable figment which sought to trace the distinguishing points of the Virginia character to the influence of those butterflies of the English aristocracy."

To this, Mr. John Fiske, with better opportunities for investigation and with larger scope of vision, says that "Mr. Grigsby's remarks are an expression of American feeling in what may be called its Elijah Pogram period, when the knowledge of history was too slender and the historic sense too dull to be shocked at the incongruity of classing such men as Strafford and Falkland with butterflies."

Undoubtedly at the early colonization of Virginia many characterless adventurers sought Virginia for the betterment of their future—many, in other words, "for their good"; and many left Old England for their country's good; and some as indentured servants. But no student of the history of the State can fail to see that there was a great emigration of cavaliers from England to Tidewater Virginia.

The great exodus of cavaliers to Virginia began in 1649, after the execution of Charles I. On the news of the death of the king, Governor Berkeley sent a message to England inviting the Royalists to the colony; and in less than a twelve-month more than a thousand had come. And from this date, 1649, to 1670 the population of Virginia had increased from 15,000 to 38,000, chiefly, no doubt, from this emigration, and in spite of the fact that there was an exodus of the Puritans to New England—as many as one thousand in 1649—on account of the treatment of Gov. Berkeley. This fact of the migration of Royalist cavaliers is further confirmed by the names conferred on the counties and settlements populated by them, which could only have been done by a people as loyal to royalty as the cavaliers were. The counties of Elizabeth City, James City, Charles City, Warwick, York, Gloucester, King

William, King George, Surry, Sussex, Prince George, Dinwiddie, Chesterfield, Brunswick, Mecklenburg, Lunenburg, and dozens of others, all derived their names from noble or royal personages.

And the population of these first-settled counties developed all the cavalier character and instinct,—in their love of horses, dogs and sporting,—and maintained these habits until the day of the sad depletion of gentle blood by the invasion of the mongrel soldiery of the North in the war between the States. Besides, by "no possible ingenuity of Constitution making or of legislation could a society made up of boors and ruffians" create and bring forward, as leaders in war, in law, in statecraft the men who made Virginia the Mother of States and the home of the highest civilization of the 18th century.

OLD BLANDFORD CHURCH.

I

"Thou art crumbling to the dust, old pile!
   Thou art hastening to thy fall;
And 'round thee in thy loneliness
   Clings the ivy to the wall;
The worshippers are scattered now
   Who knelt before thy shrine.
And silence reigns where anthems rose
   In the days of 'Auld Lang Syne.'

II

"And sadly sighs the wandering wind
   Where oft in years gone by
Prayer rose from many hearts to Him,
   The Highest of the High.
The tramp of many a noiseless foot
   That sought thy aisles is o'er,
And many a weary heart around
   Is still forever more.

III.

"How doth ambitious hope take wing!
How droops the spirit now!
We hear the distant city's din;
The dead are mute below.
The sun that shone upon their paths
Now gilds their lowly graves,
The zephyrs which once fanned their brows
The grass above them waves.

IV

"Oh! could we call the many back
Who 've gathered here in vain—
Who 've careless roved where we do now,
Who 'll never meet again;
How would our very hearts be stirred
To meet the earnest gaze
Of the lovely and the beautiful—
The lights of other days."

In referring to the authorship of these stirring lines on Old Blandford Church, we have said that they were generally attributed to Tyrone Powers, an English actor; by some others they were attributed to Mr. Hiram Haines, the editor of the *Petersburg Intelligencer;* but I have recently learned from a lady in this city, Miss Nora Fontaine Davidson, a most intelligent and vivacious lady, who still lives to great usefulness in the present, but who holds more converse with the heroic past than any other person of my acquaintance, that they were neither written by Powers nor Haines. She derived her information directly from her father, Col. James M. Davidson, who surveyed the new part of the Blandford Cemetery, and for perhaps forty years was the custodian of the grounds and records, and who was a worthy and veritable "Old Mortality." Miss Davidson quotes her father, who said: "While sitting in the old church one day in 1843 or 1844 I spied a lady standing at the south wall of the church by the door, with pencil in hand writing on the wall. Fearing my presence might be an intrusion, I remained a silent spectator. Some minutes elapsed, when, seeing me, she advanced, and I recognized in the writer an old friend and schoolmate, Miss Henning, a daughter of Chief-Justice Henning, of the Court of Appeals, and who subsequently became Mrs. Schermerhorn." Miss Davidson says that fact has been corroborated by Mrs. Schermerhorn's sister, who was with her at the time of the writing. This lady was a cousin, I believe, of the late Wm. F. Spotswood of this city.

Lately the "United Daughters of the Confederacy" and the "Daughters of the American Revolution," two distinct organizations, have both sought to get possession of the Old Church—the first to make it a Memorial Chapel of the Lost Cause, and the second to preserve it as one of the Historical Relics of Colonial Virginia, and the contest between them has been quite sharp and not always tempered with gentle concession on either side, so much so that a parody has appeared in one of the city papers—"Some more lines on Old Blandford Church," "Author still unknown"— in which the same rhythm and the same ring has been perpetuated in a production proven worthy of the original poem. But the gifted perpetrater need not hope to hide his modest merit behind the cloak of uncertainty that has so long shadowed the original. His friends will certainly recognize in "Some More Lines" the pen of the genial and talented engineer and superintendent of the Atlantic Coast Line, Mr. Morton Riddle:

I.

"Thou art stirring up a dust, old pile!
  For it's quite the proper caper
To take thee from this loneliness
  And exploit thee in the paper;
The worshipers are scattered now
  Who knelt before thy shrine,
And D. A. R. and U. D. C.
  Scrap o'er thee all the time.

Appendix

II.

"And sadly sighs the wandering wind,
　Likewise the *Index* readers,
Who have to read "Commemorated,"
　Also the Editor's leaders.
The tread of many a noiseless foot
　That sought thy aisles is o'er;
We hear the sounds of jeers and scoffs,
　The "Daughters" have the floor.

III.

"How doth ambitious hope take wing,
　How droops the spirit now!
We hear the never-ceasing din
　And envy those below.
The sun that shone upon their paths
　Now gilds their lowly graves,
Whilst we, the quick, must still endure
　This column while it raves.

IV.

"Oh! could we call this jaw match off
　And live in peace once more,
Let Johnny Reb and Colonial Dame
　Live happy as before;
How would our very hearts be stirred,
　How full would be our cup
If the U. D. C.'s and D. A. R.'s
　Would kiss, then make it up."

PERSONAL ANCESTRY

As these are personal memoirs, I will here note that my mother, Mary Elizabeth Weldon, was born in Blandford and baptized in Old Blandford Church. She was the daughter of Daniel Weldon, of Weldon, on the Roanoke, North Carolina, and of Mrs. Mary Donald Weldon, nee Fraser. Mrs. Weldon, her mother, was the daughter of Simon Fraser, of the first of Donald & Fraser (the latter a younger son of Simon Fraser, Lord Lovatt of Scotland), Scotch merchants in Blandford. She married, when very young, one of the

Randolphs, of Curls Neck, on James River, by whom she had one child, John Randolph, who died soon after coming of age. On the death of Mr. Randolph, who lived only a few years, she married my grandfather, Mr. Weldon, of North Carolina, by whom she had two daughters—one, my mother, just alluded to, and the other, Jane Weldon, who married Dr. James B. Claiborne, of Brunswick County, Virginia. My grandfather Weldon only lived a few years after this marriage, and my grandmother married a third time. Her third husband was Dr. Blunt, of Belle View, Southampton County, Virginia, by whom she had four sons and three daughters. One of these sons, Simon Blunt, displayed such courage in a fight with the negroes in Nat. Turner's insurrection (1832) that, though only a lad of 12 years of age, General Jackson, then President of the United States, made him a midshipman in the Navy. Another son, and the oldest, William Blunt, my mother's half brother, was notified in 1846 or 1847 that he was heir to the title and estates of Lord Lovatt, of Beaufort Castle, in Invernesshire, Scotland. He declined both title and estates, however, and I have recently heard that the matter was in contention for 20 years afterwards. But I suppose that another heir was finally found, as I have learned through the same source that a general officer in the British Army in South Africa is Simon Fraser, General Lord Lovatt, who, I presume, is one of my illustrious, though unknown, kin. I can only wish that, if there be such a person, he were fighting in a better cause than striving to subdue a brave people contending for the inalienable rights of home and country. But if he really represents that sturdy stock of Highlanders from which I am proud to draw my lineage on my mother's side, I am sure that, in the place of General Lord Roberts, it would hardly have taken him two

Appendix 345

years and more to reduce with two hundred thousand troops twenty thousand Boers.

I have made no reference to my father in this generalized diversion, though he was born in the vicinage of Petersburg, and his dust, with the dust of my dead for nearly two centuries past, sleeps in the hallowed old cemetery of Blandford Church. The annals of the Claiborne family are well known to all who take an interest in them. I will only say that William Claiborne, of Kent's Island, who, from 1621 to 1647 and later, played no unimportant part in the history of Virginia and Maryland, was the ancestor of all people of that name in this country. He was called at one time "Claiborne the Rebel," and his name was clouded by one or two historians; but Charles Campbell ("History of Virginia") and John Fiske ("Old Virginia and her Neighbors") have happily cleared his name and established his well-earned fame. Rev. Philip Slaughter, in "History of Bristol Parish," says that his character has been gracefully summed up by a gifted biographer, Rev. S. F. Streeter, of Baltimore. Mr. Streeter says "the hand of prejudice, prompted by personal subservience, traced on the tablet of History an inscription as unjust to the character and actions of the deceased, as unbecoming the dignity of the historic muse. It has been reserved for an humble inquirer, and a lover of the truth, to erect a new cenotaph, which displays the name of Claiborne as worthy of honor and respect; and which ranks him who planted it in this country as a man of whom his descendants have every reason to be proud—one of the earliest pioneers of civilization, the first actual settler of the territory of Maryland, and among the most active and prominent citizens in the early days of Virginia, and one of the most remarkable men of his time."

AMERICAN BASTILES.

From the organization of the Government to the administration of Mr. Lincoln we know of no case in which an American citizen was arrested without warrant, imprisoned without charge, and released after months and years of incarceration without trial. He assumed quasi plenary power to make and enforce laws without the aid, interference, or assistance of the legislative or judicial branch of the Government. "The Government was the President, and the President was the Government."

No words we could use would bring relief to or redress the wrongs perpetrated upon *thousands* of unoffending citizens by their unwarranted incarceration in American Bastiles during his administration. We contemplate the cruelties, oppressions, persecutions, and imprisonments committed during that long night of political despotism with emotions akin to horror. Hon. Jeremiah Black, writing to Mr. Quincy Adams, of Massachusetts, says "there was nothing comparable to the corruption and viciousness of the government since the days of Robespierre and the French Revolution."

The whole land of the *free* Northern States was dotted over with forts, penitentiaries, jails, barracks, and prison camps,—American Bastiles,—which contained during the short period of four years from *ten* to *twenty thousand* men, besides women and children, all citizens of *free States*, and incarcerated by the edict of one man because they did not *choose* or were *supposed* not to obey his mandates—*suspects*. The drama of the French Revolution re-enacted. When Camille Desmoulins was told during that bloody era to worship the Goddess of Liberty, he replied, "If ye would have me worship it [a statue in stone], open your prisons, set free the two hundred thousand ye have incarcerated as *suspects*. I find no such crime in the constitution or the law."

Six hundred and eighty-seven years ago the people of England, at Runnymede, an island in the river Thames, wrested from King John the Magna Charta, the great guarantee of personal liberty to every Englishman. It says: "No freeman shall be taken or imprisoned, dispossessed or outlawed, or in any way detroyed. Nor will we pass upon him nor commit him but by the lawful judgment of his peers, or by the law of the land. To no man will we sell; to none will we delay; to none will we deny right or justice."

In these words are found the monuments of personal liberty fought over and contested for in centuries of bloody wars, but ever preserved intact, the pride and the glory of the Briton of to-day.

When George III attempted to rob his colonies in America of these sacred rights, which as Englishmen they had brought over from the Fatherland, they renewed the fight on this continent and continued it until the citizen's home was recognized as his castle, from which he could only be ejected by law. The writ of *habeas corpus* could be invoked to bring him face to face with his accuser, and to guarantee to him a trial by his peers before commitment for any offense. And these rights were preserved undisputed and indisputable from the acknowledgment of independence of these United Colonies until the introduction into power of the Republican Party and the usurpation of its unscrupulous leaders. What followed then? Then "the word of the informer was the law, the sound of Seward's little bell was the signal, and the telegraph the messenger. Citizens were arrested by thousands and incarcerated without warrant. Judges were torn from the bench, bruised and bleeding; ministers of the gospel, while performing the sacred offices and holy duties of their calling, were stricken down, dragged through the streets and imprisoned. Women were incarcerated and subjected to insult and outrage. Doctors were ruthlessly taken from the bedside of the dying patient, and immured for months without warrant. Lawyers were arrested and confined to the same cell with their clients whose release they were endeavoring to effect. Post-offices were searched, newspapers seized and suppressed, and the editors handcuffed and secretly hurried to prison. The writ of *habeas corpus* was a blank, and all of our inheritable rights poor, poor dumb mouths."

After the destruction of the Bastile in Paris, which for an hundred years, perhaps, had been the horrid home of political prisoners in France, and their hidden graves, Lafayette took the key of the accursed building and sent it over to General Washington as a token of the restoration of the liberty of the citizen. This key it is said now hangs in the Mansion House at Mount Vernon. But where is the key to Fort Warren, to Fort McHenry, to Fort Delaware, to Fort Lafayette, to the old Capitol Prison, to the Penitentiaries, to the casemates and camps throughout the loyal North?

If any one thinks that in the above we have made an exaggerated statement, let us refer him to a book called "United States Bonds" and published soon after the Civil War by the Rev. Dr. Handy, a Presbyterian divine of unexceptionable truthfulness; or to "The American Bastile," a history of Prisoners of State during the Administration of President Lincoln, prepared by a resolution of a convention of the "Prisoners of State," by John A. Marshall, Esq. This note is taken largely, and sometimes verbatim, from the latter book; also from "Three Decades of the Federal Union," by Hon. S. S. Cox, of New York. But I may be asked, Why recall all of this, why reproduce so much to-day

Appendix 349

that was a disgrace and a scandal to free government not forty years ago? Alas! it is not a "recall" or a "reproduction" to many. The most of the witnesses of the scenes recounted, the most of the sufferers from the malignity of the passions of men, mad with power and drunk with blood, have passed away. The oppressor and the oppressed, the murderer and his victim have met now before the Great Assize, where wrong will be adjudicated in a light that will make bare the truth, and before that Judge who declared that "Vengeance is mine." Those for whom I write have, the most of them, no bitter memories of war, no haunting recollection of the gall and iron of the days of reconstruction. The citizen of to-day is shutting his eyes to the past; the times are prosperous, money is plentiful, big jobs are given out by the Government, and subsidies are assured to the faithful adherents of party. Why? Where is the unreturning past? Why does history never reproduce itself? What citizen would have believed in the year of our Lord 1855 that in one decade, in the induction of one man into power, that a revolution would have been sprung upon a country the happiest and freest upon earth, the hope and the haven of the oppressed of all nations, and that the Constitution would be ignored; that the laws would be declared silent; that the sovereignty of the State should be abolished; that a million of armed men should trample the fields then whitening with harvest; that brother would imbue his hand in brother's blood, until river and rivulet were stained with scarlet; that helpless women and more helpless children should be driven out into winter's cold and made to witness the conflagration of homes and of food and of clothing—and to their piteous appeal for mercy should be told by the greatest in authority, by him who alone could have helped them, that "war was hell, and the hotter he could make it the sooner it would be over." And that when some of the noblest and best of the citizens, upon whom no taint of crime or disloyalty could be established, by thousands were arrested without law and convicted without trial; that the Bastile with its dungeons, its casemates, its silent cells awaited only the order of one man to receive their hopeless victims, and that the tinkle of a little bell could summon any citizen from San Francisco to Washington, from the Pacific Ocean to the Atlantic, and that only one man could release him.

I ask again, Is history reproducing itself? Within the last few years the President of the United States, in violation of all the traditions of the Republic, and of the teachings of the Father of his Country, and of the Constitution and laws of his country, which he had sworn before the High God to uphold, not only inaugurated a war, but bought after its outcome a colony of ten millions of subjects in islands seven thousand miles from the United States—bought from a party not having right of possession, and paid twenty millions of dollars for the same, without the will and consent of the Senate. One Senator has persistently avowed that he voted for the ratification of the treaties on personal promise of the President that these islands should not be retained. How many voted under the same impression does not appear, but the islands are still held, and the inhabitants are still subjects, not citizens; subjects of an autocracy, are under civic-military rule, have no more voice in the government which imposes and collects taxes of them, and which makes the laws for the regulation of their lives, and establishes the control of them, than the subject of the Turk or of the Czar of Russia. Can these things be corollaries of a past that prognosticates no danger to the future? Is the liberty of speech secured to the citizen of to-day? If so, why

Appendix 351

not to the subject of our foreign possessions? If there be a censorship of the press at Manila, is it too much to believe that it may antedate a gag upon papers published in New York or Washington? Mr. Stephen Bonsall, a gentleman of character and observation, who spent some months in the Philippines last year, and who has published in the *New York Herald* of January 26, 1902, some of the results of his observation, says that when he advised an officer of the Government, about to return to Washington, to tell what he had seen as an officer in the field, that discreet gentleman remarked that "the very first thing that he should do when he got off the steamer would be to buy a padlock and put it on his lips, and throw the key down the deepest well he could find."

This may not have been very honest or patriotic, but it is typical of what might have been reasonably expected. "The man on horseback" evidently rules our citizens of the Philippines. How long before he shall transfer his mount to the Capitoline Hill at Washington? *Quoque tandem Cataline nostra patientia abutire!*

DAHLGREN'S RAID

The papers found on Colonel Dahlgren's body, after announcing in an address to his followers, his officers and men, the desperate but "great and glorious undertaking" before them, and advising any one who was not willing to sacrifice his life in such a cause "to step out and go home to the arms of his sweetheart, and read of the braves who swept through the city of Richmond," detailed the order of attack, with special instructions to "guides, pioneers [with oakum, turpentine, and torpedoes], signal officers, quartermasters, pickets, and scouts in rebel uniform," etc. "After getting in to the city," he said, "we hope to release the prisoners on Belle Island first, and having seen them fairly started, we will cross James River into Richmond, destroying the bridges after us, and exhorting the released to destroy the hateful city, and not to allow the Rebel leader and his traitorous crew to escape. * * * " Further on he orders, "once in the city, the men must keep together, well in hand, and the city be destroyed, and Jeff Davis and Cabinet killed."

These orders, extracts from which are here given, were written on a sheet of paper having in printed letters on the upper corner: "Headquarters Third Division, Cavalry Corps—1864," and were addressed to "officers and men." A full copy of these orders (papers they were called) which were found on the person of Colonel Dahlgren after he was killed was published in the *Richmond Dispatch* of March 5, 1864. Such atrocity of intention—imagine the reality of crime and the horrors which would have followed the sacking and burning of a city filled with women and children, whose natural protectors were absent in the army—excited an indignation worthy, if possible, of such cruel and cowardly malignity. Yet, though all of Dahlgren's immediate followers were captured when he was killed or during the following day, not one was made to pay any other penalty than that of being incarcerated in Libby Prison as prisoners of war!

Of course, indignant denial of the authenticity of these documents was made by the Northern press, which charged that they were forged by the Rebels. Rear-Admiral Dahlgren, in a memoir of his son published in 1872, reiterated the charge of forgery, and makes a statement which he supposes establishes the innocence of his son. Colonel Dahlgren's signal officer, Lieutenant Bartley, in a letter published December 24, 1864, also denies that any such "orders or address" were ever issued or made. We cannot blame an hon-

Appendix

ored and distressed father for his attempts to rescue the name of a son from such obloquy as must ever attach to it; but Lieutenant Bartley has invalidated his testimony by referring to the treatment he received as a prisoner of war, saying, "All this brutal treatment was inflicted upon us, according to the statement of the Confederate prison officials, on account of those papers said to have been found on the body of Colonel Dahlgren at the time he was killed." In his case what "this cruel treatment" was has yet to be demonstrated and corroborated. It was evidently not what he deserved, or it would not have been tempered with the mercy which permitted him to testify as early as December, 1864, and while yet a prisoner of war, that his captors were cruel and malicious. As to the authenticity of the papers taken from the body of his commanding officer, that can be established by proof as perfect and irrefragable as human testimony can make it.

On failing to unite with Kilpatrick on the contemplated raid to Richmond, Dahlgren found himself apparently left to his fate by that officer, and made a daring attempt to retreat through the counties of Hanover, King William, and King and Queen, and reach Gloucester, where he expected reinforcements or troops would be sent to meet him. Though harassed by small parties of Confederates on his way, on the second night he had gotten, with small loss, to a place called Stevensville, in King and Queen. Lieut. H. E. Blair, afterwards Judge H. E. Blair, of Salem, Virginia, a Confederate officer who had been captured two days before by Dahlgren, and who had been detained and rode with the enemy to this point, says: "I was riding with the main line, near the front, when I perceived there was some trouble ahead. Dahlgren rode forward, I heard him challenge some one; heard him snap his pistol, which was at once followed by a fire in return. That was the shot I suppose which killed him. A general fire was opened by the Confederates, and the Yankees were greatly alarmed and confused. I got off my horse and opened a fence, and they retreated into a field. I then called to our men, told them who I was, and went to them; they told me they had killed a man with a wooden leg. I said to them, 'this is Dahlgren.' They searched his person and found the papers which were afterwards delivered to the Confederate Government."

Judge Blair was witness number seven of the authenticity of the papers. The body of Confederates which intercepted and killed or captured Dahlgren and his party was described by one of their number as "a strange medley of regulars, raw troops, old farmers, preachers, school boys, etc." The man giving the description says of himself that he was an humble schoolmaster—afterwards the Rev. E. W. Halback; and that one of his school-boys, named Littlepage, was the first to reach the body of the fallen officer, though none of them knew who he was then, and who handed him the papers. They were read the following morning after they were captured by Captain Fox, Captain Pollard, Rev. R. H. Bagby, and others, and were then turned over to Captain Pollard and taken by him to Gen. R. L. T. Beale, of the Ninth Virginia Cavalry, who carried them to General Fitz Lee, and were taken by him to President Davis. They were then sent by order of Mr. Benjamin, Secretary of State, through General Stevens, to Major Albert H. Campbell, of the Engineering and Topographical Bureau, with instructions to make fifty copies. One of these "photographic fac-similes of an address to his men, and a memorandum or draft of instruction found on the person of Col. W. Dahlgren, United States Army, when killed during his raid on

Appendix 355

Richmond in 1864," was sent by Major Campbell to Colonel George W. Munford, Secretary of the Southern Historical Society, March 7, 1874. All of these gentlemen—men of undoubted character, and some of high position—testify that the copy of the papers published in the Richmond press was a true copy of those taken from the body of Colonel Dahlgren.

Any one wishing to confirm this statement will find the most conclusive testimony of the same, and a most interesting account of the whole affair, in Vol. 3, Southern Historical Papers, pages 219-221, by that gallant soldier and high-toned gentleman, General R. T. L. Beale, of the Ninth Virginia Cavalry; and again in "Southern Historical Papers," pages 215-560, by several participants in the stirring incidents of that raid; and in a letter written to the *Historical Magazine*, New York, 1870, by that peerless and chivalrous soldier, General Fitz Lee, whom none will accuse at this day of "setting down aught in malice"; and in "Lost Cause," page 504, by E. W. Halback.

Colonel Dahlgren's father complained that "nothing better was permitted to the precious remains [of his son] that a common pine box, the coarse shirt and pantaloons of a Rebel soldier, with an ordinary camp blanket for a shroud." Some of the people of the South were silly enough to believe at that time that what was good enough for a Rebel soldier was good enough for a Yankee officer whose atrocious designs placed him beyond the pale of treatment measured to an honorable enemy. General Lee, with subtle satire, says: "Let us put the shoe on the other foot. Imagine General Early's body found in the vicinity of Washington when his forces retired from there in July of the same year, with orders upon it to 'destroy and burn the hateful city' and 'to kill Abe Lincoln and his Cabinet,' exhorting long-pent-up prisoners with long-pent-up revengeful feelings to do it. I ask, would his remains have been taken up tenderly, and interred in the Congressional burying ground, and his memory be cherished as a 'martyred hero'?"

An incident of this raid showing the cruelty of which Dahlgren was capable, and leading us to believe that the infamous orders, whose authenticity we have established, were in consonance with his true character, we read in the *Detroit Free Press* of March 11, 1882. This was contributed by one of Dahlgren's staff, Lieutenant Bartley. Mr. Bartley says, speaking of the negro guard in the expedition:

> This man came down from Washington, and was sent by Stanton, who was a personal friend of the Colonel. He made a bargain with Kilpatrick and Dahlgren to take them to a ford at Davis's Mill, above Richmond, when his services would cease; and in case of any mistake or treachery on his part, he was to be hanged; and if he came out all right he was to receive a large sum of money. He took us safely through on these terms, and though he had plenty of opportunities to escape, never left us. There was no ford at Davis's Mill on the river at all; but a steam ferry, with the boat on the opposite side. When asked why he had misled us he could or would not give any satisfactory answer. The Colonel then told him that he would have to carry out his part of the contract, to which the guide assented, admitted that was the agreement, and made no objection to the execution. He went to the tree without any force, and submitted to his fate (hanging) without a murmur.

The comment made by Mr. Bartley upon this affair was that it was "mysterious." Why mysterious? Murder is sometimes mysterious, but never when done in open daylight, and in the presence of a thousand witnesses. A citizen testifies that there was a ford at Davis's Mill, to which the poor negro conducted them, but the river was swollen by rain and not fordable at the time. But what was this to a man thirsty for blood and impatient at the delay of the contemplated massacre at Richmond! The poor victim made no resistance to his cowardly executioners, of course, and he was

Appendix

hung by a halter like a dog. The same citizen said that the tree was pointed out for years afterwards.

"WHO FIRED THE FIRST GUN?"

Dr. J. William Jones gives an account in a recent number of the *Richmond Dispatch* (October 6, 1901) of a discussion which he overheard between a private soldier of the Thirteenth Virginia Regiment and a Federal colonel in reference to the origin of the war. He said that he took no part in it, as he knew that in a discussion of that character the average Confederate private was more than a match for the average Federal colonel. The Federal colonel, with a considerable air of superiority, said: "Sir, I will ask you one question, which will settle this discussion: 'Who fired the first gun in this war'?" As quick as a flash the private replied, "John Brown fired the first gun at Harper's Ferry; Major Anderson fired the second gun when he violated the agreement between himself and the authorities of South Carolina, and moved from Moultrie into Sumter; Mr. Buchanan fired the third gun when he sent the *Star of the West* to provision and reinforce Sumter; Mr. Lincoln fired the fourth gun when he violated the pledge made to the Confederate Commissioners, and sent that fleet to Charleston Harbor—and your people have been firing ever since. Now, if you will just cease firing this war will stop and peace will come at once." Says Dr. Jones, "The brave, intelligent private clearly expressed the facts, and silenced the Federal colonel, who had never before taken that view of the case."

Mr. Lincoln did not expect to bring on war when he called for seventy-five thousand troops from the different States. After the passage of the first troops, the Sixth Massachusetts, through Baltimore on April 16,

1861, which led to a collision between them and the citizens, resulting in the death of four soldiers and the wounding of thirty-six, and the death of twelve citizens (the number of wounded was never known), the city of course was thrown into the wildest excitement. The climax of this excitement was reached on the morning of the 21st, when it was reported that more troops were approaching from the North. Judge Brown, of that city, says: "It was a fearful day in Baltimore. Men, women, and children were wild with excitement. A certainty of a fight in the streets was the pressing danger." At five minutes before 11 A. M. the bell of the town clock summoned to arms, and a large part of the male population including boys and old men, thronged to headquarters, and arms and ammunition were distributed and full preparations made for a conflict. The military proper were under command of Major General George H. Stuart, and the un-uniformed under command of Col. J. R. Trimble. In the meantime, a dispatch had been received from Washington, saying that the troops had been ordered back to Harrisburg. Mr. Lincoln had wired the Mayor of Baltimore, at three o'clock that morning, to come to Washington and consult in reference to keeping the peace in Maryland. The Mayor, Judge Brown, went to Washington, accompanied by several prominent citizens of Baltimore, and an interview was held with Mr. Lincoln in the presence of the Cabinet and General Scott. At this interview the President asserted with great earnestness that the protection of Washington was the sole object of the concentrating of troops there, and that none of the troops brought through Maryland were intended for any purpose hostile to the State or aggression against the Southern States.

"In reply," Judge Brown says, "I addressed myself to the President and said with much earnestness that the disabling of the bridges leading to Baltimore was done by authority, and that it was a measure of protection in a sudden emergency designed to prevent bloodshed in Baltimore, and was not intended as an act of hostility to the general Government; that the people of Maryland had always been deeply attached to the Union, but that they, including the citizens of Baltimore, regarded the proclamation calling for seventy-five thousand troops as an act of war on the South, and a violation of its constitutional rights; and that it was not surprising that a high-spirited people, holding such opinions, should resent the passage of Northern troops through their city for such a purpose. At this, Mr. Lincoln was greatly excited, and springing up from his chair, walked backward and forward through the apartment, and said with great feeling, 'Mr. Brown, I am not a learned man, I am not a learned man'; that his proclamation had not been correctly understood; that he had no intention of bringing on war, but that his purpose was to defend the Capital, which was in danger of being bombarded from the heights across the Potomac."

No more troops were brought through Baltimore, but through Annapolis, continuously, until General Butler, on the 13th of May, entered Baltimore with two Northern regiments and inaugurated the series of outrages upon the citizens of that city—outrages of unparalleled ferocity and injustice—which continued until the war was over. As soon as that especial piece of treacherous villainy, worthy of its shameless and unprincipled author, was perpetrated, thousands of the best men of the State—twenty thousand—left it and came South, throwing in their fortunes with the cause of right as interpreted by the Confederate Government.

It is not within the province of this paper to follow farther the story of their patriotic and self-immolating

service in the Southern Armies. Literally leaving all,
—friends, fortune, home,—they laid down their lives
for principle. And wherever you find a Confederate
monument to the dead, there you will find at its foot
the grave of a Maryland soldier.

www.ingramcontent.com/pod-product-compliance
Lightning Source LLC
Chambersburg PA
CBHW070226230426
4366 4CB00014B/2232